Popular Music as Promotion

For Liv

Popular Music as Promotion

Music and Branding in the Digital Age

Leslie M. Meier

polity

First published in 2017 by Polity Press

Polity Press
65 Bridge Street
Cambridge CB2 1UR, UK

Polity Press
350 Main Street
Malden, MA 02148, USA

ISBN-13: 978-0-7456-9221-0
ISBN-13: 978-0-7456-9222-7(pbk)

A catalogue record for this book is available from the British Library.

Library of Congress Cataloging-in-Publication Data

Names: Meier, Leslie M., author.
Title: Popular music as promotion : music and branding in the digital age / Leslie M. Meier.
Description: Cambridge, UK ; Malden, MA : Polity Press, 2016. | Includes bibliographical references and index.
Identifiers: LCCN 2016023774 (print) | LCCN 2016024778 (ebook) | ISBN 9780745692210 (hardcover : alk. paper) | ISBN 0745692214 (hardcover : alk. paper) | ISBN 9780745692227 (pbk. : alk. paper) | ISBN 0745692222 (pbk. : alk. paper) | ISBN 9780745692241 (mobi) | ISBN 9780745692258 (epub)
Subjects: LCSH: Music trade. | Sound recordings–Marketing. | Music in advertising. | Branding (Marketing)
Classification: LCC ML3790 .M42 2016 (print) | LCC ML3790 (ebook) | DDC 781.64068/8–dc23
LC record available at https://lccn.loc.gov/2016023774

Typeset in 10 on 12pt Sabon by Toppan Best-set Premedia Limited
Printed and bound in the UK by Clays Ltd, St Ives PLC

Contents

Acknowledgements

I am tremendously thankful to all the people who have supported me in the development of this book and the PhD thesis from which it evolved. Jonathan Burston and Alison Hearn, my supervisors at the University of Western Ontario, provided invaluable insight, encouragement and support. I would like to extend my sincere gratitude to Matt Stahl, Jonathan Sterne and Norma Coates for their incisive input on the thesis, and to David Hesmondhalgh and Bethany Klein for the careful and thoughtful feedback they have provided as I have worked to refine my ideas in this book. I would like to thank Kate Oakley, Ted Magder, Vincent Manzerolle, Devon Powers, Jay Hodgson and my fellow PhD students at the University of Western Ontario. Thanks also to Andrea Drugan, Elen Griffiths, Ellen MacDonald-Kramer and India Darsley at Polity, copyeditor Jane Fricker and the two anonymous reviewers who provided valuable comments on the manuscript.

I am truly grateful for the generous contributions of my interviewees, without whom this research would not have been possible. The insider view on the music industries, advertising and brands during an intense period of change provided me with a one-of-a-kind education.

Thanks to the Social Sciences and Humanities Research Council of Canada (SSHRC) for its generous support of this research and to the

Canada-US Fulbright Program, which sponsored my visiting researcher post at New York University's Department of Media, Culture, and Communication. These funders enabled me to conduct indispensable interviews in New York City and Los Angeles in addition to those undertaken in Toronto.

I am also so very grateful to my family and closest friends. Thanks to my parents, Don and Judy Meier, my brother and sister-in-law, Ian and Karissa Meier, my grandmothers, Nicki Soiseth and Kay Meier, David and Carol Bonli, Melanie Preston and Jérôme Bertrand, and most of all, Liv Bonli.

Introduction: Popular Music, Branding and Promotional Culture

Today, strategically chosen popular music permeates the commercial media system, binding the work of recording artists to the world of brands. 'My Silver Lining' by Swedish folk duo First Aid Kit provides the musical accompaniment for a Renault automobile commercial, 'Nous Étions Deux' by French psych-punk rock band La Femme sets the vibe for an Apple Watch commercial, and 'Lightning Bolt' by English indie rock artist Jake Bugg has been woven into advertisements for British Airways and Gatorade. Instrumental clips or versions of 'The Universal' by Blur, 'Have a Nice Day' by Stereophonics and 'Where Is My Mind?' by the Pixies provide a quiet backdrop for British Gas, Premier Inn and Facebook commercials, respectively. No longer the sole domain of major label artists, original songs by independent artists are included in advertisements ranging from youth-oriented 'lifestyle' brands to less 'cool' brands (e.g. detergent brand Cheer, health insurance company Cigna and hardware franchise Lowe's) (Beltrone 2012). Meanwhile, in a new twist on the endorsement deal, major stars are working with brands in the roles of 'creative director' (e.g. Justin Timberlake with Bud Light and Lady Gaga with Polaroid) and 'brand ambassador' (Beyoncé with Pepsi and Taylor Swift with Diet Coke) (Barker 2013). Though such pairings take a myriad of forms, in each popular music is used as a vehicle for achieving the partner organization's marketing and promotional objectives. Music serves as a kind of cultural currency used in the service of commercial ends.

Television programmes and video games likewise feature popular music prominently, marking an extension of the well-established practice of using popular music in film. The opening credits to television programmes *Weeds* (2005–12) and *Parenthood* (2010–15) are accompanied by Malvina Reynolds's 'Little Houses' and Bob Dylan's 'Forever Young' respectively, while *House* (2004–12) opens to 'Teardrop' by Massive Attack and *Mad Men* (2007–15) to 'A Beautiful Mine' by RJD2. Canadian rock band Barenaked Ladies were hired to write and perform the theme song for the sitcom *The Big Bang Theory* (2007–). *Gossip Girl* (2007–12) and *Grey's Anatomy* (2005–) are notable for their use of original recordings by independent and lesser known artists, and *Glee* (2009–15) and *American Idol* (2002–16) for their cover versions of top hits. Popular music is not only a feature of music-related video games such as the *Guitar Hero* and *Rock Band* series (first released in 2005 and 2007, respectively), but also many others, such as *FIFA*, *MLB: The Show* and *Tony Hawk's Pro Skater*, which include songs by artists ranging from Johnny Cash to Grandmaster Flash to Gorillaz. Countless music makers participate in the now commonplace practice of licensing music for use by media and consumer brand partners – a development that has penetrated the mediascape so deeply that it almost seems unremarkable.

This book provides a critical examination of key changes that have brought together popular music worlds and brand worlds, and in so doing, ushered in what has in fact been a striking change in the fundamental tension between creativity and commerce as a site of 'negotiation, conflict and struggle' in the cultural industries (Hesmondhalgh 2013a: 82). I consider how the digital transformation of the music industries (sound recording, music publishing and live performance), combined with the emergence of an increasingly promotion-oriented culture, have contributed to shifting attitudes among industry executives and working artists regarding the appropriate relationship between music and marketing. While the participation of a broader array of corporations and brands within music-related endeavours has opened up new opportunities for musicians, it also has engendered overwhelmingly commercial and promotional understandings of and assumptions regarding popular music and its role in society. As we shall see, the music industries have grown increasingly reliant on the promotional industries – a dynamic that has influenced how record companies view recording artists and popular music not only as commodities, but also as instruments of promotion. Critically reflecting on a wide range of brand-related strategies and uses, this book asks: what is popular music used in such ways *for*, what does it *do* (or what do brand partners hope it does) and why does its promotional character *matter*? With the scales tipped firmly in favour of commercial considerations, a new system of promotional gatekeeping threatens to circumscribe the diversity of musical sounds, voices and perspectives privileged.

The Music Industries Meet the Promotional Industries

The music industries' digital transition has been widely – and problematically – heralded as a democratizing music revolution. In a fast-changing media environment shaped by the introduction of ever-new digital formats, products and services, how we learn about, access and consume music has changed and continues to change in fundamental ways. Listeners have never had more options: the digital media system boasts an overwhelming array of online media stores, streaming services and social media sites accessible via computers, tablets and smartphones, all of which have rendered popular music exceedingly abundant and instantaneously available on demand. In a culture of purportedly 'free' digital content, we have also seen the extension and intensification of property relations linked to creative works, with the music publishing and live performance industries playing key roles alongside the recording industry. Recorded music, the linchpin in the music business models that dominated for much of the twentieth century, still lies at the heart of everyday listening practices. However, the ways that the recording industry seeks to profit from popular music has undergone an extraordinary transformation. This book focuses on the central role of marketing within this commercial system. It highlights how business-to-business (B2B) licensing agreements – arrangements through which music companies sell music to a range of media and brand partners – serve as a crucial complement to the sale of music to end consumers in the contemporary music industries.

Industry cries regarding a 'crisis' in profitability set off in the wake of Napster's launch in 1999 dominated discussions of the first decade of the music industries' digital transition. Seeking to safeguard generous revenues from compact disc (CD) sales amid the advent of peer-to-peer (P2P) file sharing and the spread of unauthorized downloading, record companies initially adopted aggressively protective business strategies, including legal action. After years of stalling and deferment, the recording industry then experimented with various new business models, spearheading a period of substantive industry reconfiguration and restructuring. Figures compiled by the International Federation of the Phonographic

Industry (IFPI), a recording industry lobby group, suggest that in 2012, the value of global recorded music revenues grew for the first time since 1999, reaching US$16.5 billion, as compared with the figure of US$27.8 billion achieved more than a decade earlier (Smirke 2013). Revenues from digital formats (downloads, streaming) rose to US$6.85 billion in 2014, matching the revenues generated by physical formats (CD, vinyl) – a first for the global recording industry (IFPI 2015: 6). Moreover, if music publishing revenues are added to the equation, the worldwide music copyright industry exceeded US$25 billion in 2014, according to music industry economist Will Page (Ingham 2015a) – a staggering figure that does not even include live music, sponsorship and merchandise revenues (Peoples 2015a). The branding business – a category that includes tour and festival sponsorships, endorsement deals and synchronization ('sync') revenues for the use of music in television, advertising, films and games – reportedly generates roughly US$2 billion for the music industries (*Billboard* 2016). Although their traditional business models have been seriously undermined by digital distribution, these figures suggest that copyright owners have found ways to make money off music in the digital age nevertheless.

Despite declining record sales, the old guard of the CD era music industries, the major music companies, have proven resilient. Universal Music Group (UMG), Sony Music Entertainment and Warner Music Group (WMG), the 'Big Three' record companies, boast deep rosters that feature top-selling stars and are also powerhouses in music publishing. The continued market dominance of the majors is a result of a key shift in business strategies and practices informing the 'monetization' (i.e. converting into money) of music: what was formerly primarily a *record* business now centres on the generation of multiple revenue streams. As entertainment marketing and brand management scholar Kristin J. Lieb explains, CDs and digital music files are no longer 'the artist's primary product' but 'are instead used as brand pieces ... for artists to use as they pursue more profitable sales channels. Licensing, touring, and the sale of merchandise have become increasingly important parts of the artist's profit portfolio' (Lieb 2013: 70). Recorded music, though still essential, is now just one music product among many connected to a different product: the 'artist-brand' (see also Klein et al. 2016; Meier 2015; Stahl and Meier 2012). The recording artist 'personality' is the primary hub around which various 'ancillary' products and licensing agreements may be forged.

Technological change is only part of the story of the music industries' digital era makeover. Also crucial has been the growth of the promotional industries (advertising, branding, marketing and public relations) (Davis 2013), and the corresponding emergence of a 'promotional culture' in which communications designed to facilitate 'some kind of self-advantaging exchange' have become 'virtually co-extensive with our produced symbolic world' (Wernick 1991: 181–2; see also Aronczyk and Powers 2010; McAllister and West 2013). The enveloping logic of branding has not only shaped the range of business opportunities available to recording artists and music companies today, but also the 'common sense' that governs decision-making regarding the appropriate distance between musicians and corporations, art and commerce. The positioning of recording artists *as* brands – and the drive to pair them with partnering brands – is consistent with wider changes inside neoliberal capitalism. Amid expanding privatization, marketization and commodification, the use of branding has spread from the corporate world into the reaches of the public and not-for-profit spheres, and is applied not only to organizations but also individuals (Aronczyk and Powers 2010) – even nations (Aronczyk 2013) and 'the self' (Hearn 2008). From a music industry perspective, recording artists may be seen as 'person brands' whose 'commercial value comes from the possible extensions of their respective star "brands"' (Lieb 2013: 49) via merchandising, licensing, branding and sponsorship opportunities.

The positioning of recording artist personae as private property to be mass marketed via multiple media is not new. The case of recording, radio and film star Bing Crosby provides an early example of carefully executed cross-media promotion; more recently, music industry executives have used the language of corporate branding to describe the image cultivated by rock bands such as U2 (Negus 1992: 24, 71–2). However, the notion of the *artist as brand* as a concept, strategy and set of business arrangements has assumed greater significance in a context marked by shrinking record sales and a swelling number of branding opportunities. Furthermore, changes to recording contract terms – the introduction of the '360 deal' – have enabled record companies to take a cut of revenue streams that formerly lay beyond their reach, including endorsement branding, touring and merchandising income (see Stahl and Meier 2012; Marshall 2013). The prospects and practices of the music industries and the promotional industries have become increasingly interdependent and intertwined. As a result of brand partnerships, popular music has emerged as a dominant form of advertising music or, more broadly, promotional music.

Advertisers and brands have eagerly followed in the footsteps of consumers in the migration from old media to new and for good reason. The branding potential of popular music – online and offline – is part of a bigger marketing picture. According to Swedish brand communication agency Heartbeats International, which specializes in branding with music,

The same digital technology that changed the music industry is changing advertising as we know it. In a world where everyone is connected all the time and customers are in charge of the remote control, the rules of communication have transformed. ... Music branding ... offers a strategic way to reach consumers in ways that traditional advertising can't. (Heartbeats International 2009: 5)

In a world of 'on-demand' media, ad blocking and tremendous competition for audience attention, marketing, advertising and branding executives have turned to popular music in order to make marketing communications more inviting and even desirable. Brands' interest in popular music is rooted in its perceived ability to overcome audience distraction, signify a type of cultural authenticity and credibility, and connect with listeners on an emotional level. The top executives involved in 'marketing with music' 'don't just pair artists with trademarks – they shape the culture', claims *Billboard* (2016). Contemporary music-related marketing and branding is distinct from the well-established practice of using background music to create a desired mood or atmosphere, as in the case of standard incidental music, film scores and elevator music. Consumer and media brands[1] now attempt to take the process a step further: they seek to insinuate promotional messages into webs of positive associations tied to popular music, and capitalize on those emotions, feelings and moods through targeted marketing strategies.

From Marketing Music to Popular Music as Promotion: Key Concepts and Terminology

This book distinguishes the now conventional practices of promoting new music releases and live performances via radio, print advertisements, television commercials, billboards, music videos, appearances on talk shows and so on from what I mean by popular music *as* promotion. Marketing and marketing research have grown in significance across the cultural industries in recent decades, often eroding creative workers' independence from commerce and commercialism (Hesmondhalgh 2013a: 233–5). Marketing has become such a central consideration that music marketing and artist publicity are no longer limited to the more traditional media channels. Significantly, partnerships with brands are seen as additional sites not only for promoting music, but also for using music to market other products, services and brands. Through such licensing and branding agreements music is rendered a marketing instrument – a promotional text. Many music-related branding deals are arranged under the auspices of mutual *cross-promotion* – a notion that this book complicates by revealing the power relations that govern such arrangements.

I draw on a range of marketing and business terms in order to conceptualize the transformation of popular music into a form of promotion. Following Andrew Wernick, I understand *promotion* as a broad set of practices that 'crosses the line between advertising, packaging, and design, and is applicable, as well, to activities beyond the immediately commercial', and 'promotionalism' as a dominant cultural condition (Wernick 1991: 181). Our media environment and even physical spaces are saturated with messages designed to persuade. This broader system does not simply promote consumerism: it also endorses market values. Defining *branding* is no straightforward task, given its wide range of uses and the ever-new thinking on the subject contributed by marketers, as Liz Moor explains, but in general it 'tends to have a much more expansive notion of the appropriate *media* for communications than either advertising or other aspects of marketing, and it tends to take a much more strategic, programmatic and totalizing approach to such communications' (Moor 2007: 7–8; emphasis in original). It is closely connected to promotion in my use. In the business world, *brands* are seen as a form of private property linked to reputation, whereas branding is viewed as a type of marketing strategy and activity. According to one marketing communications textbook,

> A brand is an intangible, legally protectable, valuable asset. It is how a company is perceived by customers (or the target audience). It is the image, associations and inherent value customers put on your product and services. Brands include intangible attributes and values. ... A brand is far more than just a logo or a name. ... It is the complete customer experience (the integrated sum of all the marketing mix and the communications mix from products to customer service, from packaging to advertising, from rumour to discussion). (Smith and Zook 2011: 32)

Another claims that 'a brand represents the full "personality" of the company and is the interface between a company and its audience' (Davis 2009: 12). The fact that companies are perceived as having personalities according to this logic is one of the reasons why marketers deem certain kinds of music, and not others, to be appropriate for the image they attempt to communicate in their promotional and branding activities.

One term used to characterize advertisers' and brands' strategic use of music is sonic branding – also known as music branding, sound branding and audio branding – which 'refers to the use of sound to enhance brand awareness, appeal, and cohesion' (Powers 2010: 293). While such terminology is used primarily by executives who specialize in this area, the practice – in principle if not in name – is becoming more common-place and multi-platform. John Groves, a pioneer in this approach, cites 1995 as the first year that he 'was paid specifically for consulting and advising about the process of creating a Sound Identity and not just music production' (Groves n.d.: 1). Sound identities are used to com-municate and bolster brand identities. Sonic branding can involve the creation of 'audio logos' – brief aural hooks designed to be '[m]ore concise than a theme song and subtler than a jingle' (Jurgensen 2012). These mnemonics or 'memory trigger[s]' (Nygren, personal communica-tion, 2009) are typically two- to five-note melodic figures that do not include slogans, as in the case of the three-second Intel audio logo.

I use the terms *music branding* and *music-related branding* inter-changeably to signal a broad range of practices that involve the licensing, creation and 'curation' of popular music by consumer and media brands. Branding with music does not stop with audio logos, nor is it simply a matter of licensing music for use in advertising campaigns. There has been growing recognition among many marketers that taste in music is related to identity formation, and that this link can be mined in efforts to build and capitalize on distinctive brand identities. The strategic music-consulting world is currently advising brands to use particular types of music or sound identities as a means of uniting the many plat-forms used to communicate these brand identities. While the 'emotional powers of audio have long been understood to add storytelling value to a marketing initiative', audio branding company Elias Arts (2011) claims, music's unique power lies in its ability to function as 'connective tissue'. More than 'an audio logo or brand soundtrack', according to branding specialist Marcel de Bie, 'sonic branding is the totality of the sonic expe-rience' (quoted in Khicha 2008). For instance, a brand's sound may be communicated across television commercials, websites, retail spaces and even music on-hold (MOH) heard by telephone callers. In this way, the strategic choice of the popular music inserted within media texts and retail spaces may be used to connect virtual and 'bricks-and-mortar' brand experiences. Strong brand identities are forged not only through strategically chosen music, but also through alignment with the musi-cians, celebrities and media personalities behind the music.

When used primarily for the purposes of branding or promoting other products, services and brands, popular music becomes a type of *branded entertainment* or *advertainment*. In her analysis of the branding of female pop stars, Lieb remarks on 'the increasingly blurring lines between enter-tainment content and advertising – now called "branded entertainment"' (Lieb 2013: 53). On a basic level, marketers and advertisers regard branded entertainment as product placement within media texts and branded sponsorship of live events (Elliot 2010a). Advertainment is 'programming designed to sell as it entertains' (Deery 2004: 1). More grandiosely, such strategies are pitched as part of 'a fundamental transformation from an intrusion-based marketing economy to an invitation-based model' (Donaton 2004: 3). This decisive shift, marketers argue, offers 'the opportunity to recreate an emotional link with a consumer, for whom the brand has often lost its legitimacy over recent years' (Lehu 2007: 238). Marketing boosterism aside, content-related partnerships between consumer brands and entertainment businesses have emerged as a standard component of the marketing toolkit. The media environment is overflowing with advertisements, logos, product placements and the like, but due to their sheer pervasiveness, these promotional texts often dissolve into marketing 'clutter'. Promotion 'appears everywhere and, at the same time, we no longer notice its presence' (Davis 2013: 5). From the perspective of marketers, this tendency for promotional messages to recede into the background is seen as a challenge they aim to overcome, hence the turn to branded entertainment and advertainment. In a media environment characterized by entertainment and information 'overload', and in which audiences can evade promotional messages with ease, brands use popular music in their efforts to be entertaining, attention-grabbing, culturally relevant and, ultimately, persuasive.

As part of this pursuit of legitimacy, hip lifestyle brands have sought to position themselves as active participants in and 'curators' of culture. Advertisements, meanwhile, have been pitched as the 'new radio' – the new medium for promoting music releases – especially for independent and lesser known artists who have been frozen out of mainstream promotional channels, such as commercial radio and MTV (for an overview and critique, see Klein 2009: 59–78). Yet when placed in other audiovisual media, popular music actually assumes a decidedly different role than it does on radio. In advertising in particular, songs are played in abbreviated form, reduced to choruses or 'hooks' in order to create a certain mood or achieve the maximum 'catchy' effect quickly. As such, they arguably function much like the jingles they have replaced. By design, the music is subordinated to the brand message: from the perspective of the advertiser, it is more important that the audience remembers the brand name than the featured artist. Extending beyond just television commercials, within retail and coffee franchises we likewise have seen the privileging of soundtracks that contain music by original artists and the use of in-store music as an advertising tool (e.g. via branded compilation albums) (Kassabian 2004: 209). Fashion chains such as H&M and Topshop have featured live DJs as a way of communicating a sound identity within the retail environment. We have witnessed the saturation of both media and physical commercial environments, then, by popular music whose use abides by a promotional logic: its purpose is ultimately to reinforce the brand.

Anahid Kassabian uses the term *ubiquitous musics* to describe popular music not of our own choosing that we nevertheless encounter in everyday life – musics inserted into retail stores, films, television programmes, commercials, video games and other media, which she suggests are not 'actively listened to in any recognizable sense' (Kassabian 2002: 131; see also Kassabian 2013). It is fitting that in coining the term ubiquitous musics, Kassabian took her cue from Mark Weiser's (1991) term 'ubiquitous computing'; today, ubiquitous musics and ubiquitous computing have merged, with the mobility characteristic of both allowing for seamless integration into daily life. Elsewhere (Meier 2011), building on Kassabian's terminology, I use the term 'promotional ubiquitous musics' to describe the use of music by advertisers and brands. Whereas ubiquitous musics suggest 'a kind of "sourcelessness"' (Kassabian 2002: 137), promotional ubiquitous musics reflect strategic decisions made by a specific source: brands. The migration of popular music into new listening contexts is tied to the twin phenomena of ubiquitous music and ubiquitous promotion. It is the increasingly strategic and calculated pairing of popular music and brand partner – not the presence of popular music in and of itself – that makes contemporary music-related branding practices distinctive.

In this book, I shift my terminology to *popular music as promotion* in order to prioritize the significance not of the particular musics, but instead, of their character as promotion under this model. According to Wernick, promotion 'is defined not by what it says but by what it does, with respect to which its stylistic and semantic contents are purely secondary' (Wernick 1991: 184). When popular music is used as a form of promotion, what it actually sounds like and says is secondary to what it *does* – or is intended to do. Thus, the semiotic diversity reflected in the examples discussed at the beginning of this chapter does not alter the promotional character of the use of these songs. Cultural factors and meanings tied to music are still of paramount importance, hence the turn to popular music in the first place, but they are subordinated to the brand's objectives – to the promotional intent behind the music's use. The choice of particular songs is rooted in instrumental business thinking, even as it may reflect creative considerations.

What does popular music as promotion 'do' more broadly? In its broad range of promotional uses, popular music contributes to the aestheticization of consumerism and to the production of 'affect' – of certain emotions, feelings and moods (Hesmondhalgh 2013b: 11) – in service of capital accumulation. Inside contemporary promotional culture, consumer brands have shown interest in 'experiential' and multisensory marketing strategies designed to capitalize on the affective dimensions of popular music (Powers 2010: 288–9). This book considers how various corporations attempt to cultivate and till emotional and affective bonds with 'desirable' audiences through the use of popular music, and how recording artists are advised by music industry executives to prioritize explicitly commercial considerations. According to Jonathan Sterne, 'Programmed music in a mall produces consumption because the music works as an architectural element of a built space devoted to consumerism' (Sterne 1997: 25). In a similar way, when used as a branding tool, popular music works to foster consumer-oriented dispositions, identities, values and desires.

Popular music is a complex and much debated term – one sometimes used to label certain musics as 'inferior' or, conversely, 'authentic', as the products of mass media or, conversely, 'the people', or simply as music that is well liked and widely listened to (for an overview, see Middleton 1990: 3–6). I use the term popular music not with the intent of making judgements about the quality of music or as a way of signalling particular genres (e.g. pop music), sales figures or audience sizes. Instead, I use it as an umbrella term that designates a wide range of music produced as a commodity within the commercial music system, including pop, rock, hip-hop, R&B, country and electronica, among other genres. In the twenty-first century, the process of sound recording has become unmoored from corporate control, and it is now possible for musicians to independently produce and market recorded tracks from personal laptops or tablets virtually anywhere: the means of production are now more accessible. This analysis centres on songs by recording and performing artists that are recorded as 'tracks' and albums, either under contract to record labels or independent of record label participation, and then sold in the music marketplace (even if those tracks are sometimes given away for free for the purposes of promoting other products, such as live performances or merchandise). I am primarily concerned with professional music making and the capitalist relations of production that underpin the promotional deployment of popular music. Not all popular music is written and performed within this commercial and promotional framework, of course. Moreover, there are musics produced within the commercial music system that I would not classify as popular music (e.g. classical and art musics) that may be included in promotional texts, but which are not my focus here.

My use of the term *commodity* to describe popular music is not intended to diminish or comment whatsoever on the legitimacy or artistry of popular music. Rather, it underscores the fact that the products of the music industries are created and circulated as objects of exchange within capitalist markets. Thus, commercial considerations inform the production of popular music: the drive to turn a profit means that creativity is channelled in particular ways, although creativity is not necessarily stifled within this system. As David Hesmondhalgh argues, the commodification of culture, a process whose origins reach back centuries, is 'fundamentally ambivalent' – both 'enabling and constraining' (Hesmondhalgh 2013a: 70). The commodification of music cannot be adequately conceptualized simply in terms of capitalist 'co-optation' or incorporation. As Tiziana Terranova's analysis of digital capitalism and the internet suggests, many popular cultural forms 'originat[e] within a field that is always and already capitalism' (Terranova 2000: 38–9). What is distinctive today is the ways that popular music is being produced not just as a commodity, but also as a form of promotion intended to help sell other products, services and brands within this capitalist system – something I see as a constraining force that places decidedly commercial parameters around creative expression.

Core Argument and Approach

This book conceptualizes the promotional agreements and partnerships forged between music companies, consumer brands and media companies as an extension of previous logics of commodification. I argue that new branding strategies adopted in both the music industries and promotional industries in the twenty-first century have come together to transform popular music and recording artists who perform it into vehicles for promoting all manner of media and consumer products. While the *content* of the popular music under consideration here is cultural (i.e. primarily symbolic), the *intent* behind its use by marketers is primarily promotional. Its function and usefulness as a marketing instrument is prioritized and privileged by brands. While not all popular music is drawn into this promotional system, music and branding executives treat a very broad array of popular music as a resource that can potentially be tapped into and attached to brands.

Drawing on critical theory and political economy, I examine the tightening relationship between music worlds and brand worlds – a relationship I characterize not as a simple merger, but, crucially, as the colonization of the former by the latter. After all, the brands typically devise the strategies, select the music and dictate the rules – all significant factors when evaluating the power relations that define these pairings. Promotional industry practices have been imported into the music industries. Though not total or complete, this process of colonization is intensifying. A key product of these colliding business strategies has been record companies' reconstitution of the core popular music commodity as an 'artist-brand' to be licensed to brand partners; the logics of branding have been embraced in the music industries, with recording artists now likened to brands through and through. Given the drive to instrumentalize and rationalize popular music under the music-related branding paradigm, I consider the relevance of Max Horkheimer and Theodor Adorno's ([1944] 2002) 'culture industry' thesis in this context. Mindful of the limitations of this conceptualization, I also draw on important critiques of and advancements over this theory, especially those offered by the 'cultural industries' approach to studying the political economy of communication and culture (Miège 1989; Garnham 1990; Hesmondhalgh 2013a). In order to understand the tensions between not just creativity and commerce, but now creativity and *promotion*, I consider what might make the promotional industries and the texts they produce (Wernick 1991; Davis 2013) distinct from the cultural industries more generally.

The commercial logics in which the production and circulation of popular music are now steeped speak to shifts in the capital accumulation strategies that have accompanied what has become an increasingly 'flexible' capitalism. The promotional and music industries have begun to merge in consequential ways as a result of political, economic, technological and cultural shifts that first started to take hold in the 1970s and 1980s, and then were accelerated in the 1990s and 2000s with widespread adoption of new branding techniques combined with the digital delivery of media content. Drawing on David Harvey's (1990, 2005) accounts of 'post-Fordism' or 'flexible accumulation', neoliberalism and 'accumulation by dispossession' (terms unpacked in chapter 4), this book considers the relationship between the promotional character of popular music, the promotional culture in which music is ascribed meaning, and a capitalist system characterized by the extension of trade, markets and property relations. Following Simon C. Jones and Thomas G. Schumacher (1992) and Adam Krims (2007), I locate the shift from more homogeneous background music and jingles to more targeted and diverse promotional musics within the shift from Fordism to post-Fordism – 'a mutation in capitalist accumulation that has sufficiently inflected cultural processes as to call for new ways of theorizing music and its social effects' (Krims 2007: 94). Within the contemporary music industries, we see a complex interplay between the enduring rigidities associated with Fordism and the dynamism associated with post-Fordism, as suggested by the institutionalization of increasingly restrictive recording contracts and continued oligopolistic market conditions on the one hand, and by the proliferation of niche music markets and tremendous cultural diversity on the other. We may see considerable music production 'from below', but much of music's monetization still comes 'from above', as a handful of corporations continue to monopolize profits. The decentralization of popular musical production processes has been countered by a consolidation of corporate power. I consider troubling ramifications of the changing relationship between culture and commerce that has emerged against this backdrop.

This book uses a conceptual framework that draws on the above critiques in order to interpret my empirical research on the commercial changes that are uniting the music and promotional industries. I conducted 36 in-depth interviews with people involved in licensing music and forging relationships with brands; attended or listened to recordings of numerous music industry conferences; and analysed popular and trade press coverage of new music business models and branding strategies. The interviews, which took place between 2009 and 2011, were conducted with executives who worked for record companies (major and independent), music publishers (major and independent), artist management companies, advertising firms, sound branding firms and music supervision companies (my interviewees are listed in the reference section).[2] Almost all of these executives were based in Toronto, New York City or Los Angeles – North American cities that operate at the heart of both the music and advertising industries. Not all of these interviews are cited in this book, but each has helped me gain an understanding of the broader industrial context in which music-related branding agreements are made. My interview programme was approved by the University of Western Ontario Research Ethics Board. My interviewees consented to be interviewed and many agreed to be cited by name. I have not disclosed the names of those who indicated that they would prefer to remain anonymous.

I make no claims of developing an exhaustive and representative sample of any particular business. Rather, my wide sampling of professionals involved with connecting recording artists and brands provided the on-the-ground perspectives necessary for me to paint a picture of a larger promotional system comprised of various interlinking businesses, each with an overlapping interest in popular music. By interviewing experts in their fields, I was able to understand the business strategies and intentions behind the work that goes into, and these professionals' perceptions of, the pairing of popular music and brands.

Chapter Outline

My argument regarding the subsumption of popular music's cultural goals to promotional ones in the digital age – and the consequences of this dynamic for working artists and for music – unfolds in the chapters that follow. Chapter 1 expands on the conceptual framework introduced in the current chapter, examining key critical perspectives used for understanding the industrial production of culture and associated tensions between creativity and commerce. Beginning with Horkheimer and Adorno's ([1944] 2002) foundational 'culture industry' thesis, and then adding the necessary correctives provided by the 'cultural industries' approach (Miège 1989; Garnham 1990; Hesmondhalgh 2013a), I suggest that these two sets of critiques need not be seen as incompatible. On the contrary, drawing on critical theory to understand constraints produced by capitalism as such and cultural industries scholarship to refine the analysis on an industry-specific level productively allows for the advancement of two levels of analysis – both essential for conceptualizing the changes that have wedged culture and promotion together. In so doing, we can see the use of popular music as a marketing tool as an expected outcome of the capitalist production of music, though by no means inevitable. The primacy of marketability and sales potential have always informed which recording artists are signed by record companies and which material is recorded, released and promoted. The recruitment of artists suitable for music licensing and brand partnerships is a new extension of an old commercial logic. Chapter 1 then provides the historical context necessary to understand the intensifying relationship between recording artists and brands. It explores the origins of music's promotional uses, tracing comparable practices back to the nineteenth century and discussing the commodity character of music under earlier industrial models. It then considers the role of popular music in advertising and film in the twentieth century.

Chapter 2 investigates the music industries' digital transition. It first examines the distinctive competitive logics and corporate structures that supported and defined the 'old' music industries in order to weigh the persistent continuities against the sweeping changes that have enveloped the music industries in the twenty-first century. An unfortunate consequence of the increased access to sound recording and distribution technologies in the 'new' music industries is that more recording artists are competing for fewer dollars in a market for music copyrights still dominated by the major music companies. The importance placed on marketing – always a key force in the music industries – has only deepened. The chapter focuses on how old and new industrial logics and commercial realities have come together to produce a type of business thinking that has placed music licensing and agreements with brands at the heart of music company marketing and monetization strategies. Drawing on field interviews and trade press coverage, I discuss the latest waves of industry-wide consolidation and underscore the continuing dominance of the major music companies in marketing music and creating stars, but with a key alteration: the 'artist-brand', not the sound recording, has become the core popular music commodity today – a development reinforced by the institutionalization of 360-degree recording contracts.

Chapter 3 analyses the intensifying relationship between recording artists and partnering media and consumer brands in the twenty-first century, building on the insights provided by executives involved in forging such deals. The chapter charts popular music's colonization by brands through ever-tightening and increasingly strategic promotional arrangements. I problematize the positive light in which executives have pitched music placements in advertising, television programmes and video games, and other forms of brand partnerships (e.g. branded festivals) as a viable mode of helping musicians to make a living from making music. These relationships are not mutually advantageous in any straightforward sense. Instead, the brands are in charge and have considerable power to dictate the terms of these relationships, a sobering reality that has translated into a drastic drop in licensing fees paid to aspiring and non-star artists. Worryingly, this promotional system favours happy thoughts and upbeat attitudes: it prioritizes music that is uncritical – at the very least with respect to perspectives on brands and the capitalist system that is further commercializing culture – and thus circumscribes the diversity of ideas expressed. This analysis is by no means intended to suggest that the old music system, which was more fully controlled by major record labels, was more advantageous to working artists. Instead, it identifies new challenges and dynamics of domination inherent to the brand-driven promotional system on which artists have become increasingly dependent. Brands have become new gatekeepers of music's promotion.

Chapter 4 returns to the broader political-economic context that is shaping the morphing relationship between promotion and culture. Pulling together a theoretical framework informed by scholarship on post-Fordism and neoliberalism with the critique of cultural commodification provided by critical theory, it focuses on the instrumentalization of not only music but also affects under new music licensing approaches. To illustrate these dynamics, the analysis explores the example of music licensing software engineered to lend unprecedented efficiency to the music licensing process. This software enables music licensors to sift through music catalogues according to composer, genre, lyrics, era, instrumentation, metre, tempo, rhythmic complexity, gender, keyword and mood. This chapter demonstrates how the turn toward customization and ever more targeted marketing characteristic of the post-Fordist era does not undermine, but actually complements the push toward rationalization typically associated with Fordism. Drawing on Martyn J. Lee's (1993) terminology, I suggest that the increasingly promotional form of popular music might serve as an 'ideal-type' commodity form under post-Fordism. Given the challenges regarding recording artist remuneration discussed in chapter 3, the chapter closes with some practical strategies that music makers might consider in efforts to counter the commercial logics that have taken hold inside this capitalist system and promotional culture, including hitting companies where it hurts the most: the brand.

Overall, this book contends that the transformation of popular music into a form of promotion reflects the acceleration and intensifying logic of capital accumulation under neoliberal, post-Fordist capitalism – the latest phase in the long-term process of commodifying culture. Chapter 5 returns to the central argument and critiques advanced, gestures toward parallel instances of the spread of promotion in other cultural industries, and highlights important considerations for future research, including additional music gatekeepers that are not the focus of this book: information and technology (IT) companies. Instead, my focus is on how the cultural industries are being remade in the image of the promotional industries in consequential ways in the digital age, with the music industries serving as an exemplary case. In order to understand the significance of this shift, it is important to first examine the longer historical trajectory of cultural commodification, the rise of music-related promotion and associated critiques, which is the task of chapter 1.

1

From Commodities to Commercials? The Rise of Promotion in the Music Industries

Under capitalism, corporations produce popular music as a commodity in order to generate profits – a logic inherent to this economic system. In the twenty-first century, we have seen the introduction of a host of new music-related products and services in addition to the more customary complement of records, concerts and traditional merchandise (T-shirts, souvenirs). The music marketplace has been flooded by: digital downloads available for purchase from online digital media stores (e.g. Apple iTunes, Google Play); music streaming services (e.g. Spotify, Apple Music, Amazon Prime Music); video streaming sites (e.g. YouTube, Vevo); music-based talent shows (e.g. *American Idol*, *The Voice*); and artist-branded merchandise ranging from perfumes to karaoke 'apps'. Furthermore, pre-existing popular songs are woven throughout television programmes, films, advertisements and video games. Popular music is not only positioned as a consumer good sold to listeners, but also as intellectual property to be monetized more widely through the pursuit of various sponsorship, endorsement, branding and licensing deals. The observation that popular music is produced as a commodity within this industrial system, then, is hardly groundbreaking.

To liken popular music to promotion is perhaps a more contentious move. While each of the above examples may be characterized as commodities, not all abide by the same business logics: there is a meaningful distinction to be made between those products sold by businesses to end customers (B2C) and those that involve transactions in the business-to-business (B2B) market. Branding and licensing agreements with media and consumer brand partners – the focus of this book – belong to the latter category. Importantly, these business arrangements generate income for copyright owners and allow partnering brands to use popular music as a promotional instrument.

In order to set the stage for my examination of the expansion of music-related branding and licensing practices, this chapter establishes the intellectual and historical context that frames my understanding of the commodification of culture as an historical process. To begin, I examine key critiques of capitalist cultural production found in critical theory and critical political economy, beginning with Theodor Adorno and Max Horkheimer's 'culture industry' thesis, and then turning to the response provided by the 'cultural industries' approach inaugurated by Bernard Miège (1989) and Nicholas Garnham (1990) and extended by David Hesmondhalgh (2013a). The chapter then traces the emergence of popular music as a device for cross-promotion back to its industrial origins. After first considering music's early commodity forms and precedents for its promotional use beginning in the nineteenth century, I discuss key twentieth-century developments in the evolving relationship between popular music, advertising and mass media. I understand music-related branding and licensing practices as marking an intensification of these earlier industrial and commercial forms.

Popular Music as Commodity, Culture as Industry: Critical Theory and Cultural Production

What does it mean to describe something as a commodity? In Karl Marx's formulation, commodities meet certain human needs – they contain a 'use value' (a qualitative factor) – but, crucially, are produced for the purpose of exchange: 'exchange value' (a quantitative factor) drives capitalist production (Marx [1867] 1990: 125–31). As Hesmondhalgh points out, 'At its most basic level, [commodification] involves producing things not only for use but also for *exchange*' (Hesmondhalgh 2013a: 69; emphasis in original). While the extension of exchange relations throughout the spheres of communication and culture may now be widely acknowledged as the default reality, the consequences of the industrialization and commodification of symbolic and expressive forms have long been debated. Within cultural and social theory, a foundational but disputed account of the constraints and detrimental effects that accompany the treatment of culture as value-generating property came in the form of Max Horkheimer and Theodor Adorno's 'culture industry' thesis. These German-Jewish philosophers, originators of the 'critical theory' of society initiated at the Institute for Social Research at Frankfurt, presciently claimed that '[a]dvertising and the culture industry are merging technically no less than economically' (Horkheimer and Adorno [1944] 2002: 133). The culture industry thesis raises serious questions about the nature of capitalism and freedom, art and entertainment that continue to resonate today.

When Horkheimer and Adorno introduced their culture industry thesis in one of the Frankfurt School's defining texts, *Dialectic of Enlightenment* ([1944] 2002), the pairing of the terms 'culture' and 'industry' was polemical and intended to shock. According to this Marxian critique, the capitalist social relations and instrumental rationality that underpin commodity production had invaded what ostensibly had been autonomous from such forces: culture had been commodified. As objects of exchange and commercial calculation, Horkheimer and Adorno argue, 'the irreconcilable elements of culture, art, and amusement have been subjected equally to the concept of purpose and thus brought under a single false denominator: the totality of the culture industry' (Horkheimer and Adorno [1944] 2002: 108). From the perspective of private media corporations, the purpose of culture was to produce profits; the drive to generate a healthy return on investment was foundational to commercial interest in cultural production. As Shane Gunster sums up, 'the culture industry thesis strives to answer two questions: What specific properties does culture develop when it is produced and sold as a commodity? And what must human beings become in order to maximize the meaning and pleasure taken from cultural commodities?' (Gunster 2004: 10).

The culture industry thesis unfolds from Horkheimer and Adorno's critique of the self-destruction of enlightenment. *Dialectic of Enlightenment* and Horkheimer's *Eclipse of Reason* were born of a specific historical moment and the atrocities that era witnessed: the terror of National Socialism (Nazism) and the Holocaust. Horkheimer and Adorno conceptualize the rise of fascism and genocide in relation to a wider 'prognosis regarding the associated lapse from enlightenment into positivism' and 'the identity of intelligence and hostility' (Horkheimer and Adorno [1944] 2002: xii). After fleeing Germany for the United States, they developed a critique of American capitalist democracy and the role of mass media therein, identifying parallels between the modes of thinking dominant in the German and American contexts. Horkheimer and Adorno examine the dialectic of domination that had accompanied the progression of 'rational' thought in the modern era and conclude that capitalism had facilitated the formalization of instrumental reason. There had been a shift from 'objective reason', which is concerned with *ends*, to 'subjective reason', whose focus is on *means* – on 'serv[ing] the subject's interest' (Horkheimer [1947] 2004: 3–4). When self-interest becomes the basis for orienting and exercising reason, reason itself becomes an instrument (Horkheimer [1947] 2004: 14). Used solely in this way, rational thought can produce and problematically justify fundamentally irrational outcomes. As J.M. Bernstein explains, however, 'the key to instrumental reason is not means-end logic, but the primacy of the abstract over the concrete, the universal over the particular' (Bernstein 2001: 239 n. 3).

Horkheimer and Adorno's critique is rooted in the ways that the particular and the universal are treated as commensurate under 'identitarian thinking' or 'identity thinking'. They argue that the subsumption of diverse objects under abstract concepts works to highlight sameness at the expense of difference, as the singular and unique is problematically rendered equivalent to some universal that it is imagined to represent: 'cognition of non-identity ... seeks to say what something is, while identitarian thinking says what something comes under, what it exemplifies or represents, and what, accordingly, it is not itself' (Adorno [1966] 1973: 149). Identitarian thinking fails to account for the 'remainder' – what is unique to the individual and is not captured by the concept used to represent it. That which is 'other' and incommensurable is nevertheless assimilated, which can have deeply troubling consequences. This mode of thinking can reinforce stereotypes, for instance, and produce hostility to difference (Horkheimer and Adorno [1944] 2002: 172).

The capitalist principle of exchange is the paradigmatic form of this type of 'thinking in equivalents'. The commodity form is a powerful force of rationalization; its social relations work to assimilate difference. The culture industry thesis argues that culture is no longer exempt from these forces of rationalization and homogenization: 'The conspicuous unity of macrocosm and microcosm confronts human beings with a model of their culture: the false identity of universal and particular. All mass culture under monopoly is identical' (Horkheimer and Adorno [1944] 2002: 95). Horkheimer and Adorno do not use the term identical here to suggest that cultural commodities are exactly alike in terms of content (though they do assert that the effects of processes of standardization are evident). Rather, they argue that *as* commodities, different cultural products and practices are treated as equivalent regardless of their content; they are rendered commensurate by virtue of their exchangeability on the market. As a commodity, 'culture – no matter what form it takes – is to be measured by norms not inherent to it and which have nothing to do with the quality of the object, but rather with some type of abstract standards imposed from without' (Adorno [1960] 2001a: 113).

Horkheimer and Adorno's term 'culture industry' signals the processes of standardization, rationalization, homogenization and massification they see as inherent to commodified culture. In the United States, by the 1940s a relatively small number of publishing, film, music and radio companies had assumed an inordinate amount of control over which cultural commodities were produced, how widely they were distributed and how aggressively they were promoted – decisions made based on the profit motive. A star system was a key aspect of the culture industry apparatus: the production of fame was central to the generation of profits. Horkheimer and Adorno considered the 'controlled manner' in which the culture industry's products were assembled to be 'factory-like' (Horkheimer and Adorno [1944] 2002: 132). Taken together, this culture industry was 'infecting everything with sameness. Film, radio, and magazines form a system' (Horkheimer and Adorno [1944] 2002: 94). Adorno, a musician and composer with tremendously demanding expectations regarding the autonomy and critical orientation of art, dedicated considerable criticism to the purportedly standardized and formulaic character of popular music in particular – 'light' music he saw as driven by essentially substitutable details and hooks (Adorno [1941] 2002b).

Adorno asserted that an industrial approach to cultural production is particularly worrying because culture's critical potential had resided precisely in the individual artwork's singularity: 'Culture is the perennial claim of the particular over the general, as long as the latter remains unreconciled to the former' (Adorno [1960] 2001a: 113). He acknowledged that art had been subordinated to powerful interests even before the development of capitalism (e.g. the Church, nobility) (Adorno [1959] 1993: 20), but claimed that the shift from aristocratic patronage to market mechanisms during the bourgeois era had offered a brief window during which it was possible for artists and composers to achieve unusual degrees of autonomy and independence from society and its institutions. Aspirations to autonomy, understood as '[i]ndependence or freedom from external control or influence' (Hesmondhalgh 2013a: 414), remain a central feature of cultural work and the power relations underpinning the cultural industries today (see Hesmondhalgh and Baker 2011). The profit motive leads to the channelling of symbolic expression toward commercial objectives – corporations pursue sound investments – but, importantly, this system does not snuff out creative freedom altogether. Creativity is essential for the production of ever-new cultural commodities.

The culture industry favours those cultural commodities that will 'sell themselves', however, which means that marketing and promotional considerations do not simply take effect after cultural commodities are already produced. Instead, the primacy of marketability directly informs the types of content and the specific productions in which companies decide to invest in the first place. As Andrew Wernick suggests, 'implicit in Horkheimer and Adorno's account, though they do not consider it as an independent factor, is that one of the ways in which commodification has been a culturally homogenizing force is through the similar ways in which ... the products of the culture industry present themselves to us as objects and sites of a promotional practice. ... The marketing imperative feeds back into their actual construction' (Wernick 1991: 187). This dynamic places finite limits on cultural expression (many ideas and works are seen as unsuitable for financial support), thereby influencing the act of creation itself. Within the music industries, this commercial logic influences which recording artists are signed by record companies and which material is recorded, released and promoted. Songwriters may take into consideration the conventions of commercial radio (acceptable song length, verse-chorus form, popular lyrical themes) when composing – or may be advised to do so by record label artists and repertoire (A&R) and marketing teams.

Commodification and industrialization translate into a corporate bias toward creativity that is 'market-tested' but gestures toward originality. Given large media corporations' risk aversion, these companies seek difference within sameness, according to Adorno:

> The publisher wants a piece of music that is fundamentally the same as all the other current hits and simultaneously fundamentally different from them. Only if it is the same does it have a chance of being sold automatically, without requiring any effort on the part of the customer. ... And only if it is different can it be distinguished from other songs – a requirement for being remembered and hence for being successful. (Adorno [1941] 2002b: 448)

In Adorno's account, this dynamic translates into the production of various cultural commodities that are only superficially different from one another, despite audiences' apparent desire for difference. What he terms 'pseudo-individualization' works to mask what he sees as the standardization characteristic of capitalist cultural production: illusory differences and distinctions provide a 'halo of free choice' (Adorno [1941] 2002b: 445).

Thus far, I have discussed properties purportedly assumed by culture when it is produced as a commodity. How do these characteristics connect to matters of meaning and pleasure? This a complex question, and Horkheimer and Adorno have rightly received considerable criticism for the assumptions they made about the validity of the experiences found in the consumption of cultural commodities – and the constraints they saw as necessarily accompanying the commodity form.

While the culture industry thesis was first formally introduced as such in the chapter entitled 'The Culture Industry: Enlightenment as Mass Deception' in *Dialectic of Enlightenment*, many of the core ideas first surfaced in Adorno's 'On the Fetish-character in Music and the Regression of Listening', where he draws on Marx's analysis of the fetish character of the commodity:

> If the commodity in general combines exchange-value and use-value, then the pure use-value, whose illusion the cultural goods must preserve in completely capitalist society, must be replaced by pure exchange-value, which precisely in its capacity as exchange-value deceptively takes over the function of use-value. The specific fetish character of music lies in this quid pro quo. ... The more inexorably the principle of exchange-value destroys use-values for human beings, the more deeply does exchange-value disguise itself as the object of enjoyment. (Adorno [1938] 2002a: 296; see also Horkheimer and Adorno [1944] 2002: 128)

According to Adorno, the listener's fondness for music commodities was shaped by the star status of certain performers and the best-seller status of certain works, with economic value acting as a proxy for cultural value. He claimed that audience members' capacity to listen had regressed, as the culture industry had bred 'distracted' or 'deconcentrated' modes of listening (Adorno [1938] 2002a: 305). Radio programmes had even, in effect, imposed a process of trivialization onto symphonic works, which likewise encouraged 'quotation listening' (Adorno [1941] 2002c: 263–4) – the type of listening linked to hook-driven popular music.

Overall, Horkheimer and Adorno saw the culture industry and the forms of entertainment, cultural practices and values it promoted as pacifying forces inside the rigidly conformist industrial society of the 1930s and 1940s. Their form of ideology critique considered how cultural consumption framed capitalism as a just system and an inevitable reality. Cultural commodities need not function as explicit capitalist propaganda in order to valorize capitalism, according to Adorno:

> Radio music's ideological tendencies realize themselves regardless of the intent of radio functionaries. There need be nothing intentionally malicious in the maintenance of vested interests. Nonetheless, music under present radio auspices serves to keep listeners from criticizing

social realities; in short, it has a soporific effect upon social consciousness. (Adorno 1945: 212)

By offering representations of a seemingly preordained present, the products of Hollywood and Tin Pan Alley – the New York City-based music publishers and composers that dominated US music sales in the late nineteenth and early twentieth century – curbed audience members' ability to imagine different and more just worlds. It was not necessarily that the culture industry had the power to make people believe things that were untrue; rather, working in concert with the larger political-economic and social system, the culture industry convinced people that they lacked the power to resist that system and effect substantive change – even if they might want to (Horkheimer and Adorno [1944] 2002: 113).

While Horkheimer and Adorno's critique does pinpoint important downsides of the commodification of culture, it does not help us to understand the contradictions of capitalist cultural production, the tensions between creativity and commerce and why great artistic and cultural accomplishments have been achieved within this commercial system nevertheless. According to Adam Krims, within popular music studies, Adorno's critiques of standardization, pseudo-individualization and the regression of listening are considered 'a foundational trauma in the discipline' (Krims 2007: 91). After all, Adorno requires art to 'aspire to impossible levels of autonomy and dialectic' and displays 'seeming contempt for everyday cultural consumption in modern societies' (Hesmondhalgh 2008a: 341). His account lacks 'a sense of the potential autonomy – even in popular cultural production – of the aesthetic from the economic and institutional' and 'a place for agency' (Born 1993: 241). His stance on popular culture is pessimistic and elitist. A diverse spectrum of scholarship ranging from Birmingham School subcultural theory (e.g. Hebdige 1979) to affirmative popular culture studies (e.g. Fiske 1987, 1989) to the cultural industries approach to critical political economy – an approach I will expand on shortly – confronts the question of the commodification of culture and its effects, and comes to very different conclusions than Adorno. In stark contrast to Adorno's dismissiveness, pleasure and entertainment are taken seriously and the interpretative faculties of audiences are recognized.

Popular music is filled with rich cultural meanings and can produce powerful emotional and affective experiences (for a defence of the value of music and its potential for enriching societies, see Hesmondhalgh 2013b). Against Adorno's claims regarding standardization, the wealth of diverse and interesting music that has been produced within this commercial system demonstrates that commodification has not entirely evacuated the originality and sense of uniqueness central to cultural commodities' use value (on which see Ryan 1991: 50–5). Cultural commodities are contradictory and their use value is complex – 'almost limitless' (Garnham 1979: 140). Culture is not simply a commodity like any other; the significance and meaning of different cultural products cannot be read off the commodity form itself. In fact, it is the abundance, not absence, of meaning and emotional attachment to popular music that has motivated media corporations and consumer brands to take such an interest in it in the first place.

Horkheimer and Adorno undoubtedly make problematic assumptions about the aesthetic merits of cultural commodities, hold onto overly rigid notions of acceptable artistic and creative expression, and provide an inadequate account of reception and the capacity of audiences to be attentive and critical. The terminology employed is not only unproductively dismissive at times, but also obscures the real target of their critique: capitalism and the unequal power relations it engenders. According to Fredric Jameson, Horkheimer and Adorno 'are closer to having a theory of "daily life" than they are to having one of "culture" in any contemporary sense' (Jameson 2007: 144). The culture industry thesis and its emphasis on the problems of expanding commodification and the reinforcement of capitalist values helps to explain the emergence of a promotional culture centred on consumerism better than it offers insight into cultural commodities themselves. Even 'culture industry' is not the most apt term for capturing the thrust of their argument:

> As rhetorically productive as the term *industry* might once have been ... the governing logic of the culture industry for Adorno and Horkheimer is provided not by the organizational structures or techniques of industrial production *per se* but rather the capitalist social relations in which they are embedded. In other words, it is commodification – not industrialization – that lies at the heart of the culture industry thesis. (Gunster 2004: 9; emphasis in original)

Horkheimer and Adorno distinguish the commodity character of culture from matters related to ownership structures (Angus and Jhally 1989: 13) – an important distinction to make when evaluating the extent to which the loosening control of record companies over music production today has or has not freed music from capitalist social relations.

However, questions of media ownership *are* central to understanding capitalist cultural production and the power asymmetries that have shaped the music marketplace in the past and still today – even as new opportunities have emerged for musicians to record and release music independently. Just three music companies – Universal Music Group

(UMG), Sony Music Entertainment and Warner Music Group (WMG) – dominate an overwhelming share of the global music market. Their parent corporations wield tremendous power and reach across the mass media landscape, lending credence to Horkheimer and Adorno's argument that our culture is produced by a unitary culture industry: the interests of UMG parent Vivendi stretch across film, television, recorded music, music publishing, merchandising, ticketing and online video hosting (Vivendi 2013); Sony is a key global player in film, television, recorded music, music publishing and video games in addition to consumer electronics (Sony 2016); and WMG owner Access Industries has holdings in media and telecommunications, natural resources and chemicals, real estate and e-commerce (Access Industries 2016). In order to take the analysis a step further and adequately tend to the issues of ownership, market concentration and conglomeration, I draw on a critical lens that has provided an important corrective to Horkheimer and Adorno's lack of attentiveness to the distinctive character of capitalist *cultural* production: the cultural industries approach to critical political economy.

Despite its shortcomings, I suggest that the culture industry thesis provides a foundational starting point for conceptualizing the relationship between the commodification of culture and the collapsing boundary between popular music and promotion, and for expressing the understandable frustration felt with a system that routinely produces unimaginative and inadequate culture. Though not inevitable, the use of popular music as a promotional tool and its entrance into new B2B markets *is* an expected outcome of its commodity character and corporations' corresponding drive to maximize returns on their investments. A means-end logic and a type of thinking in equivalents inform music companies' and brands' interest in popular music. Commodification does not close off meaning and pleasure, however: music's cultural resonance and credibility are central to its appeal to brands, as discussed in chapter 3.

From 'Culture Industry' to 'Cultural Industries': Critical Political Economy and the Media

The origins of the critical political economy of culture and mass media can be traced back to the Marxian critique of the industrialization of culture forwarded by Horkheimer and Adorno (Babe 2009: 18; Hesmondhalgh 2013a: 23–4; Hardy 2014: 10, 26–8). In *The Cultural Industries*, Hesmondhalgh (2013a: 44–7) makes a helpful distinction between two political economy approaches: a North American approach associated with Herbert Schiller, Noam Chomsky, Edward Herman and Robert McChesney, and the European 'cultural industries' approach inaugurated by Bernard Miège (1989) and Nicholas Garnham (1990), and extended by Hesmondhalgh (2013a). I direct my attention to the latter approach, which draws a direct lineage from the culture industry thesis but makes significant modifications to that theory. The term cultural industries loosens the culture industry from its associations with elitism and a particular variant of Marxian economics (Garnham 2005: 18). Hesmondhalgh stresses the significance of the shift from culture industry (singular) to cultural industries (plural): it signals how '*complex* the cultural industries are', how '[t]he commodification of culture ... was a much more *ambivalent* process than was allowed for by Adorno and Horkheimer's cultural pessimism', and how the cultural industries are a '*contested* ... zone of continuing struggle' (Hesmondhalgh 2013a: 24–5; emphasis in original). The cultural industries approach accounts for the 'partial and incomplete process of commodifying culture' – entertainment *and* information (Hesmondhalgh 2013a: 45). It offers a sociological lens through which to analyse how the cultural industries are distinct from other industries; the position of cultural workers; the ways that audience behaviour complicates industrial cultural production; and historical variations (Hesmondhalgh 2013a: 45–7). Miège, Garnham, Hesmondhalgh and other scholars who fall within the cultural industries approach (e.g. Ryan 1991; Toynbee 2000) all argue that the commodification of culture seen across the cultural industries and its effects are far more contradictory than is suggested by Horkheimer and Adorno.

Cultural and media products occupy a distinctive role in societies unlike that of other commodities. The cultural industries involve 'symbolic creativity' and 'the production of social meaning' (Hesmondhalgh 2013a: 6, 16). Symbolic texts entertain, inform and move people. In some instances, they may work to pacify audiences, as Horkheimer and Adorno claim, but in others they may challenge, inspire critique and provoke action. In *The Capitalization of Cultural Production*, Miège dedicates his foreword to a critique of the Frankfurt School conception of a 'culture industry'. According to Miège, the notion of a culture industry in the singular 'misleads one into thinking that we are faced with [a] unified field, where the various elements function within a single process. ... The same model is said to be at work, levelling out the different modes of creativity and imposing common standards' (Miège 1989: 10). As he points out, the publishing model (books, records), the written press model (newspapers, magazines) and what he calls the flow model (radio, television) operate according to different logics and accumulate capital through different methods (Miège 1989: 12). Miège also criticizes Horkheimer and Adorno's 'rigid idea of artistic creation' and the fact that their approach 'is only incidentally concerned with the production process, the extension of the division of labor to the conception of artistic products, and the resulting production relationships' (Miège 1989: 10–11). Adorno does not tend to the specificities of creative cultural work.

For Garnham, the issue with the Frankfurt School critique is not a matter of disagreement over whether or not capitalist relations play a structuring and limiting role in cultural production, as he agrees they do. Rather, he contends that the lack of detailed political-economic analysis, concrete class analysis and, hence, exploration of economic contradiction translates into a flawed account of 'the industrialization of culture as unproblematic and irresistible' (Garnham 1979: 131; see also Garnham 2005: 18). As cultural industries scholarship points out, cultural sectors face a number of challenges to profitability. Cultural commodities involve high production costs (but low reproduction costs), are rarely destroyed in use (which places limits on monetization) and are particularly risky investments (Garnham 1990: 160–1; Hesmondhalgh 2013a: 27–30). Most fail to cover production costs and turn a profit. These distinctive industrial logics result in a commodification of culture that is far less seamless than is suggested by the culture industry thesis – an unevenness that media corporations seek to manage and control.

The cultural industries approach involves detailed critical analysis of the specific business strategies employed to mitigate or surmount obstacles to profitability. Briefly, the cultural industries develop large catalogues of cultural products and pursue strategies of corporate integration in order to minimize the overall impact of commercial failures; limit audience access through the manufacture of 'artificial scarcity'; use the star system and genre formats to foster market predictability; and adopt loose-tight control of the creative process vis-à-vis distribution and marketing (i.e. media companies exercise control over circulation more than production) (Hesmondhalgh 2013a: 30–3). Marketing and promotion are of paramount importance to this system:

> The bigger the perceived investment risk, the larger the role for promotional intermediaries. Marketers pre- and post-test everything. ... Promoters suck up production budgets with multiple teasers, trailers, online viral marketing campaigns, openings and press junkets. In addition, 'synergy'-obsessed conglomerates use 'cross-media promotion' to create a series of 'commercial intertexts'. ... Big budget films, television series and computer games are now conceptualized as multi-media creations, to be repackaged, franchised and sold in multiple formats. (Davis 2013: 199)

Such business thinking, informed by risk aversion coupled with the drive to maximize revenues, has also enveloped the music industries, with popular music likewise being produced with an eye to potential multi-platform 'brand extensions'.

The emphasis on marketing and marketability does not mean that all creativity has been stamped out, however. In contrast to Adorno's assertion that the '[c]ultural entities typical of the culture industry are no longer *also* commodities, they are commodities through and through' (Adorno [1967] 2001b: 99–100), cultural industries scholarship asserts that cultural commodities are distinct from *and* similar to other commodities. As Miège explains, 'Cultural commodities develop according to specific conditions and modes of production; however they are also commodities like any other because they constitute in essence a new field for the expansion of exchange values, a means used by capital to maintain a given rate of accumulation' (Miège 1989: 36). This complex dual character is often misunderstood:

> Either artistic creation … is considered as being totally separate from industrialization … or one simply refuses to acknowledge that the cultural industries possess any distinctive characteristics, and merely observes that things are now the same in this area as in others: market standardization and production concentration have gained total control. (Miège 1989: 40)

The cultural industries approach accounts for ways that cultural commodities cannot be equated with other consumer goods. Considerable creative autonomy is typically granted to cultural workers in comparison with workers in many other industries (Ryan 1991; Hesmondhalgh and Baker 2011; Hesmondhalgh 2013a), as corporations necessarily recognize '*the economic irrationality of the creative process*' (Ryan 1991: 48; emphasis in original) – at least to a certain degree. Creativity is still needed inside this system.

Hesmondhalgh identifies the core cultural industries as broadcasting (radio and television); film; music; print; digital games; web design; and advertising, marketing and public relations (Hesmondhalgh 2013a: 17). I see the last grouping – industries which 'tend to have a greater functional element as they are intended to sell and promote other products' (Hesmondhalgh 2013a: 17) – as distinct from, though intricately linked to, the cultural industries. Following Aeron Davis (2013), I classify advertising, branding, lobbying, marketing and public relations as promotional industries. These occupations are involved in the production of promotional texts, promotional practices and, ultimately, *promotional culture* – a term that signals how 'individuals and organizations have become more promotionally oriented' and 'promotional practices have spread to a number of occupations and settings which once had little or no promotional function. ... Politics, markets, popular culture and media, civil society, work and individual social relations have all adapted to promotional needs and practices' (Davis 2013: 4). My emphasis on these distinctions is motivated by my interest in questioning what music-related branding and licensed popular music are, in effect, *for*, and how such uses differ from the circulation of popular music as a commodity more generally – in exploring the consequences of music's more functional qualities as an instrument of promotion. Popular music assumes a more deeply commercial character when it becomes not just a cultural but a *promotional* commodity.

A key argument made by Garnham, which I retain in my analysis of the contemporary music industries, emphasizes how '*[i]t is cultural distribution, not cultural production, that is the key locus of power and profit. ...* The cultural process is as much, if not more, about creating audiences or publics as it is about producing cultural artefacts and performances' (Garnham 1990: 161–2; emphasis in original). The dominant position of information and technology (IT) giants Apple, Amazon and Google vis-à-vis digital music distribution (Mulligan 2014) is thus complicating the power relations characteristic of the music industries. However, it is important to clarify that 'creating audiences' is actually the work of *marketing* and not distribution *per se* – something that also remains paramount. Marketing *and* distribution continue to dictate profitability and remain the locus of power inside the cultural industries even in the digital era. Given my emphasis on examining popular music as promotion, I focus on the former – an area largely still dominated by the major music companies – in the analysis that unfolds in chapters 2, 3 and 4.

While cultural industries scholars distance themselves from many of the claims made by Frankfurt School scholars, I do not see these critical perspectives as incompatible. Much as Horkheimer and Adorno contend that '[f]ilm, radio, and magazines form a system' (Horkheimer and Adorno [1944] 2002: 94), Garnham observes that 'the cultural sector operates as an integrated economic whole', at least insofar as the different cultural industries compete with one another for skilled labour, advertising revenue, consumer disposable income and consumption time (Garnham 1990: 158). In a manner comparable to Adorno's analysis of the audience demand for difference (albeit within sameness) (Adorno [1941] 2002b: 448), Garnham stresses the importance of novelty within the market for cultural commodities (Garnham 1990: 160). The sets of concepts and critiques offered by each approach can be used in concert.

The commodification of culture refers to a long-term historical process, one that can be characterized in terms of 'extension and gentle acceleration' (Hesmondhalgh 2013a: 405). Mindful of Hesmondhalgh's advice not to overstate change at the expense of continuity, in the remainder of this chapter I chart key developments in the intensifying relationship between popular music, mass media and promotion in the nineteenth and twentieth centuries. Early precedents provide the historical context needed to situate and understand twenty-first-century business trends.

Industrial Origins: Music, Cross-promotion and 'Artist-brand' Prototypes

Music has assumed varied commercial and promotional functions since at least the nineteenth century – even before the advent of sound recording. In the Victorian music-hall and vaudeville era, music was produced as a commodity, both as live performances by professionals and as sheet music purchased and performed by amateur musicians. Within this commercial system, popular music remained accessible, participatory and communal in important ways. As John Baxendale explains, 'Within music-hall, and the later variety theatre, song was just one element in a mixed bill of entertainment, which might include comedy, juggling, acrobatics, magic, animal acts. ... But music had a particular contribution to make, through its "singalong" factor, to the general ambience of the halls, which was part of what customers were paying for' (Baxendale 1995: 139). From a business perspective, the importance of this 'singalong' factor was connected to popular music's commodity form as sheet music: the requirement of selling sheet music to fans – amateur pianists and singers – meant that catchy, melodic and relatively simple tunes were most saleable (Baxendale 1995: 138–9). Hook-based, memorable songwriting, then, has long been seen as a 'sound' business strategy. In something of a precedent for product placement, it was not uncommon for music-hall performers to 'puff' the wares of particular tradesmen during performances (McFall 2004: 116). Importantly, the 'personality', status and acclaim of the performer was central to the pursuit of profit, as ' "added value" came from the individuality and glamour of star performers, emerging from the 1870s, and assiduously promoted by impresarios, agents and the press' (Baxendale 1995: 139). Promotional texts were used not only to publicize tours and performances, but also to transform entertainers into stars.

Cross-promotion with star musicians also dates back to at least the nineteenth century, when the persona of P.T. Barnum client Jenny Lind (1820–87), nicknamed the 'Swedish Nightingale', was linked to a range of merchandise. In his account of 'Lindomania', Paul Metzner remarks on the sale of 'Jenny Lind gloves, bonnets, riding hats, shawls, mantillas, robes, parasols, combs, jewelry, pianos, chairs, sofas, sausages, even Jenny Lind teakettles' (Metzner 1998: 158). A key commodity tied to Lind – sheet music – was much more conventional, but is notable for the way it often 'featured illustrations of the singer, some quite lavish in detail, thus affording the buyer pleasure even if she did not possess the requisite ability to play the song in question' (Waksman 2011: 111). Her live performances were the main product, however, and were promoted aggressively through advertisements in newspapers and magazines (see Waksman 2011 for an examination of Lind's 1850 US concert tour, which was arranged and publicized by Barnum).

The next step in the expansion of music stardom and attendant growth in opportunities for cross-promotion, sponsorship and merchandising was the mass adoption of another commodity form: the record. With the introduction of sound recording technologies, the culture of music consumption shifted away from live performance and, as a result, the relationship between popular music and promotion also was altered. While Thomas Edison's phonograph, first introduced in 1877, was initially conceived of as a dictating device, it proved

> more successful as a coin-operated 'entertainment' machine, a novelty attraction (like early cinema) at fairs and medicine shows and on the vaudeville circuit. And for this purpose 'entertaining' cylinders were needed. Columbia took the lead in providing a choice of 'Sentimental', 'Tropical', 'Comic', 'Irish' and 'Negro' songs. (Frith 1988b: 13–14)

Recorded music, used as a means of demonstrating the marvels of this audio hardware, functioned as a tool for promoting Edison's phonographs and his competitor Emile Berliner's gramophones. By the 1920s, however, records 'ceased to be a novelty' (Frith 1988b: 15). The record emerged as the music industries' core commodity, eventually displacing sheet music.

The introduction of sound recording, the microphone and the radio underpinned the star system that emerged in the twentieth century. Radio technology allowed for mass distribution; the use of microphones allowed for the development of styles of singing that 'heightened the nuances of "personality" in each singer'; and

> the freezing of social relations as a characteristic of recordings, their congealment into commodity form, circulate[d] the human voice without physical limits, thus fulfilling one of the essential preconditions for the star system: that the star be known without reciprocation by a

mass of individuals, whose only common point lies in being represented by the same star. (Buxton [1983] 1990: 430)

The mass circulation of popular music enabled by the phonograph and radio rendered the act of listening much less out of the ordinary – and performers more extraordinary. By the 1930s, these technologies had 'brought the experience of a life accompanied by music to most Americans' (D. Goodman 2010: 38).

The business world saw the potential for musical accompaniment to add entertainment and ambience to the advertising and shopping experience. In the United States, the use of music in advertising dates back to the dawn of radio broadcasting (Kellaris et al. 1993: 114; Taylor 2012: 2). During the 1920s, corporations sponsored entire musical programmes, and in a precursor to the radio jingle, some used distinctive theme songs (Taylor 2012: 26, 74). Initially termed the 'singing commercial' during the late 1930s, the stand-alone jingle had become a standard feature of radio advertising by the 1940s, a period during which the jingle also found a home on early American television (Taylor 2012: 80, 90–8). The jingle's function was straightforward. These upbeat tunes 'should be a pleasing and intriguing form of sugarcoating the advertising pill', in the words of Alan Bradley Kent and Austen Herbert Croom-Johnson, two jingle writers from that era (quoted in Taylor 2012: 99).

In contrast to the explicit pitch of the jingle, the music used in retail spaces assumed a more indirectly promotional function. While live music had been used to create desirable (or consumer desire-inducing) atmospheres within early twentieth-century department stores (DeNora and Belcher 2000: 82), keeping apace with technological change, many stores switched to the 'canned' sounds of muzak from the mid-1930s. The shift from live performance as foreground music to muzak as background music involved a transition from in-store music as 'overt "entertainment" to more subliminal "ambience"' (DeNora and Belcher 2000: 82). In David Goodman's account, the standardized background music produced by the Muzak company, founded in 1934, 'played a part in normalizing the experience of background distracted listening to music' (D. Goodman 2010: 41). The Muzak formula produced a homogeneous soundtrack: 'Muzak's programs, from their inception, consisted of tight rearrangements of standard popular songs as well as classical and light dance music. Care was taken to remove any unique or potentially distracting rhythmic, melodic, or harmonic features found in the original versions' (Jones and Schumacher 1992: 160). After all, active concentration that centred on listening might impede the impulse to shop. Effective muzak added ambience while remaining largely unnoticed.

With the rise of sound films (or 'talkies') in the late 1920s and 1930s, popular music assumed a new prominence in film. While film scores are by design composed as background musical accompaniment, the use of original popular songs in motion pictures assigns a more complex status to film music; complicating classification as background or foreground, ambience or entertainment, popular music may elicit various modes of listening and forms of engagement. By providing mass entertainment featuring music and raising the profile of the featured artist among moviegoers, films also function as media for marketing music. Popular music's cross-promotional link with film was initially forged to bolster sheet music sales, serving as a precursor to a business strategy that gained considerable traction in the late 1980s and early 1990s, as acquisition-hungry media companies sought intra-firm efficiencies and cross-selling opportunities: corporate 'synergy'. As Jeff Smith points out, 'Although the term *synergy* is of more recent vintage, the idea that film music played an important economic function within the industry goes back at least to the early 1910s', during which time exhibitors featured 'song slides and singers as special attractions in their programs' (Smith 1998: 27–8). The tie-in between Hollywood and Tin Pan Alley was gradually formalized between the 1920s and the 1940s, during which time the movie musical – and, hence, film music by the likes of George and Ira Gershwin, Irving Berlin and Richard Rodgers and Lorenz Hart – was *en vogue* (Smith 1998: 30–1; Toynbee 2002: 150). Cross-promotion across the music and film industries laid the foundations for the launch of stars such as Rudy Vallée and Bing Crosby – actor-singers whose broad appeal could be harnessed and capitalized on within both industries.

Such cross-media promotion carried on unabated in the 1950s and 1960s. In 1954, *Billboard*'s June Bundy characterized the marketing tactic in the following way:

> Publishing firms dominated by motion picture interests have latched on to a new gimmick to push their movie tunes this year, thereby creating some new problems for artist and repertoire men and recording talent.
> The gimmick, a two-way promotion, calls for a top artist to record the title-tune from a new movie to be used as a prolog to or background for the film. Then, when the picture is released, the diskery is expected to release the record at the very same time. (Bundy 1954: 12)

At that time, cross-promotion between films and records was the domain of 'middle-of-the-road' (MOR) artists, such as traditional American pop acts Frank Sinatra and the Four Aces (Denisoff and Romanowski

1991: 10). Then in 1955, in what marked an important moment in the evolving relationship between popular music, mass media and youth culture, Bill Haley & His Comets' 'Rock Around the Clock' was featured in *Blackboard Jungle* – the first time that rock 'n' roll was used in a Hollywood film. Returning to a 'safer' sound, two versions of Henry Mancini's 'Moon River', a song written for *Breakfast at Tiffany's* (1961), cracked *Billboard*'s Hot 100 (Bundy 1961: 2). The viability of this type of cross-promotion overall motivated a tie-up between motion picture companies and radio (Bundy 1961: 2).

The practice of two-way promotion between the film and music industries has spanned decades and genres. More recent blockbuster successes have ranged from the *Saturday Night Fever* (1977) soundtrack, for which the Bee Gees composed original songs, and the Motown-filled *The Big Chill* (1983) soundtrack, to Celine Dion's 'My Heart Will Go On' from the *Titanic* (1997) soundtrack and the rock-filled *Twilight* (2008, 2009, 2010, 2011, 2012) soundtracks. Canadian advertiser and media personality Terry O'Reilly (2012) reflected on the significance of *The Big Chill*: 'There is a theory that Madison Avenue started to use songs in advertising in a big way after … advertisers saw the way baby boomers responded to the movie's soundtrack.' Toronto-based music supervisor Amy Fritz suggested that, following the commercial successes of John Hughes' films such as *Pretty in Pink* (1986), which feature popular songs, the major studios began to realize that they 'had a captive audience' to whom they could promote ancillary products and spin-offs, such as music soundtracks (Fritz, personal communication, 2009).

Popular music has been used to add entertainment value and credibility to films, while films and the promotional apparatus that supports their release have been used to drive record sales and generate marketing exposure. Similar objectives have shaped the younger trend of inserting original popular songs into advertisements, television programmes and video games, which I begin to address below and further explore in chapter 3. The objectives of producing audiences and sales – of music, media and consumer brands – has led to the conversion of various forms of popular media into marketing media.

Advertising Music: From Jingles to Original Popular Songs

Recording artists' participation in the production of advertising music – both as songwriters and as featured performers – is an established practice with a long history. Perhaps most famously, singer-songwriter and pop star Barry Manilow worked as a commercial jingle writer during the 1960s and 1970s, co-writing and performing now famous jingles for State Farm Insurance ('Like a Good Neighbor, State Farm is There'), Band-Aid Brand ('I Am Stuck on Band-Aid Brand, 'Cause Band-Aid's Stuck on Me') and others (Klein 2009: 132). Songwriters, such as Jake Holmes and Herbie Hancock, earned paycheques penning jingles during this period (Pollard 2009; Taylor 2012: 133; Hancock 2014: 89). Brands also hired a wide range of recording artists to perform jingles. According to veteran music licensing specialist Keith D'Arcy (2012), 1960s jingles performed by the Rolling Stones for Rice Krispies, The Who for Coca-Cola and Jefferson Airplane for Levi Strauss were important precedents for contemporary developments. Coca-Cola's 'Things Go Better with Coca-Cola' was performed by the Limeliters (1964), Petula Clark (1966), Ray Charles (1967) and Aretha Franklin (1968) in a campaign declared to be 'a smashing hit with the target audience' by the company's vice president and brand manager (quoted in Taylor 2012: 151). Different versions of Pepsi's 'You've Got a Lot to Live, and Pepsi's Got a Lot to Give' were performed by Johnny Cash, B.B. King, Odetta, Tammy Wynette, Three Dog Night (all in 1970) and Roberta Flack (in 1971) (Taylor 2012: 155–6). While the specific arrangements of such jingles worked to mimic the featured artists' own musical material, in them slogans were substituted for lyrics. They were original jingles, after all, and not original songs.

Coca-Cola's famous 1971 'Hilltop' television commercial marked a turning point in the crossover between songs and jingles (Klein 2009: 83; Taylor 2009: 410; Tunnicliffe, personal communication, 2010). The advertising spot featured a jingle, 'I'd Like to Buy the World a Coke', which was reworked into a popular song, 'I'd Like to Teach the World to Sing (In Perfect Harmony)', that eliminated references to the cola brand altogether (Klein 2009: 83). The song became a radio hit for both the Hillside Singers and The New Seekers (Klein 2009: 83). In an earlier but arguably less influential example, the jingle used in Diet Pepsi's 'Girlwatchers' spot (1966) was spun into the Bob Crewe Generation's instrumental radio hit, 'Music to Watch Girls By' (Klein 2009: 83; Taylor 2012: 132). Advertising music, it was discovered, could provide entertainment in its own right. The initial 'convergence' of advertising and radio, then, entailed commercial jingles becoming popular songs.

The introduction of MTV in the United States in 1981, and the attendant advertiser targeting of the youth demographic, further cemented the potent links between popular music, youth culture and visual style – and hastened the migration of popular songs into advertisements. Music videos, which were designed not just to entertain but also to advertise the songs and featured recording artists, added new emotional and affective dimensions to music, while accentuating the visual dimensions of pop and rock culture. It became apparent that brands' interest in popular music was also inextricably linked to those visual signifiers. According to musicologist Timothy D. Taylor, 'The influence of MTV can't be overstated, since it ushered in a new, fast-paced visual language to accompany music' (Taylor 2012: 185). The advertising industry started to employ a music video-inspired practice of devising commercials 'driven by music and visuals, with no hard sell', which was termed 'atmospheric advertising' (*New York Times* 1989). Whereas jingles function as sonic mnemonic devices designed to enhance brand recall (Huron 1989: 562), the rich meanings produced by popular music cannot be reduced to 'the notes': the symbolic meanings tied to popular songs and recording artists and, hence, the production of emotion and affect, are bound up with extra-musical and cultural associations. By partnering directly with recording artists, brands were able to harness the signifying power of associations tied to popular music as an audiovisual cultural form. Original music by recording artists not only provided a sound: it also lent a brand a look and a feel. In a 1986 Michelob spot, for instance, Genesis performed their song 'Tonight, Tonight, Tonight', interlaced with shots of couples embracing, women, city nightlife, a bar and Michelob beer. This television commercial belonged to the 'Night Belongs to Michelob' campaign, which also included a spot featuring Eric Clapton performing at a bar, an ill-advised pairing in retrospect; the deal was terminated after the rock star revealed to *Rolling Stone* that he was an alcoholic and had begun rehab by the time the spot was released (Robert 2010).

It was the record-setting US$5 million celebrity endorsement deal struck between Pepsi and pop superstar Michael Jackson in 1983 (Herrara 2009), however, that 'transformed the world of music and marketing' (Taylor 2012: 187). Jackson's music gave Pepsi a sound that originated in radio coupled with a visual aesthetic pulled straight from MTV. Opposite to the aforementioned 'Hilltop' case, Pepsi's 'Street' (1984) and 'Concert' (1984) commercials entailed the conversion of a hit pop song into a jingle in terms of lyrics; both feature Jackson performing a version of 'Billie Jean' in which the song's chorus is replaced with 'You're the Pepsi generation / Guzzle down and taste the thrill of the day / And feel the Pepsi way' (Herrara 2009). In terms of visuals, the spots, both of which were directed by Bob Giraldi, director of Jackson's 'Beat It' music video (1983) (Giraldi 2009), harnessed Jackson's position in youth culture as a popular cultural phenomenon. 'Street' features Jackson, clad in his fashion staples (leather jacket, sequin socks and glove), performing his signature dance moves along with the Jackson Five and a troupe of child dancers on a brownstone-lined street. 'Concert' (known for the severe burns suffered by Jackson during filming) features the Jacksons performing on stage in an auditorium filled with screaming fans. The commercials were intended to have a family appeal; this strategy 'was devised before Jackson was engaged, and he was hired because he fit that strategy' (Taylor 2012: 188).

In an interview in 1984, Allen Rosenshine, then-CEO of BBDO, the advertising agency behind these spots, explained that youth 'express themselves through music, they live through music; MTV is not an isolated phenomenon. So if we're going to be leading edge, we have to be in music' (quoted in Taylor 2012: 188). According to Rosenshine, 'There are attitudes and styles which we wish to make signals of, or synonymous with, the brand. Advertising and brands don't really create style. They take styles that exist, hopefully at the forefront ... and try to make [them] the property, proprietarily owned by a brand' (quoted in Taylor 2012: 187). Such business thinking aligns with Adam Arvidsson's more recent observation that 'brands are mechanisms that enable a direct valorization (in the form of share prices, for example) of people's ability to create trust, affect and shared meanings' (Arvidsson 2005: 236). In this formulation, ordinary people, not business executives and marketing practitioners, are the source of cultural meanings that become resources ripe for capitalization by corporations. In the Pepsi case, meanings tied to Jackson's music and his status as a pop idol generated economic value for the partnering brand. Indeed, emboldened by the success of their first campaign (Pepsi generated US$7.7 billion in sales in 1984), Pepsi signed Jackson to a second endorsement deal, valued at US$10 million, in support of his *Bad* album and tour (1987–8) (Herrara 2009). Following a template similar to the previous Jackson commercials, in 'The Chase', the lyrics to 'Bad' were transformed in order to include references to the Pepsi brand. This four-part, four-minute spot, which paired concert footage with shots of the star eluding hordes of photographers and fans via helicopter, convertible, ski jump and parachute, also featured Jackson singing (lip-synching), dancing and acting. A similar formula was adopted in Pepsi's 'Simply Irresistible' (1989) spot with Robert Palmer. Palmer's lyrics were adapted (e.g. 'she' was replaced with 'it' in order to lyrically address Pepsi rather than a woman), and the imagery mimed the aesthetic of Palmer's well-known 'Addicted to Love' (1986) and 'Simply Irresistible' (1988) music videos, in which he is flanked by a troupe of mannequin-like yet sexualized women.

A high-profile endorsement deal between Pepsi and another pop star marked the next step in the crossover between radio, MTV and television commercials: Madonna. Similar to 'The Chase', the Madonna-Pepsi spot, 'Make A Wish' (1989), was unusually long (two and a half minutes, although more standard thirty- and sixty-second versions later aired) and was launched as an entertainment event:

First, Pepsi aired a teaser commercial on the Grammys telling viewers that the *Like a Prayer* song and commercial were set to premiere a month later. ... Then, on March 2nd, 1989, Madonna's two and a half minute *Like A Prayer* Pepsi commercial aired during the Cosby Show. People in 40 countries around the world watched, giving the commercial an audience of 250 million. (O'Reilly 2012)

The advertisement featured Madonna lip-synching, dancing and acting, and drew on visual conventions found in narrative-driven music videos. In contrast to the Jackson spots, however, it showcased the song 'Like A Prayer' with unaltered lyrics, and thus serves as a key precedent for popular song's displacement of the jingle altogether.

While the Madonna-Pepsi campaign is widely known for the controversy sparked by the release of the 'Like A Prayer' music video and subsequent termination of the Pepsi deal (the video featured cross burning, stigmata and interracial love, and incited anti-Madonna fervour among social conservatives), for the purposes of an analysis of the intensifying relationship between popular music and promotion, this case is significant due to the way that consumer brand advertising was explicitly conceptualized as an alternative approach to promoting Madonna's new single. As explained in a Pepsi press release at the time, 'The groundbreaking deal is expected to change the way popular tunes from major artists are released in the future. Traditionally, new songs have been made public through heavy radio air-play. In an innovative twist, the Pepsi-Madonna deal uses television to provide unparalleled international exposure for her new single' (quoted in Siegel 1989). The commercial aired prior to the release of the 'Like A Prayer' single in stores or on radio, and prior to the launch of the corresponding music video on MTV (Siegel 1989; Klein 2009: 89). As Bethany Klein points out, 'It is interesting that this case was framed in terms of bypassing commercial radio since, at the time, US commercial radio was nowhere near the disaster it is today for young artists, with ever-narrowing playlists, a plague of payola schemes, and practical if not technical oligopoly status' (Klein 2009: 89). Furthermore, the chart-topping Madonna had not been shut out of commercial radio or MTV, but rather was played in heavy rotation. The short-lived Pepsi-Madonna campaign was an antecedent for a cross-promotional approach that came of age at the turn of the twenty-first century, which will be examined in chapter 3.

The transition from the use of jingles to the use of original popular songs in advertisements did not involve a clean break from past practices. During the 1990s, for instance, Pepsi returned to the use of jingles, though still performed by famous recording artists. Ray Charles performed 'You Got the Right One, Baby, Uh Huh', a jingle based on Prince's unreleased song 'Uh Huh' (1990–1); the Spice Girls performed 'Generation Next' (1997–8); and Britney Spears performed 'Joy of Pepsi'

(1999–2000). Similar to the approach employed in the 1960s, these jingles were produced to sound like the star artist's own material; they reflect the jingle's makeover into an imitation of the pop charts. By virtue of working with recording artists, however, these campaigns enabled Pepsi to capitalize on the cultural potency of popular music, regardless of the musical and lyrical content. In the new millennium, advertisers would become interested not only in advertising and endorsement deals with celebrities, but also in licensing original music by lesser known artists. Popular music that fell well outside the Top 40 was less expensive to license and could function as a powerful signifier of 'authenticity', themes to be examined in chapter 3.

As the above discussion demonstrates, cross-media promotion involving popular music has a long history, with popular music, mass media and advertising becoming ever more intertwined in recent decades. Reliance on comparable business arrangements and promotional practices has intensified in the twenty-first century, as music corporations have expanded their emphasis on marketing and activities across the B2B music marketplace. Cross-media promotion and music licensing have moved from the periphery to the centre of music industry thinking, as the pursuit of these opportunities has become the 'common sense' way of doing business: 'Whereas once [licensing] was perceived as simply gravy and maybe a good opportunity to pursue, it has actually now become, I think, a part of their core business' (Fritz, personal communication, 2009). This shift has caused music executives to evaluate music and musicians in ever more commercial terms. Those recording artists that promise to generate licensing and branding income are now prized assets. Worryingly, various companies compare and equate a wide range of popular music in terms of its fitness for achieving promotional objectives – not necessarily for its qualities *as music*.

Conclusion

Creating and selling music as a way of making money is not a new phenomenon. Businesses have produced popular music as a commodity since the rise of the music industries in the nineteenth century, if not before. Throughout the twentieth century and up to the present, however, we have seen the range of contexts in which popular music has been deployed by corporate entities broaden, with important consequences for the types of music prioritized: popular music well-suited to large audiences and promotional messages. From live performances to films to advertisements, music has been used not only to generate revenue but also to serve as a promotional vehicle – a development connected to the growth of the promotional industries in the twentieth century (on which see Davis 2013). The rise of promotion in the music industries has been connected to the spread of promotion more broadly, with the cultural and promotional industries serving an integral role in the ways that popular culture, ideas and human relationships have been interpreted, reimagined and remade through the lens of promotion.

The culture industry thesis offers a helpful entry point for conceptualizing the constraints that both commodification and the enveloping logic of promotion place on culture. As properties used to drive profits, varied cultural texts and practices are subsumed under and limited by the common denominator of exchange. Marketability typically becomes a precondition for financial support. However, I agree with key criticisms offered by the cultural industries approach: cultural commodities are more complex, contradictory and meaningful than the culture industry thesis suggests, and the degree to which particular cultural commodities will resonate with audiences and, hence, become profitable remains unpredictable. The culture industry system produces more uneven results than Horkheimer and Adorno's account assumes, making the cultural industries approach an important and necessary complement. Indeed, I contend that it is productive to think with both bodies of scholarship but at different levels of analysis: critical theory can help to explain the ways that capitalism necessarily circumscribes cultural production, whereas the cultural industries approach can lend critical and empirical precision to the study of different sectors of capitalist cultural production. Chapter 2 advances an analysis of the music industries that is informed by the cultural industries approach. I examine and compare the commercial pressures and industrial dynamics characteristic of the 'old' music industries, and then consider the ways these industries have undergone a transformation in the digital era – one that has reinforced and expanded the importance of marketing and promotion.

2

Capitalizing on Music: From Sound Recordings to 'Artist-brands'

During the first decade of the twenty-first century, the music industries – what largely had been a sound recording or *record* industry – were overcome by a tidal wave of change. Following the launch of Napster in 1999 and the subsequent mass popularization of various peer-to-peer (P2P) file-sharing services, the technological change that had long enveloped the commercial production of popular music was especially rapid and persistent. The recording industry's core bases of profitability and power – sales of physical album 'units' and top-down dominance over radio and music video promotion – were radically destabilized by the proliferation of unauthorized downloading, on-demand streaming media and the growth of a consumer (as distinct from a professional) market for digital recording technologies. The music industries reached a 'tipping point' (Leyshon et al. 2005: 181; see also Leyshon 2014). In fact, it has been widely held that this period of 'crisis' initiated the demise of the major music labels altogether.

However, this surface appearance of industry-wide decentralization has obscured the decisive ways that major record companies and music publishers have responded to the crisis in popular music's commodity form. In its 19 December 2009 issue, *Billboard* analysts and contributors collaborated to provide a list of the 'Top 10 Trends of the Decade', paraphrased below:

1. The recording industry's failure to keep pace with new digital platforms;
2. Consolidation across recording, music publishing, live performance, retailing, merchandising and artist management companies;
3. The transformation of ticketing companies such as Ticketmaster into marketing/sales companies;
4. The collapse of the music retail system;
5. The popularity of music reality television programmes;
6. The surge in licensing and brand partnerships and the decline in the perception of 'selling out';
7. The transformation of music videos from free promotional medium to monetized content made available online in exchange for licences;
8. The increase in the independent sector's market share;
9. The advent of the 360-degree or multiple rights recording contract; and
10. Wall Street investment in music publishing catalogues.

The trend listed at number one, the recording industry's futile attempts 'to put the MP3 genie back in the bottle' (*Billboard* 2009), has dominated industry and popular press. The prevalent view that major record labels are out-of-date 'dinosaurs' destined for failure has dangerously overshadowed the ways the music industries (recording, music publishing and live performance) have adapted to this new business climate by some of the very means highlighted further down *Billboard*'s list of trends, among them: deepened corporate consolidation; increased and expanded music licensing; the monetization of new music commodities, including music videos; and the institutionalization of all-encompassing '360 deals'.

Against overwrought claims about a radical break in major music company hegemony, we actually have seen the music industries adjust to new challenges, with those same record labels and music publishers at the helm. The sharp decline in CD sales in the digital era has propelled the recording industry's reconfiguration of popular music's core commodity form: 'artist-brands', not records, now constitute the primary basis of capitalization. These artist-brands are monetized through digital music products and services (e.g. downloads, music videos, audio and video streaming sites), music licences and other rights, endorsements, merchandise and live performances in addition to CDs. Marketing, promotion and the burgeoning market for business-to-business (B2B) licensing deals have grown in significance, motivating music companies and countless recording artists to revisit and modify their stances toward various forms of commercial and branded affiliation. As we shall see, the 'top-down' monetization of recording artists and popular music across the media environment has helped to offset the threat to profitability posed by digital change. It has also reinforced the unequal power relations characteristic of the music industries.

The 'Old' Music Industry Model: A Record Business

In order to understand the emergence of the artist-brand paradigm – or the idea that the logic of branding can be grafted directly onto recording artists and that brands, not music *per se*, constitute the foundation of revenue generation – it is necessary to evaluate the extent to which the music industries' digital transformation has disrupted entrenched ways of doing business. There was no clear break that unambiguously divided the 'old' music industry model, which was anchored by sales of physical sound recordings, from its digital successor. The backbone of the artist-brand approach – the exploitation of rights – had shifted toward the centre of industry practice long before the age of the MP3, downloading and streaming, as Simon Frith's account suggests:

> For the music industry the age of manufacture is now over. Companies (and company profits) are no longer organised around making *things* but depend on the creation of *rights*. In the industry's own jargon, each piece of music represents 'a basket of rights'; the company task is to exploit as many of these rights as possible, not just those realised when it is sold in recorded form to the public, but also those realised when it is broadcast on radio or television, used on a film, commercial or video soundtrack, and so on. Musical rights (copyrights, performing rights) are the basic pop commodity. (Frith 1988a: 57; emphasis in original)

Copyright, though routinely discussed in terms of the purported benefits for creators, actually is a mechanism used to generate huge financial gains for corporations – both before and after the digital age (see Klein et al. 2015).

The sound recording's digital format can be traced back to the introduction of the CD in 1982 (if not before), which enabled the storage of digital data, and of CD-ROM discs and drives, which made CDs playable on computers (Morris 2015: 36). However, it was the (increasingly) post-CD era that saw intensified disruption to 'business-as-usual' – changes sparked by the new ease of storing digital music files on personal computers and uploading or downloading such files via P2P file-sharing services. This period saw the emergence of what Jeremy Wade Morris terms the 'digital music commodity': 'a particular combination of data and sound that exists as an entity in and of itself for sale or acquisition in online outlets via computers or other digital portable devices' (Morris 2015: 2). In order to pinpoint the patterns of change and continuity that differentiate and unite the pre- and post-CD music industry models, I begin by examining how businesses generated profits from popular music prior to its digitalization.

Popular music's commodity form has long been dynamic and subject to change. As discussed in chapter 1, throughout the early years of music's industrialization, sheet music and live performances constituted popular music's core commodity forms. Then, during the age of sound recording and radio, the record emerged as the primary popular music commodity. A recording industry emerged alongside the existing music publishing and live performance sectors, but importantly did not displace them. While music publisher dominance continued into the 1940s (Passman 2015: 237), the recording industry was the central hub of music industry activity, profit and power for the remainder of the twentieth century. Even then, the record did not by itself 'sustain pop meaning, which has always had to draw on other forms – including posters, teen magazines, live performances, film, radio, and TV' (Goodwin 1992: 26). The sound recording, music publishing and live performance sectors largely worked in unison, although their interests did not always align.

Given the dominance of the physical recording-centred model until very recently, it is not surprising that the *recording* industry is commonly conflated with the *music* industry. According to John Williamson and Martin Cloonan, the use of the term 'music industry' in the singular is misleading overall; in addition to its imprecise use as a synonym for the recording industry (a sector often over-privileged in academic and policy writing), reference to a music industry also gives the impression of a single, unified industry, which, they argue, 'disguises conflict *within* the industries' (Williamson and Cloonan 2007: 316; emphasis in original). In their account, the plural 'music industries' provides a more precise characterization of the set of discrete sectors engaged in selling recordings, compositions, performances and associated merchandise (Williamson and Cloonan 2007: 305). After all, the recording industry has long been flanked not only by the music publishing and concert promotion sectors, but also by management agencies, music retailers and merchandisers.

Williamson and Cloonan's music industries argument echoes important contributions from the 'cultural industries' literature (Miège 1989;

Garnham 1990; Hesmondhalgh 2013a) reviewed in chapter 1. As Miège asserts, 'contrary to widespread opinion, the present situation of the cultural industries is not characterized by a sole and unique logic' (Miège 1989: 12). The music industries, much like the cultural industries in general, are marked by heterogeneity, industrial complexity and, at times, competing interests. However, as Dave Laing points out, the interlocking web of recording, music publishing, live performance and merchandising businesses within the commercial music system nevertheless functions as 'a unitary business sector, albeit one in which sub-sectors have a relatively autonomous relationship to each other' (Laing 2009: 15). The music industries *can* work together in rather uniform, seamless and synergistic ways, especially when companies in different sectors are owned by the same parent corporation, as is the case with today's music giants: Universal, Sony and Warner. Both views, then, are valid and need not be seen as incompatible. Sound recordings, compositions and live performances *are* distinct cultural commodities shaped by different industrial dynamics. At the same time, the overarching business strategies that inform corporate decision-making treat these cultural commodities *as if* they are, in essence, the same: intellectual property used to generate revenues.

Both the recording and music publishing industries, past and present, produce what Miège classifies as *highly reproducible products* compatible with industrial mass production processes (Miège 1989: 12). In their twentieth-century iterations, these industries conformed to a *publishing logic*, under which 'products generally issu[e] from the materialization and reproduction of artistic work (whose creators are paid by a system of royalties and reproduction rights), and [are] sold direct to consumers' (Miège 1989: 12). With this dynamic in mind (and to anticipate nomenclatural confusion), it is worth emphasizing here that, for Miège, the sale of records follows this *publishing* logic. Both record labels and music publishers generated profits from the sale of sound recordings to end consumers under the old system: the former through unit sales of albums or singles and sound recording (phonogram) copyrights, and the latter from mechanical reproduction rights for individual songs (musical compositions and lyrics) recorded on tapes or CDs (see Passman 2015: 229–30, 250; Price n.d.).

Then as now, however, the music publishing industry generated revenue from numerous additional sources. Music publishers exploited (a term used to describe the conversion of copyrights into revenue) print rights for sheet music and lyrics, performance rights for television broadcasts and radio airplay and synchronization ('sync') rights for the use of compositions in other audiovisual media (e.g. films, television programmes, advertisements). The recording industry also profited from such music–media pairings, because the insertion of original master recordings of songs (not cover versions or re-recordings) into film, television and advertising requires a 'master use' licence from the owner of the master recording (typically the record label) in addition.

Importantly, sync and master use licences – revenue streams central to the contemporary music industries – fall under a sales model distinct from the 'direct to consumer' publishing model identified by Miège. They entail B2B sales: instead of selling a unit to an end consumer, the music company sells a licence to another company – and the music sold can add value to the purchasing brand or cultural product. Though not an altogether new practice, forging such agreements with corporate buyers has become increasingly standard, a shift that is reshaping the music marketplace. Popular music and recording artists are being positioned as assets available to rent in order to achieve ends unrelated to music *per se*.

Under the old business model, recording industry profits generally came from the consumer market for sound recordings. Thus, capitalization strategies reflected the distinctive economics that underpinned the record business. First, the production of full-length albums entailed high production costs and low reproduction costs. The first copy of an album could be likened to a prototype, for which substantial investment was required. Once a record company reached the 'break-even' point for its investment in that album, however, very few additional variable costs accrued as sales increased (Garnham 1990: 160; Hesmondhalgh 2013a: 29). Because the costs associated with pressing and distributing additional physical albums (units) were minimal, profit margins escalated dramatically once the record company had 'recouped' the fixed costs associated with producing the first copy. Second, because the preferences and tastes of the popular music-buying public were unpredictable, the recording industry was marked by financial uncertainty (Garnham 1990: 161; McCourt and Rothenbuhler 1997: 201–2; Negus 1999: 32; Frith 2001: 33; Hesmondhalgh 2013a: 27). It was commonly claimed that only one out of every eight recording artists signed to a label sold enough records to break even – a figure that was 'hard to verify and as mythical as it is statistical', but remains at the very least 'an indication of how staff within the music industry perceive[d] their daily plight' (Negus 1999: 32). Investment in unproven talent was seen as a gamble.

To mitigate this risk and capitalize on the marginal costs of reproduction, major record labels favoured the promotion of the most commercially viable stars over investment across a broader range of smaller-scale acts. By focusing on stars, they aimed to achieve 'audience maximization' – an approach that 'favours large corporations with deep pockets who can employ economies of scale' (Garnham 2005: 19; see also Garnham

1990: 160–1). They also catered to smaller niche markets to a certain extent: different genre categories could lend a degree of predictability to the music marketplace. As Jason Toynbee explains, 'while the marketing logic of the music industry mitigates in favour of the particular and the nameable, the logic of production prefers the general – the largest possible category. The industry has responded to this situation with two strategies, for segmented and mainstream markets' (Toynbee 2002: 155). While the major labels did sign a range of new artists, it was done with the objective of acquiring a handful of stars. Because the likelihood of producing a 'hit' was higher for those companies that released more new music (Garnham 1990: 161; Hesmondhalgh 2013a: 30), record labels adopted the so-called 'mud-against-the wall' strategy, which entailed 'throw[ing] out as much product as possible in the hope that some of it [would] stick' (Negus 1992: 40). The bulk of the revenue was generated from records released by stars but also occasionally by less established talent. While commercial failure was 'the norm' for individual releases (Frith 2001: 33), revenues from the handful of blockbusters that did 'stick' enabled the major record labels to reap substantial profits overall.

Some smaller-scale and independent record labels also could maintain viable businesses in the old industrial system. Since its inception, the recording industry 'has been organized according to small-scale productions and selling to changing niche markets alongside the creation of big hits and blockbusters' (Negus 1999: 17). There even have been periods during which the hegemony of the major record labels has been tested, as was the case in the mid- to late 1950s with the influx of independent labels involved in producing early rock 'n' roll (Peterson and Berger 1975: 164; Gillett [1970] 1996; Burkart and McCourt 2006: 24). However, because profits accrue much more quickly from mass markets than niche markets, the larger companies that produced blockbuster albums were more profitable by design. There was considerable financial incentive to capitalize on international markets, which could provide 'extra income for proportionately less additional investment' (Negus 1999: 155). Indeed, international commercial success has long been considered central to profitability (Buxton [1983] 1990: 438), and major record labels with large distribution networks at their disposal were better equipped to capitalize on these markets.

The corporate strategies and structures that anchored the old industrial model reflected the major record companies' response to the huge benefits of high sales volumes weighed against the high risk of commercial failure. These corporations deployed strategies of integration in order to capitalize on available economies of scale (thereby aiming at audience maximization) and to decrease competition (toward effective risk management). Such strategies included: *horizontal integration* (acquisition of companies across the same sector in order to capture market share and reduce competition); *vertical integration* (acquisition of companies involved in different stages of production, distribution and exhibition in the same sector); *multi-sector integration* (acquisition of companies in other cultural sectors); and *internationalization* (acquisition of or partnership with companies based in other nations) (Hesmond-halgh 2013a: 30–1). Additionally, major and independent record labels routinely agreed to various joint ventures and licensing and distribution deals (Negus 1999: 35), effectively combining more than one of each of these strategies in any given instance. Within the wider commercial system, the majors sat at the centre of this matrix of strategies and smaller labels were positioned at the periphery.

Strategies of corporate consolidation helped the major music companies shore up their industry-wide dominance. Indeed, counter to a straightforward argument for industrial complexity, wherein a multiplicity of players are involved in the various commercial music sectors, only a handful of transnational corporations were at the helm of both the recording and music publishing industries under the old system. Between 1980 and 2004, the 'Big Six' record companies – Capitol/EMI, CBS, MCA, Polygram, RCA and Warner – shrank to the 'Big Four': Universal, EMI, Warner and Sony BMG (Burkart and McCourt 2006: 25). From the late 1980s to the late 1990s, the major record companies accounted for roughly 80 per cent or more of global recorded music sales (Negus 1999: 35).

Crucially, the tendency toward concentration via mergers and acquisitions has continued in the era of digital distribution. In November 2011, EMI agreed to sell its recording interests to Universal. After US Federal Trade Commission (FTC) and European Union (EU) led investigations into whether the deal violated anti-trust rules (Fixmer and Erlichman 2012), the acquisition was, in the end, approved (Mock and Smith 2012; Sisario 2012). As a result, only a 'Big Three' remain: Sony Music Entertainment, Universal Music Group and Warner. With the addition of EMI, it was estimated that Universal Music Group would control over 40 per cent of the recorded music market (Ripley 2011a: 30; Robinson 2012). As Edgar Bronfman Jr, a former Universal heavyweight before his stint at Warner, warned in his plea to stop the deal, this one 'super major' would have an inordinate amount of power over the recording industry and digital entertainment more broadly: '[Universal] would basically determine the future of not only recorded music but really any kind of digital initiative as well. ... I think it's dangerous, I think it's problematic and I think it's got to be stopped' (quoted in Christman 2012a). While *Billboard*'s Ed Christman suggests that Bronfman was possibly 'trying to shake loose some asset sales from the proposed acquisition, because the Warner Music Group would be the likely beneficiary of any regulatory enforced asset sales' (Christman 2012a), Bronfman's concerns were valid nevertheless.

Indeed, midway through 2015, Nielsen/*Billboard* figures suggest that Universal's market share was 39.2 per cent in terms of music distributed and 27.6 per cent in terms of actual label ownership (as many independent record companies work with majors for distribution) (Ingham 2015b). Sony followed with 27.6 per cent for music distributed and 20.9 per cent for ownership, and Warner trailed, putting up figures of 19.2 per cent for music distributed and 15.2 per cent for ownership (Ingham 2015b). In part on the strength of star artists such as Taylor Swift (signed to independent company Big Machine but distributed through Universal), independents captured a market share of just 13.1 per cent for distribution but 35.4 per cent for ownership (Ingham 2015b). The tremendous commercial success of a handful of independent artists can skew the data in ways that obscure the position of independents within this system overall.

Turning to music publishing, Warner Communications acquired Chappell & Co. in 1987, forming Warner Chappell Music Inc. (Warner Music Group 2011), and Sony merged into a 50/50 joint venture with the Michael Jackson estate-owned ATV Music Publishing in 1995 (Sony 2012). In 2016, Sony purchased the Jackson estate's stake in the company, ending 'what has been termed "a complicated ownership structure," giving the company sole control of the publishing operation' (Christman 2016). In 2007, Universal Music Publishing Group acquired BMG Music Publishing (Universal Music Publishing n.d.). The outcome of a separate FTC and EU anti-trust investigation has shaped the competitive landscape of the music publishing industry. In November 2011, Sony/ATV Music Publishing agreed to purchase EMI's music publishing assets. As of December 2011, the Big Four accounted for over 53 per cent of music publishing market share in this US$4.9 billion industry, with EMI Group PLC and Sony/ATV accounting for 15.8 per cent and 8.4 per cent, respectively (Ripley 2011b: 3). This deal, too, was approved with only minor concessions (Christman 2012c; Morris 2012), which placed Sony/ATV in a position to overtake Universal as the largest music publisher in the world (Robinson 2012). At the same time, BMG Rights Management became 'one of the most acquisitive players in the market. During the company's buying binge, it has picked up leading independent publishers like Cherry Lane Music Publishing, Chrysalis and Bug Music' (Christman 2012b).

The market for music publishing is dominated by just five companies, with the Big Three vying for top position. Second quarter 2015 figures suggest market shares of 19.7 per cent for Sony/ATV, 19.4 per cent for Warner/Chappell, 15.5 per cent for Universal, 12.1 per cent for Kobalt and 10.8 per cent for BMG (Christman 2015b). Together, strategies of integration and corporate consolidation intensified the economies of scale characteristic of the recording and music publishing industries, and concentrated extraordinary market share and, hence, power into the hands of just three transnational powerhouses: Universal, Sony and Warner.

Under the old industrial system, these overwhelmingly anti-competitive market conditions allowed for the entrenchment of a highly controlled, top-down system of marketing and distribution. In interview, Don Grierson, former vice president of A&R at Capitol Records, EMI America and Epic Records, spoke to this previous reality by underscoring the shift *away* from controlled promotion and distribution in recent years:

> Up until the internet, there was a system controlled basically by the majors, and ... there was traditional distribution. You had retail stores all over the place, and ... you get airplay and you get MTV exposure, and once you got the exposure then ... the sales people would get that music into the stores and then hopefully the public bought it. ... In the heyday of our business, ... the majors were rolling. (Grierson, personal communication, 2010)

The major record companies benefited from unparalleled access to the distribution network of major record retailers (e.g. HMV, Sam Goody, Tower Records and Virgin Megastores) – corporations that were 'so big that they wouldn't bother with small players' (Passman 2015: 71). In addition, the majors wielded unrivalled programming influence over commercial radio and music video promotion – media businesses also subject to oligopolistic market conditions.

Continuing a process that had begun in the 1980s, the US Telecommunications Act of 1996 further relaxed restrictions on radio ownership and removed the national ownership cap altogether (Prindle 2003: 281). From 1996 to 2002, this mass deregulation in the US ignited a 33.6 per cent reduction in the number of owners; the two largest companies, which had previously owned just 65 stations between them, quickly bought up in excess of 1,400 stations (Prindle 2003: 306). Music video promotion, meanwhile, was monopolized by MTV in the United States and by MuchMusic in Canada.

Major label dominance over marketing and distribution resulted in high barriers to market entry (Burkart and McCourt 2006: 26). Consistent with Garnham's analysis, control over these channels, not over production itself, constituted '*the key locus of power and profit*' (Garnham 1990: 161–2; emphasis in original). Overall, the dominant logics at work inside the old system actively worked against, but did not entirely extinguish, the possibilities of industrial complexity and popular musical heterogeneity.

The relatively closed system characteristic of the 'old' music industries has been challenged in important ways by digital distribution, leading to problematic accounts of major label demise. According to Tim Anderson,

> As wide-scale record retail practically vanished from its brick and mortar domains, a conventional narrative emerged: the combination of significantly compressed, relatively high-fidelity digital formats with the proliferation of seemingly ubiquitous broadband networks and personalized information control technologies through which music would now be distributed killed the music industry. (Anderson 2014: 3)

Excited proclamations regarding the death of the music industries have been premature thus far. As Anderson points out, 'the destruction by digital is only one part of the story'; a more comprehensive and precise account must also explore 'how an industry has and continues to undergo multiple experiments to create a viable set of practices to replace those that have been lost' (Anderson 2014: 3). Before examining experimentation with the artist-brand approach in particular, it warrants mentioning that the 'death of retail' has worked to tighten the majors' grip over whatever physical retail sales remain (see Rogers 2013: 44–6; Passman 2015: 69–70). As Grierson points out, 'There's very few places where you can actually go and buy music. And if you go to the Walmarts or the Kmarts or the Targets, they only carry the main titles or the main artists. They don't carry deep catalogue and they don't really support the developing artists' (Grierson, personal communication, 2010).

A record business anchored by unit sales was easier to control and manage than its digital successor in many ways. Nevertheless, the end of major label and music publisher dominance in terms of copyright ownership, marketing and the monetization of top stars has proven elusive thus far. Their longevity is largely a product of the distinctive economics of the music industries discussed above. The business logics and tendencies inherited from the old music industries still play a vital role in shaping the asymmetrical distribution of risks and rewards found in the contemporary music industries.

Digital Music Models: The Centrality of Marketing

Unprecedented access to the technological means of recording, distributing and promoting music has opened up new avenues to the recording artist interested in working outside the long-entrenched recording industry oligopoly dominated by the Big Three. Today's music audiences, meanwhile, have access not only to an abundance of musical content, but also to a range of digital audio/media players (e.g. smartphones, MP3 players, tablets) and content delivery methods (e.g. digital downloads, music streaming services). In a remarkable reversal, the audience can now choose what to listen to and when, seemingly upsetting music industry control over marketing and distribution. Television-based music video plugging largely has been displaced by streaming video services (e.g. YouTube, Vevo), and social media platforms have emerged as key sites for the sharing and promotion of music. Specialist 'direct-to-fan' sales and marketing companies (e.g. Bandcamp, Nimbit, Topspin) are available to independent recording artists seeking assistance with online 'fan management' and 'brand management'. Such expertise is invaluable in an industry that now measures popularity in terms of Facebook friends, Twitter followers and YouTube views, not simply *Billboard* charts. In the words of one record label executive,

> It used to be that the record company would decide when the single went out, when the promo tour went out, when the ... publicity hit, and how the consumer was exposed to music. Now, because everything's digital and online, the consumer sees that almost instantaneously and actually they 'pull' it. They're the ones drawing it. ... We don't control the machine anymore. We used to have to push the engine to get it going. ... Now it's pulled. (Canadian major record label executive B, personal communication, 2009)

Even the decision whether or not to pay for a recording is voluntary, although non-payment may come with the threat of legal action.[3]

At first blush, then, the new music industries bear little resemblance to their precursors. Closer examination of who continues to profit most from the commercial production of popular music, however, reveals a decidedly different reality to the optimistic vision of an industry freed from the grip of major music companies. Although the locked down industrial system has been pried open in many ways and revenues from recorded music and CD sales have declined sharply, the Big Three still dominate an overwhelming share of the music market under the digital model. The resilience of these companies is tied to the deepening importance of marketing and market-making in new business models, which hinge on the production of artist-brands ripe for monetization not only through recorded music sales, but various other revenue streams in addition.

Listeners today benefit from a remarkable abundance and diversity of popular music available, making discussions of Top 40 stars and major label dominance seem somehow out of place in a discussion of the new music industries. After all, the blockbuster approach underpinned by star artists and hit songs and albums harmonized with the marketing and distribution systems of the old recording industry model: limited access to commercial radio, music video channels and major retail chains circumscribed diversity and reinforced hierarchies between working artists. In the 2000s, a belief that the old model was antiquated emerged among many independent record label executives and small-scale music producers. Instead, it was thought, new digital models offered an open field freed from the dictates of the major record labels. Claims that the blockbuster model is on the decline in the cultural industries more generally are often linked to notion of the 'long tail' – a popular but flawed idea developed by Chris Anderson, former editor-in-chief at *Wired*.

The long tail refers to the graphical representation of a demand curve for which a handful of hits generate the majority of sales (the 'head') and numerous non-hits are sold in much lower volumes (the 'long tail'). Taking inspiration from the case of online film and television aggregator Netflix (before the company adopted its current original content-driven strategy for gaining subscribers), Anderson argued that the internet had allowed for unprecedented profitability for low-volume, niche media products, including music, which could now coexist healthily with blockbuster hits:

> These millions of fringe sales are an efficient, cost-effective business. With no shelf space to pay for – and in the case of purely digital services like iTunes, no manufacturing costs and hardly any distribution fees – a niche product sold is just another sale, with the same (or better) margins as a hit. *For the first time in history, hits and niches are on equal economic footing.* (Anderson 2006: 24; emphasis added)

In Anderson's account, falling costs of distribution have reconfigured media content profit models. It is no longer necessary to produce, distribute and retail physical media products, ostensibly a source of considerable cost-savings.

Anderson's thesis suggests a misunderstanding of the industrial logics that govern the cultural industries, including the high cost of production versus low cost of reproduction and the perennial problem of risk

– factors central to understanding why the Big Three and the top stars have been able to remain dominant amid the availability of so many alternatives. The costs of pressing, shipping and retailing physical CDs were never especially burdensome to major record companies. As Garnham points out, 'the cost of each record pressing is infinitesimal compared to the cost of recording' (Garnham 1990: 160) – an observation that still holds, according to the account provided by Ari Martin, then vice president of artist management at Nettwerk Music Group: 'The bulk of the costs are the marketing and A&R and recording, and payments to the artist and publisher. Yeah, the CD production, ... saving that cost is not that big of an effect' (Martin, personal communication, 2010). Additionally, Anderson's declaration that hits and niche products are subject to the same profit margins (Anderson 2006: 24) is simply inaccurate in the case of music. Album pricing may be somewhat standardized (although increasingly less so), but the recording contract terms that dictate record label profit margins and recording artist remuneration are not. In the United States, the album royalty rate for new artists (those who have never signed a record deal or whose previous sales fell below 100,000 albums) is typically 13–16 per cent of the wholesale price, known as the 'published price to dealers' (PPD), whereas the typical rates for midlevel artists (previous album sales of 200,000–400,000 copies) and superstars (previous album sales in excess of 750,000) are 15–18 per cent of PPD and 18–20 percent of PPD, respectively (Passman 2015: 92–4). Royalty rates are stratified and stratifying.

Even ostensibly fairer contractual arrangements do not counter the financial pressures tied to making music, and often place these risks squarely on the shoulders of recording artists. For instance, an artist might choose to sign a 'net profit deal', a type of recording contract commonly offered by independent record labels. While premised on the 50–50 sharing of net profits, under these contracts 'the label doesn't have to pay the artist anything (including, under many contracts, even mechanical royalties) until the label has recouped all costs fronted by the label', according to entertainment attorney Bart Day (2009). Even with a higher percentage of recording revenues, many independent recording artists will not achieve sales figures sufficient to pay off the initial investment required to produce an album, especially amid declining album sales. Unsigned, self-produced recording artists, meanwhile, may receive the greatest cut of recording revenue, but they must also bear all expenses and forego the marketing budgets that record labels use to drive sales. The costs associated with producing, promoting and performing popular music can impede the realization of profits.

Although the digital delivery of music has dismantled major label control over distribution channels, it has not fundamentally changed the distinctive economics of the recording industry. The substantial investment remains tied to the costs of producing and marketing the now virtual or polycarbonate plastic album, not in reproducing and distributing copies of that album. In fact, the sheer abundance of music available today makes generous marketing budgets essential to those artists hoping to be heard above the rest.

To be fair, Anderson's argument that 'millions of fringe sales are an efficient, cost-effective business' (Anderson 2006: 24) is not intended to suggest that the 'long tail' is good for the individual artist. Rather, it rests on the idea that these sales are profitable *in aggregate*; hence his focus on Netflix and not the individual filmmaker – a point overlooked by many music industry executives involved in smaller-scale and independent music production. Indeed, the position of aggregators of digital content is altogether different than that of individual creators. Unless they are involved in the production of original content (as Netflix and Amazon now are, to a certain degree), content aggregators do not need to bear the same risks as individual producers, and they are able to amass revenues from entire libraries of licensed content instead of relying on a handful of projects.

Even so, Anderson's theory has been refuted on the basis of actual sales data (see Gomes 2006; Elberse 2008; Page and Garland 2009) – and makes even less sense amid the more recent explosion of streaming and corresponding erosion of revenues for individual artists. During the period considered by Anderson, online retailers' sales closely mirrored the *Billboard* charts (Gomes 2006), and a more convincing case could be made that the 'extremely low demand for the large array of products in the tail means that simply recovering the costs of producing them will be challenging' (Elberse 2008). Put simply, in the recording industry, the head may simply be too big and the tail too small.

Nevertheless, optimistic visions of a break from the established star system circulated widely in the first decade of the twenty-first century. The '1,000 True Fans' blog post written by Kevin Kelly, founding executive editor of *Wired*, also was touted by independent labels and producers at this time. Kelly speculated that a small-scale recording artist could 'make an honest living' off the cultivation of 1,000 'True Fans' 'who will purchase anything and everything you produce' (Kelly 2008a). His thesis was based on the assumption that such fans would spend $100 every year (an arbitrarily chosen number) on their favourite act, and therefore 'if you have 1,000 fans that sums up to $100,000 per year, which minus some modest expenses, is a living for most folks' (Kelly 2008a). These expenses are not detailed. He added the caveat that this figure would only work for solo artists; larger groups would need more than 1,000 fans to make a living from making music. As Tim Anderson points out,

> Kelly's blog post was quickly seized upon by many and continues to be a popular topic for discussion with reporters, on-the-ground Internet consultants, artists, and online business gurus. ... Nowhere has the applicability of the 1,000 True Fans concept been more debated than among the independent music industry. In search of a viable economic and financial path, independent labels, musicians, and consultants have held up and criticized 1,000 True Fans as a means to middle-class achievement. (Anderson 2014: 176)

The popularity of the idea is understandable: cultivating 1,000 fans seems like an attainable goal. However, the numbers do not appear to add up to anything close to a middle-class income for the vast majority of smaller-scale music makers.

Indeed, Kelly conducted follow-up research on his '1,000 True Fans' model and his findings support a far more sobering conclusion. He conceded 'that while investigating the data for my thesis, I was unable to find much that could convince me that anyone is actually supporting themselves with 1000 or even 5000 True Fans now' (Kelly 2008b). Robert Rich, an ambient musician who fits Kelly's model of 'microcelebrities' who deal directly with fans via their websites, offered the following assessment:

> If I can make about $5–$10 per download or directly sold CD, and I sell 1,000, I clear a maximum of $10,000 for that year's effort. That's not a living. Let's say, after 20 concerts I net about $10,000 for three to four months worth of full time effort. ... I can augment that paltry income through some of the added benefits of 'microcelebrity' including licensing fees for sample clearance and film use rights, sound design libraries, and supplemental income from studio mastering and engineering fees. (quoted in Kelly 2008c)

In a streaming era in which listeners typically no longer buy CDs or, increasingly, even digital downloads, it is hard to imagine recording artists outside of famous performers (who can charge high prices for concert tickets, merchandise and so forth) generating $100 per fan per year.

Positive assessments of the ideas of the 'long tail' and '1,000 True Fans' – in spite of these problems and shortcomings – seem to be a testament to the will to believe. The dream of 'making it' has been harnessed to new technologies, not addressing the political and economic realities that produce inequalities and do not come with an easy technological fix. Major entertainment corporations have leveraged these same digital tools in the production of one of their biggest assets, celebrity, which they use to generate marketing exposure across media old and new.

The idea that 'hits are starting to rule less' is certainly appealing, as it would suggest that the foundations of the old model, including the centrality of the production of stardom, have been upended. However, the surface appearance of popular musical democratization created by the wealth of music available today actually works to veil the fact that the value of celebrity has only been heightened within the digital media environment, which has consequences for smaller companies and non-star artists jockeying for position and listeners. While digital distribution has unseated the major record labels in terms of control over the distribution of recordings, as they can no longer determine *where* and *when* *which* recordings are available, the question of what makes for cost-effective and profitable business under the new system is an entirely different matter. The majors have held fast to a proven formula, albeit with some modification, as we shall see.

If the advent of digital distribution has not substantively altered the basic economics of the recording industry, have falling costs of production reconfigured the bases of profitability? The rapid expansion of a consumer market for (relatively) affordable digital recording technology has translated into unprecedented access to high-quality recording equipment for the aspiring recording artist. As *Audiophile Review* editor and recording engineer Steven Stone points out, 'Now for under $50k US anyone can assemble the tools for a top-flight multi-channel DIY recording set-up' (Stone 2011). If a high-end set-up lies outside a recording artist's price range, 'Music production packages such as Cubase, Pro Tools, and Ableton Live deliver a professional end product and are within the financial reach of the amateur' (Young and Collins 2010: 344). In fact, Gorillaz founder Damon Albarn recorded the album *The Fall* (2010) on his iPad while on tour (Michaels 2010).

While the costs of producing an album have fallen for amateur producers, the major record companies have also benefited from these cost-savings. Furthermore, individual recording artists who choose to work entirely independently of the record label system must personally assume what can amount to considerable financial risk in exchange for the creative autonomy gained. It is still tremendously difficult to gauge potential audience interest in cultural products, and commercial failure remains the norm. As recording artist David Lowery (of alternative rock bands Camper Van Beethoven and Cracker) – a former champion of new business models enabled by digital distribution – cautions, 'The artist pays for the recording, the artist pays for all publicity, promotion and advertising. ... The artist absorbs the costs of touring. ... [T]he new model makes the artist absorb all the risk' (quoted in Resnikoff 2012a). Even with more affordable recording options, the costs associated with purchasing the required hardware and software, a computer to operate them, musical instruments, microphones and so forth, in addition to the costs associated with touring, are not insubstantial. The time and labour invested in writing music, practising and honing one's craft also figure into the cost of performing and recording music. While the costs associated with recording may have fallen, recording artists still face considerable expenses tied to producing and promoting albums and digital tracks, which consumers are increasingly hesitant to purchase.

Marketing is essential in this hypercompetitive marketplace for digital cultural goods. The ability to circumvent entrenched music industry gatekeepers has translated into a flood of new recordings, and as such, marketing costs can be prohibitively high. In stark contrast to the 4,000–5,000 new albums typically released per year during the 1970s and the fewer than 2,000 released annually during the 1980s recession years (Frith 1988b: 18), Nielsen SoundScan reported that in the US there were 60,000 new albums released in 2005, 105,000 in 2008 and 98,000 in 2009 (Peoples 2010b). Inside the new streaming economy, for the most part, the release of albums is still a necessary part of forging a career in the music industries, yet actual sales of those albums – either as CDs or as digital files – are being displaced amid the availability of various subscription and 'free'/advertising-based models. Today, listeners have a dizzying amount of music to choose from – what music industry expert Mark Mulligan characterizes as 'The Tyranny of Choice', as he points out that '[i]n 2008 the average digital music service catalogue size was 4.3 million, [whereas] by 2013 that number had exceeded 18 million' (Mulligan 2015b: 168). This might be an exciting development for music fans, but it poses substantive challenges to working artists. As *Billboard*'s Glenn Peoples observed of the new music industries more generally in 2010, the 'abundance of tools and low barriers to entry has created an inconvenient truth: More artists are chasing after less money' (Peoples 2010b) – an assessment that rings true, notwithstanding Peoples' incorrect assessment of barriers to entry. Those recording artists who lack adequate marketing budgets – non-star recording artists and especially new artists – are at a considerable disadvantage. It is increasingly difficult for even established recording artists to stand out and be heard, not to mention being remunerated in some way.

Although the oft-rehearsed story of the new music industries has been discussed in terms of the potential afforded by new technologies, the locus of power remains steadfastly located in the ability to finance, market and promote popular music, with marketing arguably assuming an even more central role in production of commercial success today than in years past. It is a cost that, in effect, keeps barriers to entry higher than is conventionally assumed. According to Ian Rogers, CEO of e-commerce and music marketing platform Topspin, 'Technology has allowed the cost of production to come down, and the cost of distribution has come down. ... But the cost of marketing has come up, because you have empowered consumers and unlimited choice' (quoted in Resnikoff 2010). Market researcher Kathleen Ripley reports that 'marketing is the largest expense for the industry, accounting for 26.3% of industry revenue' (Ripley 2011a: 25). A lower break-even point in terms of recording costs, then, is arguably offset by increased marketing costs, and the major record companies still boast the largest marketing budgets. Despite high levels of technological change, barriers to entry remain high (Ripley 2011a: 28).

Complicating matters further is the fact that recording artists are often encouraged to give away their digital music for free in order to make money elsewhere, especially from touring and merchandise sales. For some established recording artists who have opted out of restrictive major label contracts, this has been a commercially viable approach. Freed from label control and still able to generate substantial touring revenues, Radiohead, for instance, was in a position to offer a 'name-your-own-price' digital download self-release of *In Rainbows* (2007), and Trent Reznor of Nine Inch Nails was able to offer free digital self-releases of his recordings (Harding and Cohen 2008). These recording artists were already stars, however. 'There's always that good line. It's like: how do you do the *In Rainbows* release? ... The first trick is to become Radiohead', explained independent music publisher Neville Quinlan (personal communication, 2009). Other recording artists who have experimented with unconventional or free-to-consumer album releases include Jay-Z, Beyoncé and U2 – top stars among the industry elite. In the words of digital music analyst Susan Kevorkian, 'For bands who have worked with labels over the years and who have developed followings, the technology is in place to reach their fans much more directly without needing labels' marketing expertise. But for emerging groups to leverage the same technology to attract a following is a long row to hoe' (quoted in Sandoval 2007). After all, Peoples (2010b) points out, 'An unknown band is no less unknown because it gives away its music.' Established and aspiring recording artists remain on unequal footing, despite the new opportunities available.

Evidence suggests, then, that technological changes to the tools used to produce, distribute and consume sound recordings have not fundamentally disrupted the distinctive economics of the old recording industry system. This being so, it is also true that the CD is no longer seen as the primary basis of popular music's monetization. How, exactly, is music monetized in the digital era? What is the core music commodity? Popular music has not been unmoored from processes of commodification; instead, it appears in new commercial and promotional forms.

The 'Unbundling' of the Album and Proliferation of Music Products and Services

The decline of the CD format has triggered a radical transformation across what was formerly, first and foremost, a *record* business, even as those records became polycarbonate discs and then MP3s. Indeed, from roughly 1985 to 2000, the popularity of the CD album sparked strong year-on-year sales growth: it was a 'golden era' in recorded music profitability (Leyshon et al. 2005: 177). Between 2005 and 2010, however, CD sales in the United States dropped by 20.4 per cent annually, according to Recording Industry Association of America (RIAA) figures – a period during which digital download sales grew at a rate of 34.8 per cent per year (Ripley 2011a: 8). According to market research company NPD Group's statistics, 'Close to half of all U.S. teens did not buy a single CD last year [2008], while consumers ages 36–50 drove what sales there were. Since the latter group tends to prefer time-tested artists, the major labels have shied away from signing and promoting new acts in favor of relying on already-established performers' (Gardner 2009). In the first half of 2015, CD sales reportedly fell by another 31.5 per cent and digital track revenues declined by 9.4 per cent, while streaming revenues increased by 23.2 per cent (Peoples 2015b). Risk-averse record companies 'tend to bet their marketing money on the already established' (Kulash 2010), arguably even more so than in the past. In this climate, stars remain central. However, music companies monetize recording artists in a host of new ways.

Under the digital music model, the B2B market for music licences and the generation of revenue from sync and branding opportunities are paramount. The exploitation of new and expanded products, rights and markets, coupled with intensifying corporate consolidation, has allowed for extensive capitalization. Streaming services constitute one important revenue stream, but largely fall within a business-to-customer (B2C) approach that is primarily oriented toward end users (although they do involve arrangements made between third parties). Given my interest in the growing importance of the B2B market, streaming is not my focus here, even as I recognize the continuing significance of the consumer market for sound recordings in various formats. My point is not that one market has replaced the other: instead, music companies work to aggregate multiple revenue streams. All of these businesses are important.

Briefly, the *consumer* market for sound recordings is now largely a digital singles and streaming business, and the product sold is a digital track or licence to stream.[4] The music industry has largely become a service industry (Wikström 2009; Anderson 2014). Although digital revenues continue to grow, with 'streaming gains outpac[ing] download losses' (Peoples 2015b), these revenues have not in themselves compensated for the decline in album sales. 'Analog dollars have been replaced by digital pennies' is a common refrain inside the recording industry. As an executive at a Canadian branch of a major record company explained – before the mushrooming popularity of streaming: 'We've gone back to people buying tracks and that's another reason why the industry's ... had to look for ... alternative revenue models. ... You were selling a $15 CD. Now you're selling a 99¢ track, but you've got to sell fifteen of them to make up for the revenue' (Canadian major record label executive B, personal communication, 2009). These digital pennies are sliced up further when monetized not in sales but streams.

Contradicting the argument that hits matter less today, the economics of the digital singles and streaming markets, in which record labels seek to compensate for lost album revenues, provide an even stronger business rationale for the production of blockbusters. 'Don't radically alter blockbuster resource-allocation or product-portfolio management strategies', advises Harvard business professor Anita Elberse, as 'a few winners will still go a long way – probably even further than before' (Elberse 2008). In *Blockbusters: Why Big Hits – and Big Risks – are the Future of the Entertainment Business*, Elberse observes that '[r]ather than a shift of demand to the long tail, we are witnessing an increased level of concentration in the market for digital entertainment goods. ... [T]he entertainment industry is moving more and more toward a winner-take-all-market' (Elberse 2013: 163). In today's music business, 'big singles – big artists make all the money ... and that's who you need to be associated with' (Quinlan, personal communication, 2009). Major label reliance on star recording artists has actually intensified. The new blockbuster model, however, is not anchored by album sales but a host of revenue streams, only one of which is recorded music.

Because the revenue from digital music sales alone has not been able to compensate for declining revenues from CD sales, revenue streams previously seen as merely ancillary have become central to the recording industry. According to one major record label executive,

> You have to maximize all ancillary revenue. And the industry, as it evolved, was really about the primary source of exploitation, which

was the album sale, and there was a second squeeze of the orange, where you ... made compilations and that's about it. And now, of course, there's, like, fifteen squeezes of the orange, because the first squeeze isn't enough to live on. (Canadian major record label executive A, personal communication, 2009)

In fact, major record label complaints about the fragmentation of the album into the digital single belie the fact that the same process of 'unbundling' has translated into a proliferation of new digital products and rights (Ripley 2011a: 16). What is more, the growing use of popular music in advertisements, films, television programmes and video games generates substantial master-use revenues for record labels. The range of music commodities for which record companies are remunerated has multiplied.

The decline of the CD has not had nearly the same impact on business-as-usual across the music publishing industry, because these companies' core bases of monetization have not been similarly disrupted. 'The business of selling music in my world hasn't changed', explained Jodie Ferneyhough, an executive at Universal Music Publishing Canada at the time of our interview. 'I've always sold music. The record companies have always sold a disc. They've always sold a product. They've never sold music. ... Those products happen to contain music' (Ferneyhough, personal communication, 2009). More precisely, the music publisher's job has always involved the exploitation of song copyrights and the protection of that intellectual property, not the selling of units. Popular music's commodity form inside the music publishing industry, then, has not changed.

In fact, the recent proliferation of music licensing agreements with other business partners, and hence sync revenues, has been a boon to the music publishing industry. Advertising and television placement revenues in particular have flourished for these companies in the past fifteen to twenty years (they have derived revenues from the more established market for film placements for much longer). According to John Campanelli, vice president of marketing at Sony/ATV Music Publishing, 'Every year we've done better ... for the past five years ... in terms of the money that we've made. It's more volume. ... The prices are going down, but the amount of opportunities is going up' (Campanelli, personal communication, 2010). While individual licensing fees for non-star artists have plummeted, as discussed in chapter 3, sync licensing revenues in aggregate continue to grow. Furthermore, Sony/ATV garnered 'good fees' for 'catalogue songs' (Campanelli, personal communication, 2010); this catalogue features music by the Beatles, Billy Joel, Jimi Hendrix and Elvis Presley. Many independent music publishers, such as Ole and

Peermusic, are also flourishing in the music licensing-oriented music marketplace (Beavis, personal communication, 2009; Quinlan, personal communication, 2009). Indeed, music publishing and licensing accounts for 19.5 per cent of global music industry revenue (IBISWorld 2012: 13).

Today, music videos, too, are monetized products and also chiefly fall under B2B licensing models. In contrast to independent record labels and artists, which often give away music in order to generate marketing exposure, major record labels now view the model of offering music for free in exchange for promotion – the basis for the MTV promotional system – to be obsolete. In the words of one Canadian major label executive, 'What is exposure? Exposure's trying to sell more music. But we're not about selling music anymore. We're about … multi-faceted revenue streams, so that isn't our priority anymore' (Canadian major record label executive A, personal communication, 2009). Music videos constitute one of those revenue streams; what was formerly a means of promoting records is now a product for sale. Unlike under the MTV system, the major labels now have easy access to highly trafficked video channels, such as YouTube and Vevo. In fact, the world's two largest record companies now own a video channel: Vevo is a joint venture owned by Sony Music Entertainment, Universal Music Group, Abu Dhabi Media and, as of 2013, YouTube (Pham 2013). All the major labels have licensing agreements in place with the company at the helm of the new music video monopoly: Google's YouTube.

Record companies monetize digital music videos in four key ways. First, and most straightforwardly, music videos are available for purchase on iTunes – a B2C approach distinct from the following B2B approaches. Second, record companies profit from licences extracted from streaming video sites. YouTube remunerates all the major record companies by way of compensation rights per stream (Canadian major record label executive A, personal communication, 2009). Specific figures for YouTube rates are not made public, but *Rolling Stone*'s Steven Knopper (2011) reports that a top-selling artist 'might make $1 per 1,000 video plays'. Such a rate provides meagre revenues for lesser known recording artists, whose work is typically streamed in lower volumes. However, as one record label executive put it, 'When you start adding millions and millions of views, … it does add up as a significant revenue stream' (Canadian major record label executive A, personal communication, 2009). In 2012, social media data analytics company Starcount Squared reported that Universal artists Lady Gaga, Rihanna and Justin Bieber had each received over 2 billion YouTube views, collectively accounting for 6.77 billion of Universal's 6.91 billion total YouTube views (Starcount Squared 2012). For superstar recording artists and their record labels, the volume-driven music video streaming business is profitable indeed, though the major labels have been accused of inflating YouTube views (*Billboard* 2012). Nevertheless, according to Tom Freston, former CEO of MTV Networks and Viacom, the revenue generated from licences and iTunes sales for music videos became substantial enough for record labels to 'actually cover the costs of the music videos and make a profit to boot' (quoted in *Billboard* 2009). Large record companies, after all, are able to aggregate revenues generated by an entire catalogue of music videos old and new. Third, Universal and Sony sell advertising around Vevo content; the online video market is seen to provide 'valuable advertising real estate that supports strong monetization' (comScore 2012: 15). Fourth, record companies sell product placement (or 'brand integration') opportunities within the videos themselves.

Product placement in music videos can be seen as an extension of product placement in lyrics, a trend that began before the recording industry's digital transition was fully underway. The lyrics of at least eight Top 20 singles on *Billboard*'s 2004 hip-hop chart, for example, included references to the brand Pepsi-Cola (Schmelzer 2005). Niche-marketing agency RPM, with PepsiCo, even recruited DJs to 'serve as "soda ambassadors," touting the soda via on-air mentions, club events, photo shoots, block parties, Pepsi-sponsored mix tapes and cross-promotions with brands such as Launch and T-Mobile' (Schmelzer 2005). Pepsi 'multicultural marketing manager' Brett O'Brien explained that 'DJs have always been on the cutting edge. Getting into [their] minds as people who support the scene adds relevance to the brand, resulting in stronger, more credible consumer relationships' (quoted in Schmelzer 2005). Brands' interest in attaining 'credibility' of this sort will be examined in chapter 3.

Returning to the case of music videos, Rio Caraeff, (now former) CEO of Vevo, described the website as 'a conduit between the world's largest music companies and brand marketers' (quoted in Plambeck 2010). As reported by the *New York Times*, research conducted by firm PQ Media suggests that revenue from product placements in music videos was in the range of US$15 million to $20 million in 2009, more than twice the figure reported in 2000 (Plambeck 2010). In the words of PQ Media chief executive Patrick Quinn, 'That real estate – getting into the content itself – has become that much more valuable' (quoted in Plambeck 2010). Lady Gaga's 'Telephone' (2010) music video was apparently seen as particularly valuable real estate, given the abundance of product placements it features, including Beats brand headphones and laptops, Chevrolet, Diet Coke, Miracle Whip, Polaroid, Virgin Mobile, Wonder Bread and PlentyofFish.com. This pervasive trend extends well beyond pop superstars. For example, Piaget forged an agreement with indie rock outfit Florence + the Machine (now signed to Universal); the brand's luxury watches and rings feature in the music videos for 'Shake It Out' (2011) and 'No Light, No Light' (2011). Follow-up research conducted by PQ Media (2015) suggests that brand integrations in recorded music and videos continue to be an area of growth.

The availability of online music and video distribution to unsigned and independent recording artists by no means spells the end of major record label and music publisher dominance. In fact, the centrality of various inter-firm licensing agreements (as opposed to unit sales) to the rights-driven digital music industries arguably renders the administrative function assumed by these corporate entities even more important today. A Canadian major record label executive marvelled at how, despite massive lay-offs overall, at his company,

> Our royalties department downstairs has grown exponentially. We probably have eight to nine people in our royalties department now, because we used to put out ... one CD and there's ... a royalty that comes from that for the artist and the publisher and it's one product line. ... We might put out a physical single, ... maybe going back five or six years, and that would be it. Now we've got ... a digital single, a digital video, a ringtone, mobile content, we've got the full album, we've got all ten or twelve tracks on the album separately, a bunch of other unique exclusive pieces of content. We might have thirty pieces of content for every single project released. (Canadian major record label executive B, personal communication, 2009)

According to music publisher Quinlan, 'You're always going to need an administrator, but you might not need a publisher and a record label' (Quinlan, personal communication, 2009) inside the maturing digital music economy. In the near future, a recording artist's administrative associate, music publisher and record label 'might be the same person. ... To be a stand-alone publisher that doesn't sell T-shirts ... or doesn't make records or doesn't manage artists or book tours might not be viable in ten years' (Quinlan, personal communication, 2009). Clearly, a dynamic of convergence is at work.

In response to the unbundling of the CD album into the digital single and, hence, the splintering of profits, record companies launched and expanded markets for various music products, rights and licences. Miège's publishing logic is still in evidence here: in the new music industries, record labels and music publishers still produce highly reproducible products, which are sold to end consumers, and creators are still remunerated through a royalty-based system. However, departing from Miège, record labels have also become unprecedentedly dependent on the B2B market for music licensing and endorsement opportunities. Moreover, according to music industry economist Will Page, ' "Business-to-Business" revenues, or licensing income ... is likely to make up an increasing part of an increasing pie' (Page 2010). This expanding licensing business shares a key characteristic in common with the earlier record business: record labels and music publishers profit from economies of scale, because they are able to exploit the breadth of entire rosters or catalogues to generate high volumes of licence sales. Individual recording artists do not have this luxury. Importantly, the licensing market not only generates additional revenue for record companies and music publishers, it also produces a new power base for the advertisers, brands and media companies that license music – a theme examined in chapter 3.

As record labels continue to remake themselves into rights-oriented rather than predominantly units-oriented businesses, they begin to resemble music publishers, marking an interesting continuity with the pre-recording phase of music's industrialization. The continuing dominance of the major record companies unites the pre-digital record business with the digital music model, however. Also central to understanding the continuities and changes that have shaped the music industries in the digital age is the prominent role assigned to the live performance and touring industry.

The Transformation of the Live Performance Sector

In the contemporary music industries, whose financial health is sustained through the aggregation of multiple and multiplying revenue streams, the live performance sector exists alongside B2B licensing revenues as a key source of value creation. The volatility of the digital music marketplace has prompted major and independent labels alike to gear their business models around live performances and to gauge the viability of recording artists in terms of touring revenue. After all, the concert *experience* (as distinct from the actual songs performed) cannot be 'pirated'. During the first decade of the twenty-first century, the number of concerts, festivals and the like available to music fans mushroomed (Laing 2009: 19). For major and independent record labels alike, '[l]ive events are seen as a counterweight to recorded music declines' (Peoples 2010b). According to Dave Laing's assessment of figures from 2010–11, 'the live business worldwide ... may have definitively overtaken the record industry in revenue terms' (Laing 2012). To clarify, Laing's claim is specific to sales of recorded music. The recording industry now encompasses music licensing, endorsement and merchandising businesses in addition. To be sure, the affect-laden encounter with the artist-brand offered by the concert experience makes for very lucrative business in the case of a handful of stars, given rising ticket prices for top acts. However, as Peoples and numerous other industry commentators, analysts and executives make clear, the live performance sector is no panacea for the music industries more widely, especially for aspiring artists.

The new reliance on live performance revenues marks a decided shift from the old industrial model, under which concerts were viewed as promotional vehicles (Goodwin 1992: 27; Shuker 2002: 307). Writing in 1992, Andrew Goodwin observed

> a contradiction inside the music industry, between inherently mass-produced commodity forms such as records and cassettes (which produce profit but insufficient meaning) and preindustrial forms of promotion such as live performance (which help to 'complete' the package of meaning, but which until the 1980s generally failed to generate profit even when organized on a mass scale). (Goodwin 1992: 27)

While live performances may have offered the fan a popular musical experience imbued with meaning, they were primarily used in an effort to drive record sales. Touring was seen as 'especially necessary to promote a new release and build up an audience' (Shuker 2002: 305), yet those tours were often 'a loss-making activity' for all but the top star performers (Frith 2001: 45). Once already commercially successful, however, rock performers in particular could 'support careers in virtual absence of live performance, so that audiences [knew] their work only through recordings' (Gracyk 1996: 7). When concerts did generate income, these revenues were deemed ancillary.

Inside the contemporary music industries, this arrangement has flipped: recordings are increasingly seen as a means of promoting concerts and other products. The major labels are invested in monetizing all music-related products, and as such, forego opportunities to use free music as a promotional medium. However, especially outside of the major labels, it is now widely held that records (CDs and MP3s) no longer constitute the core popular musical commodity, as was the case under the old model, but instead are 'merchandise' or 'promotional items for what artists are actually doing, which is providing the service of music in the many ways that they do' (Outhit, personal communication, 2009). According to this vision of the music industries,

> MP3s and CDs are becoming viewed as promotional tools dispatched to draw fans to live performances. There, they transform into customers paying for the initial ticket and then merchandise including the traditional T-shirt, but also singles, albums, and in some cases a record-

ing of the gig they just saw – the ultimate fan memento. (Young and Collins 2010: 352)

Profitability, in this formulation, hinges on sales of music-related merchandise, and albums, reconfigured as merchandise, are sold alongside T-shirts and the like. 'Proponents of this model believe that directly charging consumers for recorded music is becoming less viable', explains legal scholar Mark F. Schultz, 'but that musicians will still produce recordings because they serve an important promotional function. ... Recording is thus seen as a necessary promotional expense for other, more profitable businesses like touring and merchandising' (Schultz 2009: 697). In what appears to be a remarkable turnaround, the concert ticket is seen to function as the key popular music commodity and the recording as the necessary loss leader.

Initially, the live performance sector was seen as the remedy for the digitalizing music industry's woes for good reason. Profits were robust. However, in stark contrast to 2009, when 'concerts were given the mantle as the savior of the music business and in large part impervious to economic recessions', the average gross and attendance per live show saw double-digit decreases on a global scale in 2010 (Waddell 2010b). Large concert promoters postponed and cancelled tours and used 'firesale'-style ticket discounting to fill venues (Waddell 2010b). Touring industry profitability was restored in 2011, however, in part due to lower ticket prices (Waddell 2011) – reductions achieved not because concert promotion behemoth Live Nation took a smaller cut, it would seem, but because the 'guarantees' paid to non-star artists fell. In the aftermath of the industry's 2010 struggles, Michael Rapino, CEO of Live Nation, reported that 'the top-tier artists are still able to demand high guarantees and the bidding remains competitive'. Mid-tier artists, however, 'are taking into account what happened in 2010' (quoted in CQ Transcriptions 2011).

Even prior to this cut to mid-tier artist guarantees, the concert business was plagued by what Schultz terms 'the superstar problem': 'The distribution of rewards in the business is incredibly skewed' (Schultz 2009: 733). Drawing on *Billboard*'s touring statistics, Schultz charts a distribution of the US$2.6 billion in gross touring earnings reported for 2007: the top 0.76 per cent (just twenty-five tours) accounted for 53 per cent of all earnings, while the bottom 99.24 per cent shared the remaining 47 per cent of revenues earned (Schultz 2009: 734–5). Most unknown artists, those who perform at a variety of smaller venues, clubs and bars, make little or no money from their performances, one entertainment attorney explained to attendees at an artist management conference in New York City (Litwak 2010). Some even pay for access to prime venues on Los Angeles's Sunset Strip or in New York City: the artist is required to 'guarantee' (i.e. buy upfront and hope to sell) a certain number of tickets (Litwak 2010; Mencher 2010).

In 2010, Topspin's Rogers reported that only 25,000–30,000 recording artists in the United States make a living from music – an estimate derived from the size and type of live music venues played, not record and digital download sales (cited in Resnikoff 2010). 'Rogers pointed to millions of MySpace bands, tens of millions of musicians, and a Long Tail that is "well, very long"', notes Paul Resnikoff (2010) of *Digital Music News*. Lowery likewise emphasizes the financial struggles associated with touring in his widely debated indictment of P2P file sharing and the new music industry (see Frank 2012; Lefsetz 2012; White 2012; Worstall 2012):

> You know only a handful of artists make a living touring right? Most artists need another job to go back to or they get tour support from the record label.
> Touring usually only pays enough to pay the crew and expenses. Touring only makes sense if it increases your sales. Artists often go on tour for free in hopes that the tour pays off in increased sales. (quoted in Resnikoff 2012a)

The healthy touring earnings routinely cited do not reflect the more telling median numbers but, instead, a grossly misleading mean.

An overall increase in competition, coupled with falling guarantees and ticket prices for non-star artists, only exacerbates the realities of touring as a costly and, hence, risky venture. Certain costs (e.g. a bus, fuel, accommodation, crew wages) are fixed, which makes it difficult for small-scale tours (under 2,500-seat venues) in general to generate a significant profit (Martin, personal communication, 2010). To mitigate this risk, the touring sector is taking a page from the record companies' playbook and becoming even more reliant on older, well-known and established artists (Schultz 2009: 733; *Billboard* 2010; Jansson, personal communication, 2010). The commercial dynamics at work inside the concert promotion business continue to favour tours that feature star artists, large venues and pricey tickets. These lucrative tours, in turn, are monopolized by mega-promoters Live Nation and Anschutz Entertainment Group (AEG). Trends in the touring business speak to an additional aspect of artist stratification inside the music industries.

The live performance sector, then, has been a saviour for only a small minority of players. Relative to the number of aspiring recording artists competing for audience attention in the touring market, very few are commercially viable, even on a very small scale. As noted above, some lesser known recording artists agree to tour for free or even pay to play. Interestingly, house party gigs have become more effective revenue generators than traditional bar venues for some smaller-scale acts in the United States (Sherbow 2010; White, personal communication, 2011). Unlike bars and clubs, house party hosts do not take a cut of ticket sales but rather pay the artist a fixed fee.

Overall, the touring business mirrors the recorded music and music publishing businesses insofar as a handful of superstars are exceptionally profitable, while most working artists struggle to break even. Consistent with Elberse's (2013) assessment of the entertainment industries more generally, *Billboard*'s Peoples characterizes concerts as a 'winner-take-all market':

> There's growing competition for concert revenue, too, and it has become a winner-take-all market. While superstars have been able to raise their ticket prices as their music sales have softened, mid-tier and up-and-coming artists don't always have that luxury. Artists who release music in order to tour – rather than tour to support new releases – can't afford two loss leaders. (Peoples 2010b)

In this context, it is increasingly difficult for unknown and unsigned artists to eke out a living. The major companies, meanwhile, reap the spoils generated by stars.

The 'Flexible' Music Corporation: Lean But Large

> The majors – I don't think they're going away. I think they're going to continue to be downsized. ... The word is, everybody believes that they will eventually, in some way, come together. The majors will consolidate more. (Grierson, personal communication, 2010)

Two particularly significant continuities between the old music industries and the new are the monopolization of popular music profits by a handful of major music companies and the persistent drive for further consolidation. The same transnational behemoths that dominated the CD era music industries still dominate the music marketplace today. The global reach and incredible economic power of media conglomerates Sony and Universal across the cultural industries as a whole run counter to the types of industrial complexity emphasized by Miège (1989), Williamson and Cloonan (2007) and others. The major record companies are starting to look different, however. According to former EMI CEO Tony Wadsworth, 'Record labels are unrecognisable compared to the 90s. They are smaller, more efficient and they have diversified and taken on many more functions' (quoted in Topping 2011). Job cuts have been part of the strategy (Rogers 2013: 42–4). While an industry performance report warned that 'CD sales are in a tailspin because the medium is quickly growing obsolete', it assured would-be investors that the recording industry is nevertheless on the mend: 'Looking forward, the picture is not so grim for the industry. Labels will benefit from their successful cost-cutting measures, new revenue streams and improvements in consumers' disposable income levels' (Ripley 2011a: 5). Notwithstanding misplaced optimism about disposable income levels, the business projections for these leaner and more diversified corporations are generally sound. As one major record label executive told me, when external clients enquired about the effect of the recession on business, his response was that after 'eleven years of recession, we're actually doing very well, thank you. We've actually worked out how we can manage our business when you literally see a 15 per cent decline [in CD sales] year on year on year on year' (Canadian major record label executive B, personal communication, 2009). Over that time span, the major record labels reinvented themselves.

To be clear, these more 'flexible' music companies are smaller in terms of staff numbers, not market share. As of July 2011, 83 per cent of US recording industry market share was concentrated in the hands of Universal Music Group (30.6 per cent), Sony Music Entertainment (27.6 per cent), Warner Music Group (13.7 per cent) and EMI Group (11.1 per cent) (Ripley 2011a: 30). Among the major record companies, industry analyst Ripley reports, 'acquisitions have been a key growth strategy' and means to revenue stream diversification (Ripley 2011a: 15). Indeed, since then, the Big Four shrank to the Big Three, as previously noted. As Giuseppe Richeri observes, 'On an international scale, the two [media] sectors in which concentration has attained the most noticeable levels are the music industry ... and the movie industry' (Richeri 2011: 132). Nielsen/*Billboard* figures reported after the first half of 2015 suggest that the Big Three controlled an 86 per cent share of the recording industry in terms of recorded music distributed (recall the distinction from music ownership previously mentioned) (Ingham 2015b). Music industry concentration is intensifying (*Billboard* 2009; Ripley 2011a: 24; Rogers 2013: 181–2). Similarly, music publishing industry concentration has been forecast to 'increase substantially' amid declines in recorded music revenues (Ripley 2011b: 22). As of the second quarter of 2015, five music publishers accounted for a 77.5 per cent share of the market (Christman 2015b). What is more, the major companies have spread their interests across 'management, merchandising, agencies and promotion, driven by a search for new revenue, not just economies of scale and higher market share' (*Billboard* 2009).

Music industry consolidation has extended beyond the recording and music publishing industries proper: processes of integration have enveloped the live performance industry (Rogers 2013: 183). After merging with Ticketmaster in 2010, concert promoter Live Nation also acquired 'management companies, promotion companies, a ticketing company, a venue owner and operator, and a company that sells photographs' (Peoples 2011b). In fact, the high-profile 360 deals (explained below) that Live Nation signed with superstar recording artists such as Madonna, Jay-Z and Shakira between 2007 and 2008 prompted considerable speculation that Live Nation would assume a growing role in signing recording artists and would begin to resemble, and compete directly with, record companies. However, the company does not currently appear to wish to become a major record label. It was reported in 2010 that Live Nation did not 'expect to recoup some of the advances it paid out to big-name artists. Investors were wary of those multi-rights deals' (Peoples 2010c). The first album released from a Live Nation artist, Madonna's *MDNA*, was, in fact, produced through a business partnership with Universal (Sisario 2011). Such initiatives are themselves commonplace, and reveal a method of profit generation that functions as a complement or alternative to consolidation for companies trying to stay flexible and lean even as they remain large: project-specific corporate partnerships.

Thanks primarily to the persistent deployment of strategies of integration and consolidation, fewer companies control more commercial music sectors across the recording, music publishing and live performance industries today. As Jim Rogers explains, 'While traditionally, record and music publishing companies have existed under the one roof, the merging of these sectors with the live sector as well as merchandising has accelerated and intensified over the past decade' (Rogers 2013: 181). 'Leaner' in the context of the flexible music corporation means fewer employees, not fewer business activities, and the diversification of revenue streams by no means leads directly to a diversity of recording artists. Rather, a new blockbuster model for producing stars as artist-brands is the flexible music corporation's preferred approach, uniting the digital music industries to their pre-digital precursors insofar as it reinforces the centrality and power of the star system.

The 'Artist-brand': 360-degree 'Monetization'

I'm not interested in selling a song. I'm interested only in selling an artist. I'm not interested in popping a song on the radio and having them go and buy the single. My job is to grasp onto the integrity and the vision that these artists have, and help them evolve their lifestyle-driven bands. (Jordan Schur, CEO of Suretone Records, quoted in Donahue 2008)

As a result of splintering profits and consequently expanding ancillary markets, the hub of the music industries' various revenue streams is now the recording artist's image and reputation, understood by record companies as the artist's 'brand'. I argue that the core music commodity is no longer the CD, but rather this artist-brand. The artist-brand is a marketing construct that speaks to a new capitalization strategy: 360-degree monetization. The resilience of major record companies has been linked to the ways they have 'innovated' or, better, 'renovated' the recording contract itself: the recuperation of popular music's commodity form is contractually inscribed in the all-encompassing 360 deal – a type of contract that enables music companies to capitalize on key revenue streams that formerly lay outside their reach, including live performance, music publishing and music merchandise, in addition to the new rights and digital products that are now essential to record label profitability.

This emphasis on generating multiple revenue streams connected to recording artists is not without precedent. Indeed, over twenty years ago, Negus observed that the recording industry had become increasingly geared toward 'developing global personalities which [could] be communicated across multiple media' (Negus 1992: 1). However, in today's marketing-driven and B2B-centred music industries and wider promotional culture, the artist-brand approach assumes new significance. More broadly, rhetoric regarding the recording artist as a brand is consonant with the rise of what Alison Hearn refers to as 'self-branding' under post-Fordist capitalism (the latter term is unpacked in chapter 4). This 'form of self-presentation [is] singularly focused on attracting attention and acquiring cultural and monetary value'; such value is 'extracted from the production of affect, desire, attention, and image' (Hearn 2008: 213–14). The notion of a 'branded self' assumes a distinctive character in the music industries. Music companies directly capitalize on affects and desires – the thread that stitches the artist-brand to various products, musical and otherwise – through encircling recording contracts that formalize and render concrete the idea of the artist-brand.

While the convention of locking down recording artist labour by way of long-term, one-way 'option' contracts is well established (Stahl 2010, 2013), the 360 deal, now more commonly (and euphemistically) referred to as the 'multiple rights' deal inside the music industries, permits labels to 'participate' in most, if not all, revenue streams linked to artists in addition to recording revenues (Stahl and Meier 2012: 442; see also

Marshall 2013; Rogers 2013: 183–5; Anderson 2014: 156). This includes sponsorship, licensing and endorsement revenues, and, increasingly, artist and fan club websites, mobile phone marketing, video streaming and artist-photo based revenues in addition (LaPolt and Resnick 2009). Although only formally introduced in 2002 (by way of the £80 million contract Robbie Williams signed with EMI), the multiple rights deal was shored up as the standard deal typically offered by the Big Four major labels by 2008 (Stahl and Meier 2012: 448–50). In a 2011 third quarter earnings call, Edgar Bronfman Jr, then-CEO of Warner Music Group, boasted that 'today nearly half of our total revenue comes from businesses that did not exist in 2004. More than 60% of the artists on our active global recorded music roster are signed to deals with a comprehensive suite of expanded rights' (quoted in Seeking Alpha 2011). For major record companies, the introduction of new music products and new recording contracts to encircle those revenues go hand in hand. The 360-degree capture of artist rights is a source of growing profits for companies, and deepening vulnerability for working artists.

The expanded reach of the multiple rights deal amplifies the rationale behind major record labels' continued emphasis on the production of blockbusters. More products attached to the artist-brand equates to more opportunities for monetization. The swelling profitability of superstars under these contracts, in turn, exacerbates stratification among working artists overall. 'Their plan seems to be swinging for the fences, how many home runs can we hit', opines Agency Group's Steve Martin, 'not how many artists can we develop from 50,000 units to 100,000 units to 200,000 units, which in this day and age should be a successful touring career' (quoted in Waddell 2010a). A notable example is Lady Gaga's multiple rights deal, which, as the driving force behind corporate partnerships with Polaroid, Estée Lauder's MAC, Virgin Mobile and others, had generated nearly US$200 million in revenue for Universal's Interscope Records as of May 2011 (Roberts 2011). In fact, due to the recent emphasis on endorsements and other new revenues, record labels approach the signing, development and marketing of recording artists differently in general. As Steve Robertson, senior vice president of A&R at Atlantic Records, joked, 'Now we're Atlantic Merchandise' (quoted in Peoples 2010a). Numerous 'squeezes of the orange' can be wrung out of 360-degree superstars.

Record label executives routinely adopt artist-brand oriented thinking to justify the use of these encircling contracts. In the words of Tom Corson, general manager of RCA, 'We've woken up and said, "Hey, this isn't fair." ... Record companies for years have funded the brand creation of artists and have only benefited through record sales' (quoted in Knopper 2007). Once these companies help build the brand value of their recording artists, they expect to capitalize fully on this investment. Countless recording artists and artist managers hold starkly different perspectives on the purported 'fairness' of these deals, however. Martin acknowledged that opinions on the 360 deal vary across the industry, but observed that a pervasive view is that this type of contract constitutes 'a land grab by the labels trying to make up for the waning CD sales. ... You would hope they'd be able to increase the overall pie, but they don't. It's generally just taking more rights to help their bottom line' (Martin, personal communication, 2010). While non-recording revenues across the music industries are growing on the whole, this does not mean that the 'overall pie' is increasing for individual artists, especially non-star artists; as we have seen, record companies aggregate revenues from entire rosters of artists. Multiple rights deals enable record labels 'to hedge their bets in a declining record market and to recast themselves as music – rather than just recording – companies' (Goodman 2008). The seizure of recording artist rights and revenues and not necessarily the growth of artist revenues, then, is the means through which record companies hedge their bets.

Amid the digital turbulence experienced by the recording industry, it is not surprising that record label executives no longer see themselves as in the *record* business at all. Not only have they recast themselves as *music* companies, but they also claim to be in the *marketing* business. According to a Canadian major label executive, who predicted that his label will remake itself into a hybrid enterprise modelled after advertising agency McLaren McCann and IMG Worldwide, a sports and fashion marketing, licensing and media rights company, music executives now function as 'brand managers doing branded things' (Canadian major record label executive B, personal communication, 2009). From his perspective, record companies' expertise will soon lie in the promotion and monetization of celebrity brands and not necessarily the production of popular music. At Toronto's North by Northeast conference, Universal Music Canada's Justin Erdman (2011) suggested that the major record companies are transitioning into boutique marketing companies, not labels *per se*. If there is merit to these claims, then what was formerly particular and distinctive about the recording industry is being seriously eroded.

Within the artist-brand era, it is increasingly the case that artist development no longer happens under the roofs of these record labels-*cum*-marketing companies. Rather, major labels expect aspiring artists to establish themselves and to 'build their brand' *before* signing (Grierson, personal communication, 2010; Erdman 2011; Nuwame 2011). According to Grierson, labels today 'have much smaller A&R staff[s]' and 'don't do artist development'. 'Because they're under such enormous pressure,' he explained, 'they don't want to sign artists that they know will need to take time to become successful – which we were able to do in the better days' (Grierson, personal communication, 2010). In effect, the major labels have outsourced the work of A&R onto the shoulders of independent and aspiring recording artists:

> They [the major labels] want somebody else to do that work, which becomes the independent community with the do-it-yourself mentality. And they look for artists that have created a buzz, 'have a story' is the word they use – a story.
>
> They want to know that that act is touring, they've sold some CDs, they've got some downloads, they've got some hits. They want to know that something's happening, or they won't take a chance. They're not making decisions on pure talent. They're basically saying, 'prove to me that something's happening and then I'm interested'. ... Plus they don't sign as many acts today, because they don't have the budgets and they don't have the staff. (Grierson, personal communication, 2010)

In this account, major label interest hinges not only or even primarily on talent, but on the existing 'buzz' around an artist.

The new metrics used to measure buzz and forecast the sales potential of an up-and-coming artist-brand include YouTube views, Facebook friends, Twitter followers and the like. Instead of sending A&R executives to Sunset Boulevard clubs to listen to live shows, the major labels might hire one person to scour the internet for emerging artists (Litwak 2010). Rather than committing to artist development, they look for artists who already have YouTube hits. Discussing the 'digital reputation economy' more broadly, Hearn argues that social media provide an infrastructure through which a person's 'total social impact ... can be measured, rationalized, and represented as their "digital reputation"' (Hearn 2010: 429–30). This is decidedly so in the case of recording artists. Digital records on and tracking of consumers' music streaming and purchasing habits lend more predictability to the sales potential of different aspiring artists, though the availability of these data does not eliminate the financial risk involved in making and marketing music.

The centrality of digital reputations to label recruitment decision-making feeds into an already stratified and stratifying system for organizing musical labour. When faced with the opportunity to sign a multiple rights deal, emerging artists, penalized for their lack of brand value, have been offered ever-shrinking advances and lop-sided contract terms on a 'take it or leave it' basis. Superstar artists, on the other hand, have received huge advances in exchange for bestowing record labels with these additional rights (e.g. Madonna, Shakira, Jay-Z). Recording contract terms reflect a recording artist's bargaining power, and the already-famous bargain from a position of strength. Much as royalty rates favour established artists, so too do ancillary revenue stream shares under multiple rights deals. As entertainment attorney Day (2009) explains, 'The label's share of those non-record kinds of income is in the range of 10 to 20 percent, but for new artists it can get as high as 50 percent.' While an examination of the politics of subordination born of multiple rights deals, which bind recording artists to one company in an unprecedented fashion, lies outside the scope of this discussion, as Matt Stahl and I note elsewhere, 'the math does not add up: lower sales volumes of recordings, concerts, and merchandise, coupled with less favourable contract terms, is a formula that promises to deepen disparities between the elite and the ranks of aspiring, increasingly disposable artists from which new stars are expected eventually to appear' (Stahl and Meier 2012: 450). Pinning the recording artist's exchange value to her or his already established digital reputation or celebrity, as opposed to talent, impedes label executives' ability to perceive value in unknown or unproven artists.

Given the decidedly one-sided terms of multiple rights deals, why do aspiring recording artists continue to sign on the dotted line? Many do not. Many others, however, recognize that the major record companies continue to boast an unrivalled capacity to market stars. According to Andrew Wernick,

> The aims and results of star-making are part and parcel of the brand-imaging of the cultural products, and companies, with which stars are creatively associated. Thus capitalists will seek to optimize the promotional value of the celebrified creators or creations they utilize through long-term arrangements which stabilize the link. *And the same ... applies in reverse: performers can only ratify their status by securing, with 'majors', a relationship of this kind.* The result is a kind of double promo. (Wernick 1991: 107; emphasis added)

While association with the majors may not be the *only* means of achieving celebrity status in this era of YouTube and social media stars, this 'double promo' logic persists nevertheless.

Although numerous new avenues are available to aspiring artists who wish to sidestep the record labels, remember that the marketing budgets afforded by the majors have become even more important to the production of commercial success than in the past. While a record deal is no guarantor of commercial success, it still works to legitimate an aspiring artist's reputation or brand. Those artists prioritized by labels (typically a select few) can benefit greatly from this marketing muscle.

The consequences of this dominant branding logic are not only felt by those artists who sign 360 deals with record labels. Promotional priorities underpin many of the alternatives to record companies available to unsigned musicians, and the artist-brand paradigm also guides the marketing of independent artists. Aspiring artists who seek marketing support but are not interested in signing a restrictive label deal may choose to partner with a 'lifestyle' brand. In recent years, brands such as Mountain Dew and Bacardi started offering record label services, as discussed in chapter 3. Consumer brands typically offer 'short-term deals with few strings' that many recording artists and artist managers therefore consider 'fairer and more favourable than traditional label contracts' (Sisario 2010). However, partnering brands are actually less invested in marketing *music* because they have less of an ownership stake in the artist. Instead, music is a device for marketing these brands. In other words, helping build careers and drive sales for artists is not the priority of lifestyle brands.

The new industry 'common sense' regarding artists as brands also has penetrated many independent labels. In the words of Toronto-based independent music consultant Allison Outhit,

> The most important thing for artists to understand and for everybody in the music business to understand right now is that artists, bands, musicians are a brand unto themselves. ... [T]he most important thing that we do is to continue to develop the brand in a way that grows their audience, that grows their consumer base, so that we can leverage their brand against every other possible opportunity, whether it's licensing and so on. (Outhit, personal communication, 2009)

In fact, Emily White, a New York-based independent artist manager, asks her artists to submit lists of brands that they would feel comfortable promoting and then seeks out appropriate band–brand pairings. According to White, both artist longevity and the success of brand partnerships are tied to 'being genuine': 'When the branding thing works for an artist, it's when it's something they genuinely like or use' (White, personal communication, 2011).

Under these arrangements, brands do not simply promote independent recording artists. Rather, these artists are advised to promote their various brand partnerships. In order to curry the favour of brands, for instance, White publicizes the promotional agreements she organizes through recording artist and social media websites:

> So, every brand that we deal with – even if it's just Gibson guitars or something. ... Whenever we get free stuff, like gear – and that's, like,

the most basic level of branding for musicians – we're, like, 'Cool. Thanks. We'll post this on [the artist's] site and Twitter and Facebook.' And brands are psyched. You know, they just want to see that we're working to push them out as well. And, like, everything is a brand. It's not just H&M or whatever. ... I really look at things so that it benefits both parties as much as possible. ... I think that our artists are so authentic and genuine they might often pick a brand or a stylist or a vegan cookie company or whatever and then I have to reach out to this small company and explain what we're doing. Once they get it, they're, like, 'Wow, this is really cool.' (White, personal communication, 2011)

While the substance of such 'authenticity' is addressed in chapter 3 (see also Meier 2011), what is important here is how increasingly difficult it is becoming for independent recording artists to opt out of this music licensing and brand partnership approach amid dwindling revenues for recorded music. When I asked White if the notion of 'selling out' has any cultural resonance today, she responded: 'I don't hear it from my colleagues, because for my colleagues, it's all "branding, branding, branding, sync, sync, sync" [synchronization rights]. ... I hear it from the bands a little bit more' (White, personal communication, 2011). While most of her recording artists remain 'open' to branding opportunities, they draw the line at 'animal cruelty-related, fast food ... nothing anti-women, nothing anti-gay, which to me are very obvious things, I think, especially for artists' (White, personal communication, 2011).

Today, consumer and media brands present themselves as an important gateway to a music-buying audience. What industry commentators refer to as the 'new DIY' involves a new degree of dependence on such brands; it is increasingly oriented around selling what Hearn (2008) terms the branded self in any and every way. According to independent recording artist Damian Kulash, whose band OK Go is championed as a successful example of this DIY model, 'making a living in music isn't just about selling studio recordings anymore. It's about selling the whole package: themselves' (Kulash 2010). OK Go, formerly signed to EMI and now independent, is reliant on brand partnerships for revenue and exposure. 'Now when we need funding for a large project', explains Kulash, 'we look for a sponsor. A couple [of] weeks ago, my band held an eight-mile musical street parade through Los Angeles, courtesy of Range Rover. ... A few weeks earlier, we released a music video made in partnership with Samsung, and in February, one was underwritten by State Farm' (Kulash 2010). Chevrolet sponsored the band's music video for 'Needing/Getting' (2010), in which the Chevrolet Sonic car features prominently. More recently, OK Go were shot in zero gravity in a parabolic aircraft for their 'Upside Down & Inside Out' music video – an epic stunt sponsored by Russia's S7 Airlines (Reynolds 2016).

Amanda Palmer, an independent solo artist and former member of The Dresden Dolls, is also widely seen as a new DIY success story (Anderson 2014: 173–4). She spearheaded a massively successful Kickstarter campaign (see Powers 2015 for an analysis of this form of cultural entrepreneurship), and she has used her Twitter account and personal blog to monetize her connection with her fans, as *Billboard*'s Cortney Harding reports:

> Palmer, 34, can't sell lots of albums in a record store. But she can spend a few hours on a Friday night in front of her computer, drinking wine and tweeting, and wind up rallying her followers to drop $11,000 on T-shirts. (The numbers Palmer reports are all gross, but even so, 440 $25 T-shirts less production and shipping costs is still a nice number.) She can spend a few more hours in front of Twitter and auction off postcards and miscellaneous junk from around her home and bring in another $6,600. And she can release an album of Radiohead covers played on her ukulele and gross $15,000. (Harding 2010)

Palmer offers fans a performance of a more private self – not a (straightforward) stage personality – and even sells her own personal items. 'Not every musician takes the project of selling themselves literally', according to Kulash, 'but the personality and personal lives of musicians are being more openly recognized as valuable assets' (Kulash 2010). Kulash (2010) commends the entrepreneurial creativity of drummer Josh Freese, who has sold lunch dates with fans for US$250 each and even offered a premium US$20,000 option: a miniature golf date with Freese and his circle of friends. The monetization of recording artists' private lives, always a facet of the music industries' star system, is rendered more explicit, intensive and personal.[5]

Major label artists, too, are offering fans more intimate access to who they 'really' are. According to sponsorship agent Laura Huftless (2010), country star Zac Brown, an avid cook, has prepared brand-sponsored meals for his VIP fans before his concerts, and Michael Bublé, a table tennis enthusiast, participated in a sponsored ping pong tournament with fans prior to a show. 'Finding what the artist likes to do', she advised attendees at the 2010 Billboard Touring Conference, 'always makes it a better experience for the fans and for the brands who are sponsoring, because that gives them something different' (Hutfless 2010). In order to function effectively as a lifestyle-driven brand, it seems, an artist must represent more than just music. She or he must offer and monetize a snapshot of the whole person, at least as defined by hobbies and non-music interests. The path to 'independence' for working artists who rely on brand support demands new depths of commodification and promotionalism.

The sum of the industrial dynamics and developments discussed above has facilitated the centralization of tremendous influence and power into the hands of a few transnational corporations, thereby presenting working artists with formidable obstacles. Those interested in signing with the major companies are faced with an ever-narrowing range of potential business partners, upon whom they will become overwhelmingly dependent once signed to a multiple rights deal. Those who choose to opt out of this system altogether, on the other hand, are forced to compete for audience attention and dollars not only with the stars backed by these global giants but also with countless others attempting to forge a similarly independent path. As a result, many aspiring artists covet corporate assistance with marketing activities, a factor that has led to business partnerships between artists and brands.

Conclusion

In a 2007 interview with the *New York Times*, Paul McCartney relayed his record producer's assessment of major record label struggles in the digital era: 'as David Kahne said to me about a year ago, the major labels these days are like the dinosaurs sitting around discussing the asteroid' (quoted in Kozinn 2007). It is a familiar cliché. While the shift away from the CD would seem to signal the loosening of major record company dominance, these companies ceased discussing how they might stop the digital juggernaut and took decisive action to ensure that they would adapt to and profit from new commercial opportunities: they reinvented themselves as diversified marketing-oriented companies that sell artist-brands.

Against understandable excitement regarding the purported 'consumer revolution' in the music industry and the 'widespread feeling that the major record labels are becoming redundant' (Young and Collins 2010: 340), this chapter calls attention to the worrisome business strategies that have enabled the majors to retain a tremendously powerful position in the global music marketplace to the detriment of most working artists, including intensified, cross-sector consolidation and the institutionalization of encircling multiple rights recording contracts. The embrace of the multiple rights deal suggests that the artist-brand terminology commonplace inside both major and independent record companies is not simply a matter of marketing hype, but rather speaks to a larger reconfiguration of record company monetization and accumulation strategies. As the popular music commodity mutates in the digital age, so too do the contractual terms and marketing strategies devised to wring surplus value out of musical labour. An abiding continuity between the old and new music industries is the egregious disparity in power between music companies and recording artists, which, in turn, seriously threatens the autonomy of working artists. As *Billboard*'s Peoples points out, 'The ability to create, which has never been easier, is confused with the ability to be heard and especially the ability to gain sales' (Peoples 2010b). The new music industry resembles its pre-digital predecessor insofar as a handful of stars continue to yield a disproportionate share of profits. Overall, the corporate trends surveyed above have allowed for popular musical production 'from below' to be frustrated by monetization 'from above'.

The artist-brand paradigm affects the recruitment and marketing of even those recording artists who choose to work outside of the major record companies. Under the new model, activities that were formerly seen as vexing or even alienating, such as selling music to advertisers, have become standard practice. A perhaps unforeseen consequence of the open-armed pursuit of music licensing agreements by record labels, music publishers and recording artists has been the dynamic of dependence that has emerged amid this shift toward B2B revenue generation models. Music companies have become unprecedentedly reliant on partnering with consumer brands and media companies, which, in turn, have joined entrenched major music corporations as new music industry gatekeepers, as we shall see in chapter 3. Even if the 'artist-brand' language proves to be a fad, both brands and music companies are unlikely to cede new levers of control afforded by this approach.

3

Brands: The New Gatekeepers

The new 'common sense' within the contemporary music industries is that partnerships with brands and music placements in advertisements and popular media constitute standard modes of music marketing. In interview, Don Grierson, a former A&R executive, relayed an oft-repeated phrase: 'They call it the new radio. It's exposure, right?' (Grierson, personal communication, 2010; see also Hau 2007; Barnhard and Rutledge 2009; Klein 2009: 59–78). When inserted into an advertisement, an abbreviated version of a licensed song is intended to stand in for and promote the song as a whole and, by extension, the featured artist's singles and albums, live performances and merchandise. From the perspective of consumer brands or producers of films, video games and television programmes, the purpose of music placements and other branding initiatives is decidedly different: to transfer positive feelings and associations over to the brand or media text in an effort to set it apart from its competitors and make it distinctive and 'credible'. Popular music is used as an instrument of brand differentiation (Barnhard 2009). Brands are typically more interested in what particular sounds and associations *can do* – facilitate the strategic mobilization of emotion and affect – than in popular musical content as such. According to Andrew Wernick,

Those who shape and transmit its [advertising's] material have no intrinsic interest in what, ideologically, that material might mean. Advertising is an entirely instrumental process. You promote to sell. You sell to get money, in turn to get more money or else to exchange for something else. In this, the mobilization of affect through the invocation of values is strictly a tool, an incidental side-effect of what advertising is instrumental for. (Wernick 1991: 25–6)

Music-related branding works in service of this instrumental process. The generation of affect is intended to deepen the cultural relevance of and build emotional bonds with the consumer or media brand promoted.

Advertising and music industry executives, however, have pitched the relationship between musicians and brands in terms of 'mutual benefits' (Knight 2015) – as a 'symbiotic relationship' (Beltrone 2012). In 2016, the Austin, Texas-based South by Southwest (SXSW) festival featured industry presenter-led conference panels on 'Shaping Brand Identity: Creating Music for Brands', 'How to Seduce a Brand and be Seduced' and 'The "Brand" New Patrons' – the last of which promised to discuss the 'shift in attitude toward commercialization of artistry' and how 'the evolving partnership landscape benefits artists, brands & fans alike' (South by Southwest 2016). These telling panel titles reveal how a straightforward account of reciprocity does not capture the power relations underpinning the various pairings of recording artists and brands: it is incumbent upon artists, it would seem, to pursue brands and position their music as up to the task of branding.

This chapter charts what I characterize as an intensifying relationship between recording artists and brands, and discusses the consequences of the music-related branding and licensing paradigm for working artists and for music making. I challenge the assumption that 'everybody wins' through music placement and other promotional and branding agreements. While the 'erosion of meaningful distinctions between the advertising and music industries' largely has been framed as 'a convergence of content and commerce' (Taylor 2009: 413), the term 'convergence', which suggests a mere union or merger, does not capture the actual dynamic at work: popular music is subordinated to advertising and branding objectives. Music companies' and artists' increasing dependence on music licensing and brand partnerships for marketing exposure and revenue has paved the way for what I argue has been popular music's *colonization* by new industry gatekeepers: brands. Achieving brands' goals and building brand value is what popular music is *for* under this approach – a far cry from the language of 'collaboration', 'partnership' and 'patronage' routinely used in relation to these arrangements.

Furnished with an inordinate amount of power vis-à-vis aspiring and lesser known artists in particular, consumer and media brands have been placed in a position to exercise considerable control over the definition of desirable popular musical content and to drive down licensing fees. In seeking to avoid the Scylla of the major music companies, I suggest, recording artists have fallen into the Charybdis of brands.

Music Placements in Advertising, Television and Video Games as Promotion

These big brands want to be ubiquitous. They want to be absolutely everywhere, and because they're ubiquitous, people don't react to it anymore. ... I think people are becoming more and more and more desensitized to the corporate branding. At the same time, I think that makes the corporation's job more difficult, because it just becomes background noise. You just tune it all out. ... The big corporations, in order to get noticed, ... they're now finding the cool, indie cultural things that have a hip value to them. (Danzig, personal communication, 2009)

Between roughly 1998 and 2008, the notion that music placements in audiovisual media constitute the 'new radio' went from novel idea to established convention. The dividing line between the worlds of popular music and advertising began to fade, as music companies and recording artists sought new ways of generating income, in part due to the industrial changes examined in chapter 2. 'Brands have always been interested in co-opting hit songs', according to sonic branding executive Bill Nygren, but whereas rock bands had rebuffed advertiser advances in the 1960s and 1970s, artists since have become considerably more 'open to letting brands ... grab the ... equity out of songs that were well loved and attach them to their products' (Nygren, personal communication, 2009). 'When we started in the '90s, it was still considered sacrilegious for bands to work with brands', recalled Jon Cohen, co-CEO of lifestyle marketing firm Cornerstone (quoted in *Billboard* 2009). The first decade of the twenty-first century, by contrast, witnessed a new 'openness from artists when it comes to branding. Licensing and brand partnerships have [become] part of the marketing mix alongside radio promotion, press and other things', he continued (quoted in *Billboard* 2009). During this period, licensing agreements characterized as 'brand–music integrations' by advertising and brand partnership expert Mike Tunnicliffe (personal communication, 2010) grew in popularity. Such licensing and music placement arrangements were often forged under the auspices of mutually beneficial *cross-promotion*, not celebrity endorsement: the 'new radio' purportedly served the dual purpose of promoting both artist and brand. Within this system, music supervisors – the executives responsible for selecting and clearing the rights for music placements – played a key role in bringing together music and audiovisual media (see Klein and Meier forthcoming). According to Tim Anderson, 'gaining the ear of a well-placed music supervisor has not simply become important, but a key to breaking new music' and is 'indicative of three specific changes in music industry systems as they have responded to a climate of crisis and change: the reassertion of the role of publishing in the music industry, the change of what it means to be a "record label," and the strategic need for media branding in the new media environment' (Anderson 2014: 120). If music placements are the new radio, it would seem, music supervisors are the new A&R.

In this chapter, I demonstrate that such a characterization of music placements and music supervisors is problematic for a number of reasons, as I consider the practices of licensing music for use in advertising, television programmes and video games in turn. Briefly, music placements are a decidedly more indirect method of marketing music than radio. Radio stations play entire songs (or radio edits), not clips of main hooks, catchy riffs, or emotion-saturated measures. Furthermore, on radio, songs do not simultaneously compete for audience attention with brand messages, storylines and dialogue, or gameplay: airtime dedicated to songs is kept more separate. I identify a *possessive* promotional logic at work in music placements: by creating distinctive sound identities, consumer and media brands attempt to 'possess' the symbolic force and credibility of the chosen music. There is typically more emphasis placed on achieving the partnering brand's objectives than on promoting the featured artist's music. Whereas A&R personnel are responsible for the development of artists' careers, music supervisors are not; the relationship with the artist typically ends after the song has been licensed and delivered to the client (Fritz, personal communication, 2009).

Although I pull together a diverse range of music licensing practices – all of which have been pitched as sites for promoting music – there are notable differences between the specific uses to which music is put in each medium. 'The function of music in ads is to sell a product', explained music supervisor Amy Fritz, whereas 'the function of music in a film is to help tell the story of the film' (Fritz, personal communication, 2009). In television, popular music is used to aestheticize particular moments (Donnelly 2002: 331) – a role it also assumes in film. Video game music, on the other hand, is typically 'a focused compilation of music … for a particular demographic', which serves the function of 'wallpaper' or entertainment 'environment' (Fritz, personal communication, 2009).

These differences aside, all music placements generally involve a strategic production of affect ultimately tied to commercial goals: they are used to target audiences seen as desirable in an effort to improve sales, ratings or reputation. Note that the licensing of popular music for use in film was already a well-established practice during the timeframe of interest and therefore is not the focus here.

Writing in 2002, professional branding expert and former Harvard and Oxford marketing professor Douglas Holt observed how advertisers' increasing use of popular music as a tool of differentiation had obliged forwarding-thinking agencies to cast the net wider in their search for attention-grabbing or affecting music:

> Now that ad agencies have mined the most accessible music, they are forced to search out more esoteric tracks that are still perceived as pristine. Leading creative agencies now use music from the distant past, from obscure genres, and from independent bands that are known to only a few thousand fans. ... Postmodern branding is now running a fine-toothed comb through the culture industry's dusty closets and countercultural dead ends to mine the last vestiges of unsponsored expressive culture. (Holt 2002: 86)

The use of popular music in and of itself already had become expected. Advertisers' turn to lesser known, 'unsponsored' culture was intended to create the perception that brands are 'without an instrumental economic agenda', and in so doing, appeal to consumers wary of commercialism (Holt 2002: 83). Popular music was believed to help camouflage brands' actual commercial motives. In the years since, brands have turned to independent and lesser known music more and more, as they have attempted to add a musical dimension to their brand identities. At the same time as advertising firms were experimenting with new branding tactics, the expansion of P2P file sharing and growing uncertainty about viable revenue streams meant that many smaller and independent record labels were hunting for new marketing outlets and means of generating revenue. Brand and music industry interests seemed to align.

In order to appreciate the gravity of the shift away from longstanding, though complex and at times problematic, beliefs regarding the inherent tensions between culture and commerce – beliefs that Simon Frith argues lie at 'the core of rock ideology' (Frith 1981: 41) – it is important to understand the broader historical-industrial context that has informed this shift. As mentioned in chapter 2, in the United States, the Telecommunications Act of 1996 shored up oligopolistic market conditions and ever-narrowing playlists for commercial radio – a development that effectively compelled recording artists and record labels to seek alternative means of exposure (Klein 2009: 62–3; Taylor 2009: 407–8; Anderson 2014: 122). The inaccessibility of radio arguably instigated a re-evaluation of the idea of 'selling out' altogether, leading Timothy D. Taylor to argue that 'the old stigma about allowing one's music to be used in commercials … evaporated almost overnight' (Taylor 2009: 408).[6] The popularization of P2P file sharing and resulting destabilization of established modes of monetizing popular music further fuelled this change in thinking: amid declining CD sales, record label executives, major label artists and even independent artists sought new revenue streams and promotional channels. As aspiring artists began seeking 'alternative routes to market without signing to major record labels', licensing deals with brands were positioned as a way 'to help them gain their new independent status' (Tunnicliffe 2008). Advertisers presented themselves as 'hero to the damsel-in-distress of the struggling artist' and, perhaps surprisingly, were 'portrayed as a champion of music that might otherwise be unheard' (Klein 2009: 60). Seemingly paradoxically, deals with brands were cast as a vehicle for circumventing the restricted major label/commercial radio/MTV system.

Citing Madison Avenue's use of music by the Crystal Method, Stereolab, Spiritualized and others, *The Washington Post*'s Frank Owen suggests that '1998 may go down in pop history as the year in which the really cool music wasn't heard on MTV or the radio but on TV commercials' (Owen 1998). In his account, advertisers had become 'convinced that pop music classics no longer guarantee audience attention', and, as a result, had started to use 'electronic and alternative music as a way to stand out from the pack' and attempt to 'out-hip one another – aiming for postmodern surprise and novelty' (Owen 1998). The sonic and formal attributes of electronica, rather than the celebrity personae of pop and rock stars, were becoming increasingly desirable to advertisers interested in targeting youth audiences. Advertisers favoured electronica's dramatic qualities and expansive sonorous range, and more importantly, the fact that it typically did not feature vocals, which they worried could 'distract from the ad' (Taylor 2007: 247). Underground techno was effective for 'ambient advertising' strategies that used 'mood and setting to attract the youthful media-cynical audience' (Owen 1998). The timbre and vibe of electronica made for a cool atmosphere.

The licensing of all eighteen tracks on electronica artist Moby's album *Play* (1999) for use in commercials, films and television programmes was a milestone in the move toward using music placements as promotional media (Taylor 2007: 240; Klein 2009: 59; Tunnicliffe, personal communication, 2010). 'On a purely accidental level', Moby told *Wired*'s Ethan Smith in 2002, 'I have managed to develop my name and self into a brand' (quoted in Smith 2002). 'On the contrary: It's no accident',

Smith (2002) correctly informs the reader. Moby's managers sought out music placements in advertising and media as part of an aggressive marketing plan explicitly designed to sidestep commercial radio promotion (Sanburn 2012). The approach worked. After signing in excess of 100 licences in North America alone, the independent artist earned in the range of US$1 million in licensing fees, gained access to radio and MTV (promotional media previously closed to him), and sold over 7 million copies of *Play* (Leland 2001). Moby's style of electronica lent brands an unthreatening yet distinctive sound. His music 'sounds cool – but not too cool', Smith wrote at the time, '[w]hich is precisely why it's so appealing: To corporate America, Moby offers an easy shorthand for cutting-edge cachet' (Smith 2002). Moby 'made electronica (read: edgy, intimidating, next big thing) safe for the mainstream (read: mass exposure, mass audience, massive sales)' (Smith 2002). As noted above, advertisers' turn to electronica and independent music had already begun. 'I think that by the time Moby did it', recalled advertising sound designer Ray Loewy, 'it was almost like the floodgates had opened. ... The wave was already moving' (quoted in Sanburn 2012). However, the widespread licensing of Moby's techno tracks 'got more advertisers interested in less-known acts whose contemporary sound could resonate with consumers' (Fixmer 2012).

Another key case that entailed licensing original music to an advertiser in a campaign explicitly designed to bypass radio and MTV promotion involved a star artist who had previously benefited greatly from that closed promotional system. Sting's 'Desert Rose'/Jaguar spot (2000) is widely viewed as a landmark example of the integration or convergence between music and advertising (Donaton 2003; Taylor 2009: 409; Tunnicliffe, personal communication, 2010). Despite Sting's prior commercial successes, his 'Desert Rose' single had received little radio airplay after its release. Miles Copeland, his manager, believed that the corresponding music video, which features scenes of Sting in a Jaguar, resembled a car advertisement, leading him to pitch the idea of a cross-promotional television commercial to the automaker (Donaton 2003). Jaguar agreed, and the resulting spot – which includes clips from the music video and captions that promote Sting, the 'Desert Rose' single and the *Brand New Day* album – reportedly catapulted album sales from an anticipated 1 million to 4 million within the United States alone, and injected the single into the playlists of 180 Top 40 radio stations (Donaton 2003). Notably, unlike the Michael Jackson and Madonna deals with Pepsi discussed in chapter 1, this was not a formal endorsement deal; Sting was not paid to promote the car and Jaguar was permitted to use music video clips at no cost (Donaton 2003). Instead, the Jaguar spot was a site of promotional synergy in which Sting's celebrity and music was a type of currency exchanged for the marketing exposure it might garner.

The newer approach to integrating music into advertising was markedly different than the pop endorsement deals of the 1980s, which had placed star artists at centre stage as a way to bolster the profile of the sponsoring brand. In contrast, advertisers began avoiding prominent promotion of artists on the grounds that it might impede effective brand messaging. The explicit marketing of music was not a primary consideration, despite the rhetoric of cross-promotion. Instead, 'different' sounds were used as a means to target audiences seen as generally resistant to marketing. The subordination of music to the brand message is one of the reasons that I characterize this promotional dynamic as 'possessive' rather than reciprocal.

Advertisers' use of more conventional pop and rock star endorsement deals did not cease altogether in the first decade of the twenty-first century, however. One of the more high-profile licensing deals of 2002 was between Cadillac and Led Zeppelin – a campaign intended to speak to an older demographic, not a youth audience. As General Motors' John Howell explains, 'Led Zeppelin and the song "Rock and Roll" appeals to our target market. You know, the 45 to 59 group grew up with that group. It's a piece of music and genre that does very well in terms of appealing to them' (quoted in LeBeau 2003). In terms of the artist's perspective, given the fame and commercial success of this band, it would seem that money rather than otherwise unavailable marketing exposure was the primary motivating factor, unlike the above examples of brand–music integration or advertising as cross-promotion.

The well-known but decidedly unrepresentative cases of Sting and Moby would problematically come to stand in as evidence of the viability of this newer promotional approach for aspiring artists more broadly. It is important to remember that Sting was already a star, and Moby's case was remarkable in terms of the unusual volume of licences sold. Furthermore, when these deals were engineered at the turn of the twenty-first century, the music industries' digital transition was not yet fully underway. Still under the sway of the old promotional model, record companies and artists saw music licensing 'as not only an alternative avenue for reaching the ears of potential buyers, but also a way to reach the ears of radio programmers' (Klein 2009: 64). The commercial success of these two anomalous examples was a product of record sales, radio play and access to MTV – the bulwarks of a soon to be obsolete business model. It is also important to remember that these deals garnered considerable attention because this practice was still novel; similar 'buzz' could not be banked on once such arrangements became standard.

The licensing of popular music to advertisers became increasingly commonplace during the first years of the twenty-first century. However, at the time, 'it still seemed relatively uncool for musicians, especially newer bands, to hawk products – until Apple changed things' (Sanburn 2012). Apple's much lauded, music-driven iPod and iTunes commercials gave this practice a new credibility, cementing the notion that advertising was the new radio, and the accompanying assumption that this shift was to the benefit of independent and aspiring artists. After initially licensing songs by star artists, such as U2's 'Vertigo' (2004) and Eminem's 'Lose Yourself' (2005), Apple began licensing less known tracks, including 'Ride' by the Vines (2005), '1234' by Feist (2007) and 'Shut Up and Let Me Go' by the Ting Tings (2008). In the cases of Feist and the Ting Tings, exposure through an iPod commercial translated into a spike in sales: '1234' jumped from 16,000 the month before the spot to 249,000 during the month of the advertisement's release, and 'Shut Up and Let Me Go' (unreleased prior to the Apple spot) sold 1,000 during the month of the advertisement's release, and shot up to sales of 116,000 the following month (Hampp and Netherby 2011). Apple's interest in lesser known or emerging artists, rather than Top 40 stars, was widely celebrated as a positive development for independent music. Deserving musicians were finally receiving the spotlight and the sales, or so the argument went.

Indeed, the commercial success of artists such as Feist, the Ting Tings and Yael Naim (whose song 'New Soul' was used in a MacBook Air advertisement in 2008) translated into a widespread belief across the music industries that Apple had a unique ability to 'break' artists, shoring up the business rationale behind the use of advertising as a means of marketing music. 'It's the ultimate way to win', Nygren told me in interview in 2009, because the already hip Apple brand 'gets to be that much hipper' by tapping into the credibility of independent music, and Feist gets a wide audience 'listening to the hookiest part of her tune' (Nygren, personal communication, 2009). An advertising creative director based in Toronto (personal communication, 2009) championed Apple as 'probably more powerful than MTV, in some cases, in making a star', and Canadian independent music executive Allison Outhit characterized iPod commercials as the 'holy grail' of advertising opportunities for emerging artists: 'Not only does Apple benefit from the great music and from whatever brand that artist has as being a kind of a cool insider, but absolutely the reverse happens, too, which is that the artist benefits from the brand of Apple' (Outhit, personal communication, 2009). A sync placement in an Apple television commercial ranked number one in *Billboard*'s 'Maximum Exposure' list in 2008 (Harding 2008b) and 2009 (Bruno 2009), before falling to number two, behind a performance on the Grammy Awards, in 2010 (Bruno et al. 2010). These rankings of the 'best ways to generate sales and buzz' are based on surveys of record label and music publishing executives, artist managers, publicists and branding experts (Bruno et al. 2010). Exposure on MTV, by this time, was tied to starring roles on reality shows, sync placements on *The Hills* (2006–10) and performances on award shows, not music videos (Bruno 2009). In addition to serving as a form of cross-promotion, the Apple spots would seem to suggest a type of 'co-branding' between musicians and the partnering company (see Taylor 2016: 56–9), wherein associations connected to each 'brand' are (at least in theory) transferred to the other, ostensibly to the benefit of both.

Much as MTV was (and remains) a restricted institution, access to these prime Apple advertising spots was limited to a select chosen few. By 2009, *Billboard*'s Antony Bruno had already observed a winnowing down of Apple's music playlist: 'So far this year, Apple has relied on only four songs for its TV ads in the United States, down from seven songs licensed last year and the eight licensed in 2007. And none of the ads featured artist performances the way previous commercials presented Feist and U2' (Bruno 2009). His second point is also significant. In contrast to the iPod commercial template – Apple's signature iPod-wearing, dancing silhouettes – the Feist iPod Nano spot (which promoted the video capability of the device) quite atypically featured clips from Feist's music video. Her colourful video played on the Nano, rendering her image uncharacteristically prominent and effectively pulling the music from background to foreground. Similar to the Sting-Jaguar case, this spot was unusually cross-promotional: Apple also pitched Feist. It is for good reason, then, that Ben Swanson of independent record label Secretly Canadian Records warned that 'everyone looks at someone like Feist and thinks they can do that, but she's really the exception, not the rule' (quoted in Harding 2008a). For those few artists selected by Apple, the conversion of this marketing exposure into robust sales was by no means a given, even at the height of Apple's influence. In 2008, while touting the significance of the Apple spots, *Billboard*'s Cortney Harding also cautioned, 'more often than not, the increases are modest' (Harding 2008b). The Vines, for instance, saw sales from 'Ride' crawl from 3,000 to a mere 7,000 during the month their spot aired, before falling back down to 3,000 the month after the commercial's release (Hampp and Netherby 2011; see Harding 2008b and Hampp and Netherby 2011 for sales figures for artists who have appeared in Apple commercials).

Although Apple has been trumpeted as a supporter of independent music and aspiring artists, the emergence of Apple commercials as a medium for promoting music did not free recording artists from media conglomerate involvement. Instead, Apple, a transnational corporation whose iTunes store dominated digital music distribution, simply joined the ranks of the music industries' old guard – the major record companies – in terms of the power it wielded vis-à-vis artists. As recording artists began to seek an endorsement from Apple and not the other way around, it became clear that Apple, not the artist, was firmly in charge. Crucially, the majority of promotional capital was accrued to Apple, as the sum of these music-driven commercials helped the brand create a distinctive indie 'sound identity'. If these commercials served as the new radio, then the station, Apple, was the real beneficiary. Grey Group's Josh Rabinowitz used the term 'neojingle' to describe Apple's approach: 'Instead of literally singing about the product, the music becomes the sound of the product and in essence the product becomes inextricably connected to sound. It feels not as if they borrowed or even stole the music, *but that the music belonged to the Apple brand*' (quoted in Hampp and Netherby 2011; emphasis added). This possessive promotional logic undermines any straightforward notion of cross-promotion.

The central role of iPod advertising in music promotion reached its zenith in roughly 2007–9. Apple's interest in licensing popular music for its iPod and iTunes spots largely aligned with the function of these music-related digital media technologies. As Apple switched its focus from iPods to iPhones, the importance of music to its marketing, and therefore its relevance as a cross-promotional vehicle for recording artists, lessened. Placement in an Apple commercial was not even included in the listing of the top sixty-five ways to promote a single or album in *Billboard*'s 'Maximum Exposure 2011' (Mitchell 2011). However, a 'song in a TV commercial that runs during a special event with significant viewership', 'synch placement in a high-rotation TV ad for a leading athletic shoe brand (Adidas, Converse, Nike, Reebok, etc.)', 'synch placement in an ad for Coca-Cola' and 'synch placement in an ad for Pepsi' ranked number eleven, twenty, twenty-four and twenty-seven, respectively (Mitchell 2011).[7] Advertisers credit Apple with 'pav[ing] the way for many other brands that would later incorporate indie music into their marketing efforts, from Converse to Kia to Verizon Wireless' (Hampp and Netherby 2011). In the late 2000s, as a result of the influential Apple spots, the indie advertising soundtrack inaugurated by Moby and others a decade earlier emerged as a new standard rather than a novel exception to the rule.

During the same decade, television programmes also were pitched as cross-promotional vehicles that could break aspiring artists. As K.J. Donnelly observed in 2002 in relation to the British context, 'Pop music is now dominant as stock music on television, filling the expansion of continuity and advertising spaces, and indicating the degree of industrial integration and collaboration between the television and music industries' (Donnelly 2002: 331). Original popular music had likewise become a dominant type of incidental or stock music in television programmes in North America. From the original recordings inserted into programmes such as teen drama *Gossip Girl* (2007–12), comedy-drama *Parenthood* (2010–15) and crime comedy-drama *Bones* (2005–), to the cover versions performed by the cast of musical comedy-drama *Glee* (2009–15), popular music came to permeate contemporary television.

The practice of licensing popular music performed by original artists, rather than hiring studio musicians to create sound-alikes, has a long history, with *WKRP in Cincinnati* (1978–82) serving as a notable example (Butler 2007: 249). *Miami Vice* (1984–90) was also significant, as it 'set a precedent of having stylish visuals accompanied by contemporary pop music' (Donnelly 2002: 332). According to Canadian music publisher Jennifer Beavis, the first iteration of Aaron Spelling's *Beverly Hills, 90210* (1990–2000), which featured Top 40 R&B and pop, marked a decisive moment in the formalization of this practice: 'Previous to *90210*, ... TV producers didn't feel that they needed original music to carry the narrative – to make ... the viewer ... feel that they're actually looking at reality' (Beavis, personal communication, 2009). She describes the shift toward licensing original popular music for use in television programmes as the '90210 effect' (Beavis, personal communication, 2009). In an important television benchmark, alternative rock band The Flaming Lips appeared in a 1995 episode of *Beverly Hills, 90210* (McFarland 2005). A handful of teen dramas from the 1990s set the stage for the licensing of music by aspiring artists rather than stars. 'Music-driven' shows such as *Dawson's Creek* (1998–2003), *Felicity* (1998–2002) and *Party of Five* (1994–2000) were also instrumental in the development of the independent music 'formula' (Kenzer, personal communication, 2010) – and each released soundtrack albums.

However, *The O.C.* (2003–7) and *Grey's Anatomy* (2005–) are routinely credited as pioneering in their use of lesser known or independent music and, hence, for breaking artists (Garrity 2007; Hau 2007; Tunnicliffe, personal communication, 2010). The programmes feature music selected by prominent music supervisor Alexandra Patsavas, who has also been responsible for selecting music for *Mad Men* (58 episodes, 2007–15), *Numb3rs* (63 episodes, 2006–9), *Private Practice* (95 episodes, 2007–13), *Without A Trace* (118 episodes, 2003–9) and the *Twilight* films (2008, 2009, 2010, 2011, 2012) (IMDb 2016). Death Cab for Cutie featured extensively on *The O.C.*: this pairing was touted as a key cross-promotional music placement success story (Tunnicliffe, personal communication, 2010). Much as Feist's iPod spot was more explicitly cross-promotional than most, Death Cab for Cutie's relationship to *The O.C.* was unusually close. While a standard music placement in television would entail the insertion of a song into a scene, and a prominent placement would occur in a particularly important scene or episode (e.g. a season finale), Death Cab for Cutie were actually written into the storyline: they were a main character's favourite band, their poster was included in his bedroom, and the band was a topic of discussion in the drama (McFarland 2005).[8] This explicit promotion undoubtedly helped to raise their profile. Hence, the excitement stoked regarding the viability of television as a non-traditional promotional channel was understandable.

The music placements of Snow Patrol and The Fray in *Grey's Anatomy* are also cited as evidence of television programmes' effectiveness as sites for cross-promotion (Tunnicliffe, personal communication, 2010). Snow Patrol's 'Chasing Cars' (2006) shot up the iTunes charts after appearing in an emotional scene (Tunnicliffe, personal communication, 2010), selling 1.8 million digital downloads and achieving a number five position on *Billboard*'s pop charts (Hau 2007), and a prominent placement of The Fray's song 'How to Save a Life' (2006) is credited with helping the band achieve platinum status (Hau 2007; Ben-Yehuda 2008). Not only was the song used in 'a really critical moment in the show', but it was also promoted in a music video featuring clips of both TV show and artist (Canadian major record label executive B, personal communication, 2009). Notably, 'How to Save a Life' reportedly was selected by Patsavas after The Fray's record company arranged for the band to perform a private acoustic set at her house (Canadian major record label executive B, personal communication, 2009). The music supervisor was actively courted by the record label. Unlike most music placements on television, the above cases involved an unusual emphasis on cross-promotion.

The influence of Patsavas was perceived as so great – and music placements were seen as so central to music promotion – that she even opened her own label (Garrity 2007; Coffing, personal communication, 2010). Chop Shop Records was launched in partnership with Warner's Atlantic Records: 'it is fantastic that we have her dialed into our company', averred Atlantic president Julie Greenwald (quoted in Garrity 2007). While it could be argued that Patsavas assumes 'an A&R function that has been a longstanding element for the music industry' (Anderson 2014: 119–20), her own description of her role seems at odds with such a characterization: 'Music supervision, at its core, is really about helping the producers define a sound for their show' (quoted in Anderson 2014: 119). Popular music is folded into the television programme's 'sound' and, in effect, becomes part of the programme's brand. Any considerations regarding promoting the music itself are typically secondary. As

Louis Hau points out, 'commercial success stories like the Fray and Snow Patrol ... tend to be rare exceptions to the rule' (Hau 2007).

Nevertheless, the minority of placements that did lead to commercial successes helped to solidify the notion that television programmes offer a way to break new artists and get ahead in the competitive music marketplace. Record companies and artists desperate for exposure and revenue started to aggressively pursue television placements as promotional opportunities. Songs by aspiring artists began to flood music supervisors' inboxes. As music publisher Peter Jansson explained, 'people are submitting music to music supervisors all the time via email or MP3s', and as a result, 'music supervisors quite often get overwhelmed' (Jansson, personal communication, 2010). The successes of the few have fuelled the work of countless musicians dreaming of 'making it' ever since the star system was introduced, if not before. What we see here is how the winner-take-all dynamics of the music industries have not disappeared: they have simply migrated elsewhere.

The use of music placements in television as an attention-grabbing promotional strategy must be understood as an historically specific phenomenon. This does not mean that this practice has ceased: the opposite is true. Licensing popular music for use in television has continued to grow, and precisely because it is now so common these placements no longer garner the audience and media attention they received only a few years ago. Interestingly, *Gossip Girl* was the only television programme cited in *Billboard*'s 2011 listing of 'the best ways for emerging acts to get the word out', which had switched its focus to YouTube, Pitchfork and Twitter promotion (Mitchell 2011). While by no means the final authority on music marketing, the ranking does reflect the thinking of music industry and branding experts.

During the first decade of the twenty-first century, video games also were pitched as the new radio. The popularity of *Grand Theft Auto III* (2001) and subsequent versions (which featured in-game radio stations), *Guitar Hero* (first released in 2005), *Rock Band* (first released in 2007) and various karaoke games produced excitement across the music industries about the music marketing potential of video games. Music-based games in particular have had an 'incredible' impact on back catalogue sales for established bands, such as Kansas and Queen (Coffing, personal communication, 2010). As might be expected, stars have benefited most from these music placements in terms of music sales. The priority of video publishers is not the promotion of unknown music. 'Our priority is selling games', indicated Andrew Hanley (2011), a music supervisor at Rockstar Games (publisher of *Grand Theft Auto*). Video game publishers license original songs in order to make games 'more expressive and vibrant and exciting', according to one video game licensing executive (director of licensing at video game publisher, personal communication, 2010). Cross-promotional campaigns with recording artists are rare: if his company does choose to develop such a campaign, it is because 'obviously it's a big-name artist and ... you want to integrate their name [into] ... some sort of marketing initiative. ... Mostly for us, though, ninety plus percent of the time, ... it's really what works best, what we think fits the game the best' (director of licensing at video game publisher, personal communication, 2010). A video game can benefit from the media and audience attention garnered by stars. The purpose of lesser known music, by contrast, is atmosphere or a cool vibe: if video game publishers' strategies are effective, the music used becomes part of the game's distinctive sound – again, what I characterize as a possessive dynamic.

Today, music licensing is seen 'not only as a revenue generator, but an extremely important part of exposing an artist' (director of licensing at video game publisher, personal communication, 2010). Music companies' and recording artists' pursuit of music placements in advertising, television and video games has become the new baseline – the new normal. In the words of Nygren, 'It's no longer uncool, unhip, you know, traitorous to license your music. It's just smart, because one, you get paid, but two, you open up a new media channel, because radio is so static and so stale and so safe' (Nygren, personal communication, 2009). Some even argue that '[t]he idea that licensing music is somehow different from selling music through iTunes isn't taken seriously anymore' (Sanburn 2012). According to this logic, because the intent of those involved in the commercial production of popular music is to sell music, the specific commodity form or buyer is of no consequence. A type of thinking has emerged that suggests that 'by participating in any way in the business of music, i.e. selling your records and so on, you're in the machine. You are in the music-selling machine' (Outhit, personal communication, 2009). As I note elsewhere, executives seem to frame 'taking' licensing money as savvy and holding onto concerns about 'selling out' as naïve (Meier 2011: 402). Although the 'smart' approach has yielded commercial success for some, the wholesale adoption of music licensing and branding as independent music's saviour has been based on a false promise. By 2008, aspiring recording artists were faced with a conundrum. 'If you're a recording artist and you think you can make it financially without exposure via other media, like TV, film, advertising or videogames, you're almost certainly wrong', pronounced Grey Group's Rabinowitz (2008), but 'if you think associating your music with a brand is going to secure your future, you're definitely wrong'. For aspiring artists, licensing agreements with brands had become the price of admission to the competitive music industries. Given the ubiquity of popular music across media today, in order to maximize the promotional effect, it is now necessary to do more than simply place popular music in commercials.

Under endorsement deals, brands capitalize on the promotional value of popular music and recording artists. By contrast, the examples of music placements as cross-promotion or brand–music integration discussed above involve recording artists capitalizing on the promotional muscle of advertising and media companies. As Taylor observes, whereas 'once manufacturers of commodities attempted to make their goods seem cool or desirable, it now seems to be increasingly the case that musicians will try to link themselves to a brand in processes of cobranding' (Taylor 2016: 57). This shift is significant: it indicates a central change in the balance of power. As recording artists, record labels, artist managers, lawyers and music publishers began to realize 'the power of promotion through associating yourself with a brand', they also began 'chasing' these opportunities (Tunnicliffe, personal communication, 2010). There is 'more of a supply than there is a demand', according to Sony/ATV Music Publishing's John Campanelli, and 'there are tons of small acts that are … totally up for licensing their music for … very low fees' (Campanelli, personal communication, 2010). Today, brands have a new source of leverage vis-à-vis recording artists: access to a highly sought-after media audience.

The widely held belief that music placements offer effective cross-promotion, and are therefore mutually beneficial, actually has helped fuel the growing gulf between the fortunes of a sea of aspiring recording artists and a comparatively small set of brands. Unlike the handful of highly publicized cases, most music placements do not place explicit focus on cross-promotion. Instead, if an artist happens to experience commercial success after appearing in an advertisement, television programme or video game, it is typically a happy but not strategically planned outcome. The examples discussed above capture an important phase of the tightening relationship between popular music and brands. In the years since, new strategies and approaches have emerged.

Marketers now argue that media content is so abundant that the discovery, sifting, presentation and overall *curation* of this content have become the new site of value creation: 'content isn't King because it isn't scarce. It's everywhere, it's overwhelming, and it's gone from quality to noise' (Rosenbaum 2010; see also Sisario 2010; Seybold 2011). This view has affected related trends in music licensing and branding. According to Taylor, 'advertising agencies are increasingly producers of popular music, not just its brokers; the boundary between "advertising" and "not advertising" in the realm of popular culture is even more porous' (Taylor 2007: 235). No longer content with renting culture, brands pursue opportunities to create their own original content (advertising creative director, personal communication, 2009). Within this promotional system, 'the gold standard for an advertising agency is for its client's brand to become part of popular culture, not simply to emulate it' (Taylor 2012: 227), and the ultimate aim is to transform the brand itself into the media content sought by audiences (Hanlon 2012). After all, while 'licensing offers the opportunity to leverage celebrity brands', the creation of original works 'allow[s] advertisers to create 100% brand equity' (Barnhard and Rutledge 2009). The persistent drive to build brand equity has produced a shift from the brand as broker to the brand as creator or curator model, the next phase in popular music's colonization by brands.

Brand Partnerships and 'Content Curation' Strategies

The proliferation of music placements has had a curious effect: from the perspective of advertisers, the use of popular music in and of itself no longer achieves the objective of brand differentiation, yet music remains a rich source of cultural meaning and, hence, value to brands. While 'music is not unique anymore as far as breaking ... through the cluttered marketplace', one advertiser explained, it remains 'a way for brands to help touch different cultures' (lifestyle advertising account executive, personal communication, 2011). Tunnicliffe uses the term 'brand–music partnerships' to describe a more recently introduced set of strategies and business partnerships that bring together music and marketing (Tunnicliffe, personal communication, 2010). 'Brand/music partnerships truly [came] of age in 2008, with a raft of increasingly innovative deals between brands and musicians appearing on what seems like a daily basis', according to Tunnicliffe. 'A number of brands [are] striking deals that go way beyond traditional music licensing for TV commercials or standard endorsement deals' (Tunnicliffe 2008). While these business partnerships do not follow a set template, they are underpinned by a common logic: the creation of targeted, strategically paired and therefore seemingly 'credible' matches between consumer brands and 'artist-brands'. In the 'brand–music partnership' era (c.2008–present), we have seen increasing use of 'authentic' popular music and novel business arrangements as a result of strategies designed to grab attention, 'touch' audiences and build value for brands.

The foundation of brand–music partnerships remains brands' interest in mining the associations tied to popular music and recording artists in order to reinforce brand identities and build brand equity. However, as advertisers have detected consumer resistance to blatant commercialism, the particular associations sought have changed. In the words of Steve Stoute, CEO of advertising agency Translation, 'The biggest mistake is that they [brand marketers] try to bring the artist into the brand's culture and what they really need to do is get their brand into the artist's culture' (quoted in High 2009). According to a strategist at a New York City-based advertising firm, 'Brands are trying to be more lifestyle oriented. ... They're trying to step away from being super commercial. ... They're trying to feel more authentic. They're trying to feel like they're a part of your life. ... That's the kind of emotion they want to evoke in you' (advertising strategist, personal communication, 2011; see also Holt 2002: 83–5). As music supervisor David Hayman observes, 'gone are the days of jingle houses. ... [M]ore and more these days the brands want a song that actually really exists that they can reference in the real world, so it's "authenticity" ' (Hayman, personal communication, 2009). Under contemporary marketing strategies, brands 'use' recording artists to 'talk to' fans, but 'in a subtle way' (Tunnicliffe, personal communication, 2010).

From the perspective of advertisers and brands, popular music can lend brands authenticity (Hayman, personal communication, 2009; Tunnicliffe, personal communication, 2010; advertising strategist, personal communication, 2011; Gutstadt, personal communication, 2011; lifestyle advertising account executive, personal communication, 2011; White, personal communication, 2011). In fact, an 'indie' soundtrack is now the default setting for many brands. According to Jared Gutstadt, CEO of music licensing firm Jingle Punks,

> Authentically, nowadays, you can't just put a Britney Spears video in a Pepsi commercial and expect people all of a sudden to go, 'oh yeah, I love Pepsi.'
>
> It's more like the idea of subversively trying to convince people things are cool without it seeming like overt commercialism. ... You're basically sneaking in the back door of culture by ... creating a cool sound to go alongside what they're doing. (Gutstadt, personal communication, 2011)

The nascent trend that Holt (2002) had identified years earlier is now in full force. Independent music can 'bring a feeling and ... an emotion' to an advertising campaign (advertising creative director, personal communication, 2009). It can also confer distinction. 'Indie-inflected music serves as a kind of Trojan horse', claims Grey Group's Rabinowitz: 'Consumers feel they are discovering something that they believe to be cool and gaining admittance to a more refined social clique' (quoted in Sisario 2010), or so brands hope.

The use of popular music to lend cultural relevance and credibility to a brand is not new in principle. After all, Pepsi used its deals with Michael Jackson and Madonna to tap into the cultural currency of MTV within youth culture. Advertiser interest in electronica also reflected a response to growing audience cynicism toward marketing. Today, however, we have seen a growth in business rhetoric about, and strategies geared around, the use of cultural beliefs about authenticity as a tool for achieving brand differentiation (see Banet-Weiser 2012 for an analysis of the cultural dimensions of branding and authenticity). Business consultants and authors James H. Gilmore and B. Joseph Pine II, best known for their work on the 'experience economy', argue that the *management of the customer perception of authenticity* is a 'new source of competitive advantage' and 'business imperative' (Gilmore and Pine 2007, 3; emphasis in original). 'Rendering authenticity', they argue, can be likened to 'controlling costs' or 'improving quality' (Gilmore and Pine 2007: 3). As I observed elsewhere, this produces a paradoxical dynamic: 'Having a link with the world *outside* brands, a world itself ever-more constituted *by* brands, seems to be the substance of "authenticity" in this context' (Meier 2011: 409; emphasis in original). The relentless hunt for authenticity actually leads to what Holt terms 'authenticity extinction' (Holt 2002: 86).

Brands' interest in authentic popular music and in developing credible relationships with recording artists is by no means limited to independent or unknown artists, however. They routinely seek out star artists. For instance, branding strategist Michael Baylor engineered the 2005 partnership between British pop star Robbie Williams and T-Mobile: 'Music and music associations are a great way of forging meaningful cultural connections with a consumer who has never moved faster, never been so elusive, or so resistant to brand messaging' (quoted in Tunnicliffe 2008). The key to the effectiveness of these partnerships, in Baylor's account, is that they are 'put together in a credible and meaningful way that allows the brand to slip behind the consumers' "firewall" but at the same time produce some form of quantifiable return on marketing' (quoted in Tunnicliffe 2008). Here, the credible link between the music or artist and the brand is of more importance than the music as such. For advertisers, authenticity hinges on the perceived 'fit' between recording artist, brand and audience, as the management of perception rests on believability. According to a *Billboard*/Nielsen white paper, for instance, 'The successful use of music in branding relies on the strength of links between the artist or event and the product. Weak alignments – caused by lack of relevance or differences in the perceived value of artist and product – threaten to spoil the transfer of one brand's image and affinities to the other' (Peoples 2009: 4; see also

Tunnicliffe 2008). Strong alignments make for persuasive promotion, and authenticity or credibility is defined in terms of the salience of these alignments.

The contemporary music industries cater to the demand for customized, targeted and strategically chosen popular music and recording artists, with record companies developing departments dedicated to fostering brand partnerships (Koren, personal communication, 2009; advertising strategist, personal communication, 2011) and music publisher websites offering tools designed to increase the efficiency of sync licensing. Warner Music Canada boasts a Strategic Marketing division – a 'dedicated in-house entertainment marketing consultancy', which helps brands 'use our music as a marketing tool' and 'provide[s] advice on tailoring entertainment concepts to match the consumer profile of the product or service being promoted' (Warner Music Canada 2015). Universal Music & Brands, a 'music & media agency', offers 'experiential' marketing (including access to artists), product placement, video content, data and intelligence, and strategic media planning services, among others (Universal Music Group 2015). Record labels are being remade as retailers of music for brands.

It is the increasingly refined calculation and marketing rationales behind the matchmaking process that sets brand–music partnerships apart from earlier music-driven branding approaches. 'If we're going to use anybody – celebrity, … musician, whatever – it's not just an endorsement deal', a New York City-based advertising executive explained: 'It's: *These* are the core values of each brand: Brand Rihanna, brand, you know, Kodak or whatever. The reason it would make sense is *this*. The reason why we should partner is *this*. The reason why it makes sense to do it over a certain amount of time is *this*' (lifestyle advertising account executive, personal communication, 2011). Under this logic, brands perceived as having complementary values become the best match. The partnerships that are most compelling to brands are justified with consumer data on already existing audience interest: 'Brands look for a proven fan base. … So the more measurable fans [sic] base in hand, the better artist–brand partnerships are formed' (Bruno 2010). Thus, stars remain central. 'Brand Rihanna' could be exchanged with another recording artist, so long as that artist had a similar level of credibility with the target market – and boasted a similar audience size.

The case of Rihanna is paradigmatic of the new brand–music partnership model and correspondingly dubious language about authenticity. 'We've worked hard to build me and my name up as a brand', Rihanna attests. 'We always want to bring an authentic connection to whatever we do. It must be sincere and people have to feel that' (quoted in Creswell 2008). She has signed an abundance of promotional agreements, including deals with umbrella brand Totes Isotoner, Procter & Gamble's Secret, Nike, J.C. Penney, Nokia, Fuze and CoverGirl (Creswell 2008) in this effort to aggressively, yet 'sincerely', promote her name as a brand. Nevertheless, according to Marc Jordan, one of her managers, 'We said no to so many deals. Either the fit wasn't right – it was more about a check than extending Rihanna's brand – or there was a disconnect between the brand and Rihanna' (quoted in Creswell 2008). Mindful of the power of what different consumer brands signify, music industry executives, like advertisers, are becoming increasingly strategic as they pursue music licensing and endorsement opportunities, even if the calculus involved in determining fit may be subjective.

A key factor is consumer 'lifestyle'. Within many brand–music partnerships, the consumer brand must be seen as authentically linked not only to a recording artist's music, but also her or his (perceived) personal lifestyle or star persona. Marketers have touted Jeep's sponsorship deal with Faith Hill and Tim McGraw as a particularly authentic brand–music partnership, for instance, due to the country singing couple's personal history with the Jeep brand (Tunnicliffe 2008; Peoples 2009: 10). The 'My Jeep Stories' advertising campaign was anchored with the following pitch: 'It was during a ride in a Jeep in 1996 in State College, Pa., that country music's reigning first couple Tim McGraw and Faith Hill decided to build a life together. That's their Jeep story. What's yours?' (PR Newswire 2007). The campaign, which invited fan participation, was deemed a success due to the 'high degree of functional relevance' between artist and brand, and the 'value derived from deeper personal meaning' (Peoples 2009: 10). Personal meaning, so understood, was a source of surplus value for the brand. In another lifestyle-driven example, Brita forged a sponsorship deal with singer-songwriter and surfer Jack Johnson in its efforts to brand Brita water filters as the eco alternative to bottled water. Brita offered free water at Johnson's concerts as a means of promoting its Hydration Station product (Brita 2012). Johnson was considered a good fit, explained Drew McGowan of Brita/Clorox, because he 'lives and breathes a green lifestyle' (quoted in Elliot 2010b). Brita attempted to gain credibility by associating itself not just with Johnson's music, but also with his star persona and environmental advocacy work.

Lifestyle-driven strategies are often tied to advertisers' (often problematic) perceptions of and assumptions regarding the link between genre and ethnicity. For instance, in a brand–music partnership orchestrated by Translation, an influential advertising firm, Wrigley partnered with R&B singer Chris Brown, because 'the company's consumer research showed that African-American consumers prefer Doublemint to other gum brands' (Smith and Jargon 2008). Wrigley helped launch Brown's new single, titled 'Forever', which features the Doublemint slogan 'double your pleasure / double your fun' (Smith and Jargon 2008). The song became a hit before it was revealed that it was actually commissioned by Doublemint: 'This is a song placement in reverse and the first time that a song has been seeded into popular culture before it has been used in a commercial. ... [T]his is the first time that a branded song such as this has been served up to the public in such a covert fashion' (Tunnicliffe 2008; see also Smith and Jargon 2008).[9] Indeed, opposite to the early examples of converting jingles into pop hits (e.g. 'I'd Like to Teach the World to Sing' discussed in chapter 1), the slogan-driven song was launched prior to the commissioned jingle. This strategy suggests that for Wrigley it was important not only that the song appear to originate in popular culture, but also that the brand itself assume an authorial role.

Under lifestyle-driven brand–music partnerships, brands have taken on roles formerly served by music companies. By 2010, the notion that 'lifestyle brands are becoming the new record labels' (Sisario 2010) had gained traction. Mountain Dew and Red Bull had opened record labels, and 'Levi's, Converse, Dr. Martens, Scion, Nike and Bacardi ha[d] all sponsored music by the kind of under-the-radar artists covered in Pitchfork and The Village Voice, and they blitz[ed] the blogosphere with promotional budgets fatter than most labels could muster' (Sisario 2010). Label-like arrangements with aspiring artists enable brands to glean cool credibility from independent music (Sisario 2010; sound branding executive, personal communication, 2010), but are also business ventures. In some cases, brands take an ownership stake in recordings and live performances, while in others artists are permitted to keep full ownership rights. I will briefly review key examples.

In 2008, TAG Body Spray partnered with Def Jam to launch a record label in the hope that it would 'establish even more credibility for TAG with the important urban/African-American market' while also securing 'a return [on investment] over and above the promotional benefits of being associated with an artist' (Tunnicliffe 2008). Artists would receive promotional support and the label would share in the revenues generated (Tunnicliffe 2008). The label signed aspiring Brooklyn rapper Q Da Kid and hired noted record producer Jermaine Dupri (Sisario 2010). The marketing push for Q Da Kid included the insertion of his song 'I Am Him' in a TAG commercial and the airing of a documentary about the artist on MTV, but his single 'On a Mission', which was released September 2008, had only sold 2,000 units by December 2008 (High 2008). TAG Records collapsed in less than a year (Sisario 2010). 'I was with a company that didn't understand the music business', Q Da Kid offered. 'They're used to their brands flying off the shelves like it ain't nothing, and they thought, "If we put enough money behind this, he'll be big." And it wasn't like that' (quoted in Sisario 2010).

Also in 2008, Bacardi partnered with an already established act: Groove Armada. The rum brand signed the British electronica duo to an exclusive one-year record deal, which covered the release of a four-track EP (Brandle 2008; Tunnicliffe, personal communication, 2010). This '360 deal' also covered touring and audiovisual content (Brandle 2008). Bacardi took a cut from all revenue streams, but Groove Armada retained ownership of their masters and copyrights (Brandle 2008; Tunnicliffe 2008). According to Groove Armada manager Dan O'Neil, 'They are looking at it from a point of view of association, and they're getting access to a license to use the music to implement their strategy world-wide' (quoted in Brandle 2008). Bacardi was able to introduce its customers 'to a musical experience ... with an artist that had great credibility, ... that was really well known, but quite cool still' (Tunnicliffe, personal communication, 2010). While the duo was seen as a 'snug fit' for the brand (High 2008), the deal was not renewed.

PepsiCo brand Mountain Dew also started a record label in 2008: Green Label Sound, run by Cornerstone, a prominent lifestyle marketing agency (Sisario 2010). Mountain Dew's Hudson Sullivan (2011) indicated that the label's artists keep ownership of all revenue tied to their music (see also Barshad 2011). Under this model, Mountain Dew seeks to build brand equity not through direct ownership, but rather through credible participation in cultural creation. 'Consumers are smarter', according to Sullivan. 'The last thing we want is to look like we're paying someone to drink our product on-camera. We want to create genuine loyalty' (quoted in Barshad 2011). 'Chromeo, Cool Kids, Theophilus London, MNDR', all artists who have worked with Green Label Sound, 'they reflect our sensibility. They define their own genre', he continued (quoted in Barshad 2011). Under such hands-off arrangements, it is understandable why some artists, such as Chromeo singer David Macklovitch, would argue that multiple rights deals with major labels (discussed in chapter 2) are 'way more of a sell-out than doing a collaboration with a brand where you have full creative control and you give free content to your fans' (quoted in Sisario 2010).

Mountain Dew's record label is not a stand-alone endeavour. Rather, it is part of a much broader marketing strategy designed to target youth culture:

Instead of being a sponsor to anything, instead of sponsoring an event or sponsoring a concert ... they're being creators. ... So, they created a label. They created an art project: Green Label Art. And they created a platform to let consumers speak for themselves. It's called

Dewmocracy. ... They created a tour with extreme sports and music and everything. ... They are present at all those passion points of youth culture. (advertising strategist, personal communication, 2011)

Mountain Dew does not want to function as mere sponsor or 'wallpaper' at festivals, according to Sullivan (2011); the brand seeks collaborations with, not endorsements from, artists. By 'collaborating' with recording artists, the brand seeks to entrench itself within the web of meanings produced by fans. As such, Mountain Dew's strategy exemplifies the shift from brand as licensor or sponsor to brand as content curator.[10]

The notion that lifestyle brands would become the new record labels had waned by 2010. As Tunnicliffe explained to me,

Whilst for a while people were saying ... brands are going to become the new record labels ... that's not really what brands want to do. ... Brands are not in the business of music. Brands are in the business of brands. Alright? And that's a very important thing to remember ... and a very important distinction. (Tunnicliffe, personal communication, 2010)

According to New York Times reporter Ben Sisario (2010), 'Tag Records' fate points to the reality that sneaker and soda companies are ultimately in it to sell sneakers and soda, not music'. Brands' interest in music is decidedly different than traditional labels': brands are interested in music fans as would-be purchasers of consumer products, not recordings and other music products. Many advertising executives now express reservation about the music business overall, which one sound branding executive characterized as 'a giant hole that people pour money into' (sound branding executive, personal communication, 2010). Even while they might be dissatisfied with simply licensing music, brands do not necessarily want to be investors in a turbulent industry. Instead, following a content curation-inspired strategy, it appears as though lifestyle brands have become more interested in the production of music festivals.

From Coke Live and Virgin Festival/V Festival to the more recently launched Budweiser Made in America Festival, corporations do not simply stamp their brands on but also curate line-ups for live music events. Brand-curated music festivals are less risky investments than record labels (remember that concert 'experiences' cannot be 'pirated' in the same way as sound recordings), and in terms of marketing, they enable brands to position themselves as the headliner. In her study of an Irish music festival, Witnness, run by Guinness (2000–3), Liz Moor argues that such 'experiential' branding tactics are intended to expand the 'perception and practice of what constitutes a marketing "space"' and thereby 'achieve a much more proximal relationship between consumer bodies and brands' (Moor 2003: 45). Music, 'perhaps the most portable and simultaneously the most affect-laden of all cultural products', is of particular utility in strategies designed to socialize and spatialize the links between brands, experience and memory (Moor 2003: 50). According to Nicholas Carah, whose analysis of Coca-Cola's and Virgin's music festivals draws on interviews with young people, musicians and marketers, 'The audience's festival experience creates brand value. … The mediation of social life that unfolds at music festivals embeds brands within everyday cultural practices and webs of meaning' (Carah 2010: 122). Situated at the heart of a site of collective meaning making, the brand 'extracts value from social actors' (Carah 2010: 143). In the case of Budweiser's Made in America, the brand has a direct and explicitly proprietary stake in music-related cultural practices.

Budweiser's two-day concert, whose 2012 inaugural line-up featured stars such as Pearl Jam and Drake in addition to lesser known, credible artists such as Passion Pit, Odd Future and Dirty Projectors, was 'headlined and "curated" by Jay-Z' (Logan 2012). The 2015 bill featured Beyoncé, The Weeknd, Death Cab for Cutie, Modest Mouse, De La Soul, Santigold and many others (Roc Nation 2015). The festival, designed to target younger consumers, was the product of a change in branding strategy initiated by Anheuser-Busch vice president of marketing, Paul Chibe (Logan 2012). Stoute of advertising agency Translation united Budweiser with Live Nation and Jay-Z (an artist signed to a Live Nation 360 deal) (Hampp 2012b). 'We started with the music, but it's more than that', according to Budweiser vice president Rob McCarthy. 'It's a *property* – Budweiser Made in America – that celebrates the diversity of young adult culture and experience' (quoted in Logan 2012; emphasis added). In 2012, approximately 45,000 people attended the festival (Greenburg 2012a), paying from US$75 (an early-bird, single day special) to US$175 for tickets, according to the festival website (Made in America 2012). Budweiser also commissioned a film, directed by Ron Howard, about the event and not the performances *per se*, as Stoute's pitch suggests: 'The narrative of this film is not a concert. The narrative is everything Made In America stands for, and the music is a backdrop. Budweiser has been a partner from the beginning because they own the trademark for "Made In America." You're gonna start seeing brands become much closer to the content' (quoted in Hampp 2012b). In this example, the brand positions the music as a 'backdrop' for its broader branding ambitions even at a music festival. Importantly, as brands embed themselves ever more deeply into content and create content themselves, these corporations profit more directly from popular music and also benefit from the marketing exposure and cool associations this content cultivates.

The increasingly branded character of concerts and live events is now generally accepted as an unavoidable reality. As Zack O'Malley Greenburg of *Forbes* reports, 'the musicians who played at the Budweiser-backed affair didn't appear to be fazed by the notion of "selling out" that could arise from appearing at such a heavily-branded festival. Indeed, many suggested that there's no such thing these days' (Greenburg 2012a). Given the pervasiveness of branding now with live music, it is difficult for working artists to be too selective about gigs. Even Lollapalooza 2012, which is not a lifestyle brand festival *per se*, featured 'fully-branded stages by Sony, PlayStation, Bud Light, Google Play, BMI and Red Bull' in addition to 'a bag check from State Farm, free T-shirts from The Gap and two different activations from Toyota (a Free Yr Radio lounge and a Prius Family Playground)' (Hampp 2012a). The SXSW festival likewise involves active involvement from major brands and corporations (see Klein et al. 2016). According to Howlin' Pelle Almqvist of The Hives, a band featured at Made in America, 'Maybe ten years ago, we could go on tour and play nothing that was sponsored. But nowadays, if we said, "We don't play anything that's sponsored," we'd get no shows. ... It's hard to fight the dragons and pay the people' (quoted in Greenburg 2012a).

Lifestyle brands have even appropriated a critique of the cynical, hits-driven recording industry as a part of their pitch – an approach consistent with the move toward 'authenticity'-oriented marketing strategies. For example, the 'Right Music Wrongs' manifesto, penned by Virgin for its 2009 V fest, censures 'the insincerity of reality pop stars and pre-fabricated, formulaic, celebrity seeking, silicone enhanced lip sync-ers', which it distinguishes from 'real music', which 'isn't about the instrument, it is about the intent. ... It can be quiet and considered, or loud and obnoxious but is not artificially sweetened, mass produced, celebrity seeking mediocrity with a marketing plan at its core' (quoted in Carah 2010: 21). As Carah observes, 'Virgin, like other brands, savvily appropriated mythologies of real and authentic popular music and engaged the live performance of music to legitimate their claims to authenticity' (Carah 2010: 20). Virgin positioned itself as a champion of 'real' music and distanced itself from the idea of marketing plans – an idea that was also no doubt the product of a marketing plan intended to help sell Virgin products (for further discussion of the invocation of the 'spirit of independence tied to popular music' suggested by these examples, see

Hesmondhalgh and Meier 2015: 108). Brands' interest in recording artists and popular music is ultimately based on commercial factors and is an exercise in branding, advertising and public relations.

During the era of brand–music partnerships, we have seen a proliferation of new approaches to music branding, which nevertheless mark persistent continuities with more conventional approaches. The same advertising impulse that produced brands' interest first in pop star endorsements and later in independent music is behind more recent experimentation with branded record labels and music festivals: the thirst for something new. As Owen observed in 1998, 'With advertising, there's always the need to break through the media clutter by coming up with something fresh and surprising. Since most rock-and-roll is neither one anymore, consumers are currently hearing a lot more unusual sounds in advertisements' (Owen 1998: G01). By 2010, even unusual sounds were no longer fresh or surprising. So-called 'world music' and songs with 'weird instrumentation' were sought by brands, according to one music publisher, who referred to ambient post-rock band Sigur Rós as an indicative example of one such sound (Campanelli, personal communication, 2010). Toronto-based music supervisor Hayman had even licensed the music of a yodeller and of throat singers in order to differentiate his clients' brands (Hayman, personal communication, 2009). As advertising agencies continue to 'mine the last vestiges of unsponsored expressive culture' in an effort to render consumer brands more authentic (Holt 2002: 86), difference – in terms of either content or approach – has emerged as the new standard.

In a shift away from more conventional music placement and licensing deals, some brands have expressed a desire for a more 'ownable' sound. The rationale behind the decision to commission a Willie Nelson cover version of 'The Scientist' for use in a Chipotle Mexican Grill commercial captures this new thinking: 'If you were just simply to use the Coldplay version, you don't really get the same equity as if you kind of make it … ownable by Chipotle and specifically by that film [commercial]. *It didn't feel like it was anything that totally special to rent the song*' (Nashel 2012; emphasis added). 'Renting' music is now so common that brands seek something more novel and strategic; they demand more from recording artists and appropriate more from culture. Because the Chipotle spot offers a critique of the industrialization of livestock production, and because Nelson's work with Farm Aid is well known, the fit between the music and the message is ostensibly credible and authentic. Under this strategy, the restaurant franchise attempts to place its stamp on this web of positive associations, feelings and even political dispositions.

My intent in the above section has not been to provide a comprehensive catalogue of the myriad and multiplying array of brand–music

partnerships but, rather, to identify a key logic: the increasingly calculated pairing of recording artists and lifestyle brands under authenticity-
oriented marketing strategies. Brand–music partnerships forged in an
effort to provide brands with 'credible' content have further eroded the
distinction between popular music and promotion. The term 'partnership' is a misnomer, as it suggests a business arrangement wherein two
parties work together to advance mutual interests. In reality, outside of
rich endorsement deals with star artists, one party is firmly in charge:
the brand. Brand–music partnerships work to entrench brands more
deeply into popular music cultures, accelerating the colonization of
popular music by brands. Next, I examine some of the effects that the
sum of these music-related branding strategies have had on working
artists and on popular music itself.

The Bottom Line: Recording Artist Remuneration

Recording artists agree to work with brands in the hope of making a
living from making music – a prospect that, as always, comes with
serious obstacles. In a post-CD music marketplace, record companies
and artists have become increasingly dependent on sync licensing and
branding opportunities as a source of revenue, as we have seen. Though
positioned as a solution to problems tied to achieving fair remuneration
in an era of free and inexpensive music, the widespread pursuit of such
deals as a standard practice among even independent artists actually has
produced yet another set of challenges. Prior to the post-2008 context
analysed here, some independent artists were able to secure – and in
some cases turn down – offers reaching six figures (see Klein 2009: 71–2,
131). Such rich offers are now rare. A growing power imbalance between
brands and (especially aspiring) artists has translated into deteriorating
fees for most artists. Against hype about brands as 'patron[s] of the rock
arts' (Sisario 2010), we have seen the rise of a type of *reverse* patronage:
the artist supports and champions the brand.

Fierce competition for these sought-after music placements has made
them increasingly difficult to secure (Beavis, personal communication,
2009; Ferneyhough, personal communication, 2009; Kenzer, personal
communication, 2010). Music licensing is 'kind of a closed world'
(Outhit, personal communication, 2009) – a claim affirmed by entertainment marketing executive Marcus Peterzell:

> We just don't have the time. ... I have my brief. I'm going to the seven
> major labels, my three favourite independents, ASCAP and BMI, my
> three management companies, and my five publishers. That's it. ...

That's fifteen people. They're going to give me five suggestions. That's seventy-five suggestions I have to look through. ... We just go to the low hanging fruit. (Peterzell 2010)

A striking power imbalance between artists and consumer brands has placed the latter in a strong position to dictate the terms of these relationships and agreements.

With respect to fees, music, media and advertising industry executives tend to shy away from pinpointing specific dollar figures, and often state that all deals are different and depend on the particular artist, song and use. Therefore, this overview is not intended to be comprehensive or incontestable; it is a mapping of rough fee ranges and general trends. In 2007, it was reported that 'TV producers might shell out upwards of $50,000 for the use of a song by an established artist on a major label, but can sometimes pay as little as several hundred dollars for the use of a song by an unknown talent' (Hau 2007). As of 2012, according to *Time* business reporter Josh Sanburn, 'An emerging indie artist can get $10,000 for a song for a 30-second ad' (Sanburn 2012) ('can' being the operative word), and more recently, Rhian Jones (2015) suggested a range of US$5,000–15,000 for films, television commercials and series. In 2013, music supervisor P.J. Bloom, known for his work on *Glee*, *Nip/Tuck* and *CSI: Miami*, provided the following response to a question regarding artist revenue from sync placements:

If you expect nothing, then you'll probably be very pleased. If you expect to get one of those $50,000 sync fees then you're probably going to be quite disappointed. There was a good moment years ago when the retail record business was starting to fail and sync was starting to take over in a lot of ways. We were spending a lot of money: our budgets were higher, the notion of licensing music had much more value so the fees were much higher. Fees have systematically gone down and down over the years and that's going to continue to happen.

Personally I'm shocked that [labels] don't pay [studios] to get your music in there. I don't say that to piss anybody off, I'm just saying that it's amazing to me that we still pay anything for it. To me the potential disclosure opportunity is immense and potentially a great thing. (quoted in Pakinkis 2013)

Media companies trumpet the promotional value of these opportunities as part of a rationale for negotiating lower prices. While fees vary by medium, a downward trend is affecting films, television programmes, commercials and video games, with payments to independent and aspiring artists in particular plummeting. Because fees are directly tied to the celebrity status of the recording artist or the hit status of the song, stars can still earn big paydays, however.

The power of the recording artist influences the terms of the deal. Music attorney Steve Gordon (2015) cites a figure of US$100,000 or higher for a pop hit versus a range of US$10,000–25,000 for songs by indie writers and artists used in major motion pictures. Indie filmmakers may pay US$5,000 or less: 'Don't be surprised if they offer you no more than a credit' (Gordon 2015). The figures reported in *Film Music Magazine*'s '2011–2012 Film & TV Music Salary and Rate Survey' suggest that a 'high-end popular song' in a medium budget studio feature may fetch US$20,000–75,000 – a figure that drops to US$5,000–25,000 for a 'mid-line popular song' and to US$1,500–3,500 for a 'generally unknown or unreleased song' (Global Media Online 2011). For a medium budget indie feature, music comes with a price tag of US$500–2,000 (Global Media Online 2011). In a high budget studio feature, the report suggests a range of US$2,000–15,000 plus for a 'generally unknown' song – a stark contrast with the US$125,000–150,000 plus that a 'high-end popular song' might command (Global Media Online 2011).

As of 2011, for a placement in a television episode on network television, the rates reportedly ranged from US$500–2,000 for low budget to US$5,000–15,000 for medium budget to US$15,000–25,000 plus for a high budget series – rates that were only slightly different for premium cable (Global Media Online 2011). Turning to national advertisements for 'major products', *Film Music Magazine*'s survey suggested rates of US$5,000–10,000 for low budget, US$10,000–175,000 for medium budget and US$100,000–250,000 plus for high budget advertisements – all of which typically shrink by 40–50 per cent for regional or single market advertising (Global Media Online 2011). According to Rabinowitz (2010), Grey Group's director of music, during the 'glory days' an artist might be paid US$30,000 for a thirty-second spot, whereas by 2010, US$5,000–15,000 was more typical, and some brands paid no fee at all to unknown artists based on the stance that it is 'a privilege to have your song on a commercial'.

In Canada, fees for advertising and television placements also dropped dramatically, in part, due to unsigned bands' willingness to license music at bargain rates (Quinlan, personal communication, 2009; Potocic, personal communication, 2009). According to Canadian music publishing executive Beavis, many independent artists are willing to clear all rights for $500 CAD to secure such licensing opportunities (Beavis, personal communication, 2009). As Canadian music publishing executive Jodie Ferneyhough observed, the advertising industry 'has figured the trick out, so they're going to indie artists a lot more. ... They'll a lot of time say "Okay guys, here's your $500, off you go" and the band is thrilled.

They're starving artists – of course they're thrilled' (Ferneyhough, personal communication, 2009).

The downward trend in fees, particularly for unknown artists, is mirrored in the market for popular music in video games. Whereas artists were formerly paid tens of thousands of dollars, even up to US$100,000, fees plummeted during the first decade of the twenty-first century, with many video game publishers offering 'five grand "all in". ... Take it or leave it' (Coffing, personal communication, 2010).[11] 'The leverage changed', explained Los Angeles-based music supervisor Barry Coffing. 'Before, bands didn't want to be in video games. ... Once the bands wanted to be in there, then they [video game publishers] said, "Well, we're not going to pay that"' (Coffing, personal communication, 2010). Unknown and aspiring artists hungry for music placement opportunities have little bargaining power. In fact, a primary source of lesser known music's value to brands is precisely the substantial cost savings reaped (Fritz, personal communication, 2009; Coffing, personal communication, 2010). Remember that these licensing fees are split between group members, the artist manager and so forth, and for signed artists, the label and music publisher often take a cut in addition. Four-figure sums do not amount to much per person.

Interestingly, advertising executive Cheryl R. Berman (2010) advised against licensing music to advertisers for no money in exchange for marketing exposure, as this approach might set a troubling precedent that could be eagerly adopted as an industry standard. It is telling that Berman (2010) stressed how the very real potential for brands to exploit unknown artists' desire to 'be big and be famous' and to get their music 'out there' 'scares' her. Of course, her concerns are not unfounded. Unknown artists desperate to catch a break are routinely advised to be 'flexible' (Nagi 2010), a term seemingly used to suggest a willingness to accept very little money from brands and even to tailor lyrics to brands' messages. As Bethany Klein laments, 'musicians desperate to be heard and survive financially by any means possible make for easy marks to an advertising industry that will pay as little as possible to license music' (Klein 2009: 121).

Corporations' impulse to shop for bargains has extended to music festivals. For example, the band Ex Cops was invited by McDonald's to play at a branded showcase at the SXSW festival in spring 2015 – for free. Band member Brian Harding (2015) expressed his concerns in an open letter posted on Facebook:

> Their selling point was that this was 'a great opportunity for additional exposure,' and that 'McDonald's will have their global digital team on site to meet with the bands, help with cross promotion, etc.'

I don't, and doubt that they know what this means either.

Getting past that rhetoric, at the very least a big corporation like McDonald's can at least pay their talent a little. Right?

'There isn't a budget for an artist fee (unfortunately)' ...

In lieu of being paid like a real artist, or anyone who is employed to do a service, McDonald's assures us that we will 'be featured on screens throughout the event, as well as POSSIBLY mentioned on the McDonald's social media accounts like Facebook (57MM likes!).'

McDonald's claimed that what they were proposing was nothing out of the ordinary: 'We follow the same standard protocol as other brands and sponsors by inviting talented and emerging musicians to join us at the SXSW Festival. We look forward to serving McDonald's food, drinks and fun in Austin. #slownewsday' (quoted in Grow 2015) – a glib hashtag seemingly intended to undermine serious discussion of an important issue. Ex Cops singer Amalie Bruun pointed out that on the contrary, smaller corporations *had* offered to pay them (Grow 2015). The band decided to express their concerns on Facebook 'so people know what the music industry is like today', Bruun explained. 'If we're not going to get paid for our live shows, what are we going to get paid for?' (quoted in Grow 2015). Perhaps feeling the heat of media scrutiny and negative publicity, McDonald's changed their policy and agreed to pay artists for performing at their showcases (Hampp 2015).

Although I identify an overall trend of declining artist fees, a handful of superstar artists still receive rich endorsement and licensing deals with consumer brands. For instance, in 2012, hip-hop stars Lil Wayne and Nicki Minaj signed seven-figure endorsement deals with Mountain Dew and Pepsi, respectively (Greenburg 2012b, 2012c). Lady Gaga's headlining performance at a Doritos-branded SXSW stage in 2014 reportedly was tied to a seven-figure payday (Hampp 2014a). Note that Mountain Dew and Doritos, a Frito-Lay brand, are both owned by Pepsi, demonstrating just how powerful a select group of consumer brands are in the marketplace for music-related branding deals.

When brands are willing to pay a premium for celebrity recording artists, it is because they expect a return on their investment. By signing deals with stars, brands are not paying for music *per se*. Rather, they are 'buying the fame' (Coffing, personal communication, 2010). Indeed, while popular music is abundant today, stars remain scarce, and still receive considerable media attention. Superstars can lend a brand 'instant recognition' and can command considerable publicity: 'If you work with Madonna, you are banking that the commercial you spent $1 million [on] is going to get $10 million in added value from P. R. and that's why you pay Madonna 5 [million dollars]' (advertising creative director, personal communication, 2009). The artist's fan base, an additional audience to 'pay attention to your brand', is a source of 'added value' (digital marketing project manager, personal communication, 2011). Deals with brands facilitate 'borrowing some of the equity and the relationship that artists or celebrities have got with their fans' (Tunnicliffe, personal communication, 2010). As always, stars are used to draw the attention of the widest possible audience. Interestingly, speaking in 2010, Katrina McMullan, senior counsel for music and entertainment at Mattel, pointed out that 'what cost me a million dollars two years ago doesn't cost that anymore. Only about five artists are in that [top-tier] category that can command that kind of money' (quoted in Bruno 2010). The effects of the overall collapse in fees have penetrated even the upper reaches of popular music stardom.

The ways that brands and music companies appraise the value of recording artists are cloaked in the business jargon of 'equity'. From the perspective of major music companies, fees reflect 'an equity balance' (Campanelli, personal communication, 2010). In some cases (e.g. stars such as Lady Gaga), 'the brand borrows the artist's equity', and therefore the cost can be very expensive, whereas in other cases 'the artist has no equity' in popular culture, and benefits from any exposure afforded by the brand (Campanelli, personal communication, 2010). The following record label executive's explanation of the 'artist triangle', though hyperbolic, illustrates the gross disparity born of this type of thinking:

> The artists at the top are those like Beyoncé or Bruce Springsteen ... or Coldplay or Radiohead, for example, and they bring to the table very, very high equity ...
> But those are going to be the ones that are most expensive and most fussy and difficult to work with, because they have a very specific ... mindset of what they should be associated with, what their vision is ... and they can afford to be picky and choosy. Of course, there are ... fewer of those. The ones at the bottom are all completely unknown developing bands that no one's ever heard of. They have no equity whatsoever. They would literally jump off this building naked ... just to get lunch at McDonald's, because they have a six/seven hour journey in a minivan with eight other guys – [and] they haven't washed for three days – to earn two hundred bucks in the kitty. (Canadian major record label executive B, personal communication, 2009)

The 'laws' of supply and demand reign in these industries, and the power of consumer brands and media companies is routinely exerted at full force.

Music licensing deals largely operate on a 'take-it-or-leave-it' basis, and brands are in a position to dictate self-advantaging, not mutually beneficial, terms. According to Martin,

> If the artist is successful enough where they're not relying on that money and they're not relying on that association ... then the leverage is on the side of the artist and they can command a lot more money. But on the other side of the spectrum, there's so many unsigned and independent musicians that are clamouring to get on TV that ... the prices are pretty low, if not free. (Martin, personal communication, 2010)

Canadian independent label and distribution executive Tim Potocic described a competitive pricing strategy imposed by some companies, which involved a fee proposal process that impelled artists to underbid one another (Potocic, personal communication, 2009).

Those recording artists desperate for a chance and unwilling to say 'no' have little leverage. For brands hunting for cost savings, exploitation of aspiring artists' lack of 'equity' constitutes business-as-usual. This is a system clearly founded on domination.

Where has this logic of domination taken us? Now that independent music is readily available for little to no money, low cost (underbidding one another) is no longer a source of competitive advantage for individual artists interested in piquing a music supervisor's interest. One entertainment marketing executive provided the following instruction to aspiring artists and artist managers seeking to stand out from the pack and secure a brand partnership:

> Take stock of everything you like and own – your shirts, your pants, your skirts, your makeup, your sunglasses, the car you drive, the liquor you drink, the beer, the milk, everything you have that's not a ridiculous brand, ... all of the small things that you're passionate about, whether it's ten or twenty – and go to those brands, find them on LinkedIn, and just say: 'I'm a singer-songwriter and I love your sunglasses. It's all I ever wear. They never leave me. They're unbelievable. There's great quality and I'd love to just tell my fans.' You're going to get brands [responding with] – 'Really? Thank you. Let me send you a pair. Let me tell you' – and it starts a conversation. So you can't reverse engineer. You can't go to a brand and say, 'Hi, I'm doing a tour, can you sponsor me?' Not going to happen. You've got to give them a reason. Say: 'I love your product. I am genuinely passionate about it. That's all I'm saying and I'm happy to tell my fans, because I think it's the best jeans or the best sunglasses.' (Peterzell 2010)

The perversely one-sided courtship between artist and brand revealed by this advice provides evidence of the utter substitutability of non-star artists to brands – and of the ways those artists, in turn, must perform a deep internalization of their prospective sponsor's brand identity. From the point of view of brands, with little 'authenticity' left to glean from independent music *per se*, it seems, artists must not only be corporate-friendly, but must also prove their utility as pitchmen. The race to the bottom has taken on a new hue. Harding of Ex Cops (2015) pre-empted the 'No one is holding a gun to your head!' rebuttal. 'I'm aware that to achieve any exposure is a Herculean task in 2015, but the Boethian Wheel is a real thing, and this will continue to exist if we, as artists, keep saying yes in exchange for a taste of success.'

Increasingly dissatisfied with the older music sponsorship model, many brands ask for endorsements from artists, yet refuse to pay fairly for those endorsements. However, the promise of music placement and branding deals has not necessarily been pinned to the paycheque. Amid dwindling fees for independent and lesser known artists, the promise of sync licensing and branding partnerships largely hinges on the promotional value of these opportunities. The assumption is that the marketing exposure can help with sales, though it is really difficult to tell if it actually does (Potocic, personal communication, 2009). After all, music placements offer only 'possible exposure': 'It's not like anything is proven out there' (sound branding executive, personal communication, 2010). One practice that can heighten the promotional effect of a music placement is the inclusion of captions that identify the artist and song featured in television programmes and commercials. When included, these 'chyrons' or 'dead cards' are often offered in exchange for a lower fee (Hayman, personal communication, 2009; Campanelli, personal communication, 2010; Coffing, personal communication, 2010; Martin, personal communication, 2010). Brands typically are not interested in such arrangements. Contrary to the widely accepted notion that 'everybody wins' through music branding deals, it is clear that brands, new music gatekeepers, are the real winners.

Unfriendly 'Syncs': Constraints Placed on Musical Content

Given the diverse range of popular music licensed, produced and curated by consumer brands and media companies today, it may seem curious to argue that brands function as a rationalizing and even standardizing force in the music industries, yet I contend that brands' emergence as key music gatekeepers has had precisely that effect. With respect to capitalist cultural production more broadly, Shane Gunster argues that 'the polysemy of the sign has become both functional for *and* a function of capitalism itself' (Gunster 2007: 310; emphasis in original). In the case of the 'different' sounding musics that interest brands, they are desired because they help to produce surplus value. Although a wide range of musics may circulate within popular media as a result of sync licensing practices, they are characterized by a homogeneity or sameness in terms of the range of feelings that advertisers in particular attempt to evoke. While niche-specific sad, aggressive or sexy songs may be used in advertisements to a certain degree, there is an overriding bias toward music perceived as happy.

One interviewee described the type of music that works well within this system as 'sync-friendly': a sync-friendly song for use in advertising offers 'upbeat happiness for fifteen to thirty seconds' and employs lyrical references to cheerful words such as 'sunshine' (independent label licensing executive, personal communication, 2011). As Lynn Grossman of independent artist management company and music service Secret Road explains, 'We get approached by people usually looking for positive messages in songs. Things like, "I feel good," "Life is great," "I'm the man," "I feel good about myself," or something about coming home or feeling at home. They're all pretty similar' (quoted in Sanburn 2012).

Music licensing software used by music supervisors and other licensors sorts music according to various moods and keywords – a topic examined in chapter 4. A search of Sony/ATV Music Publishing's catalogue yielded the following results within the mood/style category, underscoring the premium placed on happiness: 3,339 songs tagged as upbeat, 2,593 as happy/feel good and 2,348 as energetic, compared with 512 tagged as aggressive, 320 as angry and 1,499 as sad (Sony/ATV 2013). Some sentiments are clearly more popular among or relevant to licensors than others. The fact that the market for happy thoughts is bullish is not surprising. As Wernick argues regarding the 'bias' of advertising, promotion 'is determinedly positive and upbeat. ... [I]magistic advertising may build on the values, desire and symbologies that are already out there, but by no means does it simply reflect them. It typifies what is diverse, filters out what is antagonistic or depressing, and naturalizes the role and standpoint of consumption as such' (Wernick 1991: 42). Advertising professionals are typically interested in using popular music as a tool for eliciting and directing 'pleasant' feelings toward their products and brands. Cheery music helps to naturalize lifestyle-driven consumption.

Happiness is not the only emotion targeted, of course. After all, as that same search of Sony/ATV's catalogue demonstrates, there is still scope for the use of sad sounds. Furthermore, a sync-friendly song for television programmes follows a different formula than that appropriate for advertisements. It typically starts low, builds and leads to a climactic ending, and features general lyrics: 'You want someone to say that "it was a great night" as opposed to "it was a Tuesday night"' (independent label licensing executive, personal communication, 2011). The exploration of specific themes and ideas reduces popular music's utility to television producers; the use of vague words assures the widest appeal and, hence, largest number of bidders.

Because music licensing is considered a key way for aspiring artists to build their audience today, songwriters may face pressure to write material tailored to the requirements of brands. At an artist management conference in New York, entertainment attorney Stephen T. Erwin (2010) stressed that appropriate business planning for recording artists and managers starts from the very beginning; artists ought to write about marketable themes and think of opportunities to license. At the same conference, sonic branding expert Paul Nagi (2010) advised artists to write songs that are 'useable' – to 'sell their souls to the devil', he said jokingly. This advice reflects a new industry reality. Even within independent record labels, the centrality of licensing has translated into a strong interest in music that is 'sync-friendly' (independent label licensing executive, personal communication, 2011). Many labels are interested in signing those artists who write material compatible with the demands of brands.

I asked music publisher Jodie Ferneyhough if this trend might impact on songwriting – whether he might potentially say to songwriters, 'Write a song about sunshine', if he kept getting requests for songs about sunshine. He responded:

> Yeah, absolutely. We never tell them to write a song *about* ... I can't dictate the terms of the single he writes or doesn't write. That's a jingle. ... But I say to them, 'Look, when you're writing songs ... think about writing about a happy day or ... write about sunshine or write about smiles ... How can you incorporate those words, those thoughts?' It doesn't even have to be the word smile, but it could be, you know, a theme around it. ... I've never been, 'You should write this kind of a song', but just 'these are the key triggers', because there [are] key triggers – sunshine, smile, happy, glad, joyful ... that especially advertisers are looking for. (Ferneyhough, personal communication, 2009)

Singer-songwriter Helen Austin provides an artist's view: 'After being a songwriter for many years ... I decided that my next "job" was going to be getting my music licensed' (Austin 2010a). Due to her successes in this area, a music promotion website invited her to give advice to artists. 'Produce targeted content', she recommended: 'instead of just having songs that I think I can submit, I have started writing with placements in mind. Taxi [an 'A&R' website] had a listing that was looking for a song with the word "happy" in it, so I wrote a song called Happy, which was picked up and is one of my most successful songs' (Austin 2010a). The lyrics in the chorus of 'Happy', which is undoubtedly an extreme example, contain the word 'happy' in all but two lines, totalling six mentions (Austin 2010b). It should come as no surprise, then, that Pharrell Williams' top hit of the same name was licensed for use in a Beats commercial (Adams 2014), a global Fiat advertising campaign and the *Despicable Me 2* soundtrack (Cobo 2014).

The dictates of sync-friendliness even result in outright lyrical restrictions. The use of K'Naan's 'Waving Flag' in Coca-Cola's 2010 FIFA World Cup campaign is instructive. In order to make his political song compatible with Coca-Cola's campaign, the Somali-Canadian hip-hop artist agreed to record a 'Coca-Cola celebration mix', as *Billboard*'s David Prince reports:

> Coca-Cola loved the song but noted that lyrical references to 'a violent prone, poor people zone' and people 'struggling, fighting to eat' didn't fit the campaign's themes. 'The crucial moment in the discussion came when K'Naan said, "I can take that song, refashion some of the lyrics and give you an exclusive version," ' [A&M/Octone Records president/CEO James] Diener says. 'That's an attempt on K'Naan's part to revitalize the song in the spirit of the World Cup.' (Prince 2010)

The conversion of K'Naan's song into advertising music necessitated the removal of lyrical content that reflected a social conscience. In order to effectively serve the purposes of advertising, threatening political content must be scrubbed and muted, resulting in an edgy vibe, aesthetic or feel that is devoid of specific referents.

The case of Mark Foster of chart-topping band Foster the People may give us a glimpse into the future of popular musical production under this paradigm. He wrote Foster the People's breakthrough hit, 'Pumped Up Kicks', while working at Mophonics, a sound design and licensing firm (Fixmer 2012). The song garnered advertising, television and film placements (Peters 2011).[12] Following in the path of Barry Manilow, Foster is both a recording artist and jingle writer. Despite the commercial success of his Grammy-nominated band, Foster intended to return to his advertising day job after touring: 'Foster the People wouldn't exist without Mophonics. Mophonics is kind of a creative home for me' (quoted in Fixmer 2012). The music he writes there often conforms to the parameters of sync-friendliness. His safe, indie-sounding, acoustic guitar-driven advertising song 'Beautiful Day', for example, hits all the keywords: 'Hey sunshine / Let me see the smile / In your eyes / I said wait sunshine / There's something I should say / You're beautiful to me / Yeah, Yeah' (Mophonics 2012). Music licensing software is geared toward precisely these types of keywords, as discussed in chapter 4.

Given the success experienced by Foster and many other artists, is advertising really the new radio? Margarita Alexomanolaki, Catherine Loveday and Chris Kennett characterize music featured in television commercials as 'a *collaborative sign*, since it reinforces the meaning of what is depicted and also has a secondary attentive role, since the focus of the viewer's attention is on the visual track' (Alexomanolaki et al. 2007: 52; emphasis in original). While this account of the function of advertising music may be accurate, the use of the term 'collaborative' to describe this dynamic is misleading. Music, they continue, may be used to 'attract attention, carry the product message, act as a mnemonic device, and create excitement or a state of relaxation. *Music functions, not only semantically but also in the viewer's memory, as an index of the advertising spot*' (Alexomanolaki et al. 2007: 52; emphasis added). While the particular tactics may vary, popular music explicitly functions as a means of executing advertisers' goals: this is a dynamic of semiotic subordination. The possessive promotional logic characteristic of music branding strategies overall undermines the parallel between advertising and radio. If it is true that 'there is no longer a meaningful distinction to be made between "popular music" and "advertising music"' (Taylor 2012: 229), it is because artists are playing by rules devised by brands.

This is not to uncritically champion commercial radio. The demands of 'radio friendliness' also have contributed to predictability and homogeneity; radio, after all, favours 'repeated exposure of "typical" or "non-objectionable" songs' (Rothenbuhler and McCourt 1992: 113). Radio stations, too, cater to the demands of advertisers, as advertising sales are the basis of music's monetization for commercial radio. Radio is not as focused on happiness, however; anger, sadness, introspection and heartbreak can also prove to be lucrative. Advertising and promotion, and the associated management of consumer perception, are tied to attempts to target and harness a very narrow range of emotions. They set a decidedly uncritical tone.

Contrary to the notion that the brand-driven music promotion model is far more open and free than the previous, locked-down major label system, the new system carries with it a different bias instead. In effect, to be sync-friendly is to be corporate-friendly. While brands may take interest in a broader range of genres than is typical for major labels, it is because they can empty a song or genre of its specific content if it poses a threat, and convert it into an 'authentic'-sounding aesthetic. When brands have too much influence over content creation itself, according to a Toronto-based advertiser, it is cause for concern:

> It is scary, because as much as I say that brands can be creative, they're also controlling, so when they dictate content ... it gets a little scary. ... The fact is there needs to be a balance between art and agenda, right? Brands have an agenda, they always do, and that's to sell more product, so there has to be a balance where there's always content being made for the sake of content. (advertising creative director, personal communication, 2009)

It is telling that even advertisers seem to fear brands' hijack of popular music. Whether aspiring artists write with the demands of brands in mind or impose a type of self-censorship regarding the themes they explore, the 'new indie' does not look so independent. Unfortunately, it is increasingly difficult for aspiring artists to opt out of the still-expanding music licensing and branding system altogether.

Conclusion

Routinely hyped as the new radio, music placements in advertisements and media are considered key revenue generators and marketing vehicles not only for stars, but also for aspiring and independent artists. Music licensing can be likened to radio only in its most negative sense, however: a handful of gatekeepers have an inordinate amount of control over popular music's promotion, to the detriment of the vast majority of recording artists and their fans. Against claims that this is a cross-promotional model, popular music is not so much *marketed* as it is used as an instrument for *marketing*. In music supervisor Coffing's experience, 'The thing that makes you a great artist makes you probably not ... good at film and TV. Like big hit songs, nine times out of ten I can't place them, because you're supposed to be playing in the background. ... Licensing is about setting a mood and a vibe and a feeling – and staying there' (Coffing, personal communication, 2010). Advertisers are not even looking for a particular sound *per se*:

> As a creative, when you get a strategy, you're not looking for a piece of music. You're looking for an idea. ... What's the emotional connection of the idea? If you have an idea, then you can say, 'O.K. Here's how I want to execute this idea and here's the role that music plays in

it.' … From my experience, clients aren't out there looking for a piece of music. They're out there looking for an idea that they can put on all different kinds of mediums, that is going to build their brand. (Berman 2010)

In this system, the brand strategy or 'idea' comes first. More often than not, the overarching idea and corresponding mood is an upbeat one.

Today, aspiring artists are presented with a choice between two evils. The major record label system was – and remains – no ally to unknown and independent artists, but neither are the new brand-run alternatives. Deals between recording artists and brands have, in some cases, produced marketing buzz and helped launch careers. However, my analysis of the intensifying relationship between recording artists and brands reveals the deepening subordination of the former to the latter. The power imbalances at work have produced alarming consequences, including falling fees for artists, severe restrictions on the creative process, and a resulting homogeneity: this promotional system privileges happy and upbeat feelings and vibes. The larger story that emerges is about the domination of recording artists and the colonization and control of cultural content – dynamics that have accelerated as the brakes keeping the excesses of capitalism's profit orientation in check continue to be lifted. The system and processes sketched above are thoroughly instrumental: from attention-grabbing advertising music to background music in popular media, popular music is used as a type of promotion.

4

'Flexible' Capitalism and Popular Music: Branding Culture, Designing 'Difference'

Music, it seems, to be worth something right now, requires a purpose. ... The aesthetic should be free. (advertising creative director, personal communication, 2009)

Colliding and coterminous changes implemented across the music industries and the promotional industries have come together to transform popular music into a form of promotion in the digital age. Taken together, the reconstitution of recording artists as artist-brands in the post-CD music marketplace, the escalating involvement of media and consumer brands in the licensing and production of culture, and the attendant proliferation of brand partnerships have transformed popular music into a more thoroughly instrumentalized commodity. When used in promotional contexts, popular music is *for* building brand identities: it is used to mobilize affect as a means of achieving brand objectives. Popular music remains a rich site of expressive culture today, and the meanings that we derive from listening and watching are complex and cannot be determined by brands. Nevertheless, I contend that when used as an instrument of brands, the promotional intent driving these uses trumps their cultural content. If promotion 'is defined not by what it says but by what it does' (Wernick 1991: 184), I argue, what is most important is not what these musics *mean* but rather what they *do*: valorize and, in effect, *produce* consumption. Under the music-related branding paradigm, potential promotional opportunities and effects are more influential in terms of who gets signed, which types of music are privileged and so forth, than what the music actually sounds like and says.

Thus far, this critical analysis has focused on one set of cultural industries – the music industries (chapter 2) – and the development of a key business trend that is shaping decision-making about the production and marketing of popular music: music-related branding (chapter 3). By drawing on trade press, industry conference discussions and interviews with a range of executives involved in and knowledgeable about the new union of recording artists and brands, I have provided an account of the music industries in the digital age informed by practitioners' explanations, perspectives and perceptions. Having advanced an examination attuned to distinctive cultural industry logics, I can now turn to the influence of capitalism as such and structural changes therein over the emergence of popular music as a form of promotion. The changes seen in cultural production and branding were set in train long before the World Wide Web disrupted entrenched music distribution channels. Dynamics of exploitation, domination, control and colonization originate in capitalism itself, a system whose growth orientation and drive to maximize return on investment have always produced detrimental effects for workers – cultural or otherwise. Beginning in the early 1970s, however, economic changes fostered by new technologies, production systems and labour processes began to generate new sites of and strategies for capital accumulation, allowing for the widening and deepening commodification of culture. This chapter explores the political-economic context that has shaped popular musical production and capitalist cultural production more broadly, focusing on the ideologies, policies and practices associated with 'post-Fordism' and 'neoliberalism'.

As we saw in chapter 1, popular music has been subject to processes of commodification and industrialization since at least the nineteenth century. As a result of the range of media placements and business partnerships examined in chapter 3, much popular music has been transformed into a form of 'advertainment' or 'branded entertainment' – terms I use to describe the various content 'partnerships' between music companies and brands. The promotional system I have described enables popular music not necessarily created with a promotional intent in mind to be treated as a reservoir on which branding executives, advertisers and music supervisors can draw, potentially pulling all manner of music into these branded worlds.[13] This development has been the next step within the larger trajectory of the commodification of culture. In this chapter, drawing on Martyn J. Lee's (1993) characterization of the 'ideal-type' commodity forms that can be paired with the Fordist and post-Fordist regimes of capital accumulation, I consider what popular music's new commodity form – the 'artist-brand' – and associated promotional pairings can tell us about capitalist cultural production in the digital era. To examine existing and emergent commercial dynamics, I focus on the music licensing software available to music supervisors and other corporate licensors in the B2B market for recorded music – software whose capacity to categorize and sort popular music according to the purpose or effect sought illustrates quite concretely how the turn toward post-Fordist customization and 'difference' does not undermine, but actually complements, the processes of calculation and rationalization typically associated with Fordism. It contributes to the instrumentalization not only of popular music, but also of the affects that music is intended to harness. While this analysis presents an account of a malleable, powerful and perhaps overwhelming capitalist system, it is important to remember that this system is a product of history, of decisions made by people, and not nature. This chapter closes with suggestions for creating progressive changes that might help to improve working conditions for recording artists.

Post-Fordist Capitalism, Commodification and Culture

The restructuring of capitalism witnessed in the post-Fordist era has fuelled a tightening feedback loop between the spheres of production and consumption, with increasingly sophisticated marketing strategies and techniques serving as a vital link. The term 'Fordism' speaks to the rationalized system of mass production underpinned by a detailed and regimented division of labour or Taylorist Scientific Management – a system that propelled mass consumption and the development of a consumer society in the twentieth century (Harvey 1990: 125–40; Lee 1993: 73–85; see also Braverman 1974). The Fordist period began (at least symbolically) in 1914, with the introduction of Henry Ford's five-dollar and eight-hour day for assembly line workers, and lasted until the recession of the early 1970s (Harvey 1990: 125, 140). The term 'post-Fordism' most commonly refers to a matrix of social, cultural, political and economic shifts that deviate significantly from the processes of Fordist capitalism. Adam Krims identifies two shortcomings of the term post-Fordism: 'First, ... it defines itself mainly negatively, not offering a unique characterization of that which it claims to describe. And second, and more damagingly, it implies a clean break from Fordism, when in fact ... [m]any if not most of the aspects of Fordism continue, even in some respects predominate, in the period of so-called post-Fordism' (Krims 2007: xxii).[14] Stephen Kline, Nick Dyer-Witheford and Greig de Peuter, on the other hand, suggest that 'the ambiguous nature of the term "post-Fordism," as it teeters between the old (post-*Fordism*) and the new (*post*-Fordism), has its merits. It emphasizes the paradoxical nature of change' (Kline et al. 2003: 65; emphasis in original). Here, I adopt the latter perspective, using the term post-Fordism to describe a regime characterized by the employment of new *and* well-worn strategies for managing production and consumption – an increasingly 'flexible' capitalism capable of generating profits through a variety of means.

These theorizations of the crisis tendencies and attendant transformations of capitalism stem from the scholarship of the Regulation School (e.g. Aglietta 1979; Lipietz 1986; Boyer 1988). Their works examined distinct systems of production and consumption, or 'regimes of capital accumulation', and the corresponding formal and informal/social laws that govern societies, or 'modes of social and political regulation' (see Harvey 1990: 121–2). The Fordist regime was maintained with assistance and intervention by the state via Keynesian economics. This system of government regulation has been largely dismantled during the post-Fordist era as a result of the entrenchment of a neoliberal governmental ideology and set of policies whose 'fundamental mission ... is to create a "good business climate" and therefore to optimize conditions for capital accumulation no matter what the consequences for employment or social well-being' (Harvey 2006: 25). Harvey's political-economic analysis demonstrates the ways that post-Fordism, or what he calls 'flexible accumulation', 'is marked by a direct confrontation with the rigidities of Fordism. It rests on flexibility with respect to labour processes, labour markets, products, and patterns of consumption' (Harvey 1990: 147). Technology-driven production processes (e.g. automation and computerization) have enabled 'flexibly specialized' production: small-batch production and 'just-in-time' inventory management facilitate efficient targeting of highly segmented niche markets (Harvey 1990: 156). Practices of sub-contracting and outsourcing enable 'better labour control' and significant cost-savings (Harvey 1990: 155). 'Flexibility' for corporations, then, is contingent on and produces precarious conditions for labour. Together, the international division of (often underpaid and exploited) labour and flexible specialization, and the resulting drop in prices for consumer goods, have directly affected the realm of consumption: an accelerated turnover in production has created shortened consumption times, especially for trend-oriented products such as fashion and consumer technologies (Harvey 1990: 156). Post-Fordist production processes are uniquely intense, dynamic and fast, but such developments mark only 'shifts in surface appearance' in capitalism overall (Harvey 1990: vii).

Especially relevant for an analysis of popular music as promotion is how post-Fordist capital accumulation strategies produce, respond to, reinforce and rely on consumer trends, and are geared around the production of information, symbols and affects. Harvey famously argued that the economic shifts described above, and ever-multiplying cultural practices, media texts and lifestyles, exist in dynamic, generative relation to one another (Harvey 1990: vii, 285, and *passim*). As a result, '[t]he relatively stable aesthetic of Fordist modernism has given way to all the ferment, instability, and fleeting qualities of a postmodernist aesthetic that celebrates difference, ephemerality, spectacle, fashion, and the commodification of cultural forms' (Harvey 1990: 156). Cultural commodities have assumed increasing importance as value generators for corporations. What is distinctive here is how flexible production systems cater to and commodify a tremendously diverse range of cultural practices. Unlike in Horkheimer and Adorno's 'culture industry', we have seen an accommodation of heterogeneity alongside homogeneity – but the flipside of this cultural fragmentation and proliferation of niches is the expanded reach of capitalism itself.

Considering the case of the digital music industries in relation to this wider context, it is apparent that instantaneous distribution (e.g. iTunes, streaming services), digital marketing strategies and an abundance of consumer data allow for targeted tracking of and catering to tastes in ways that seem consistent with dominant accounts of post-Fordism. The music industries appear to offer an exemplar of the dynamism, difference and niche-specific customization characteristic of these capital accumulation strategies. For instance, as Jeremy Wade Morris and Devon Powers explain, 'curation'-driven music streaming services quantify and potentially shape listening practices, as they draw on behavioural and 'social' data and attempt to differentiate the 'branded musical experiences' they offer (Morris and Powers 2015: 117). Algorithms further lubricate the feedback loop between production and consumption, with online advertising taking the precision and depth of market research to a new level. Corporate brands likewise use social media and the consumer data they generate both to engage with and respond to the cultural worlds inhabited by music fans, and to render sociality productive by aligning it with the logic of algorithms (Carah 2015). This appears to be a system geared toward finely segmented niche tastes.

Yet as we have seen, against a backdrop of unauthorized downloading and, hence, financial risk, music companies have become ever more reliant on mass markets and star artists: mass consumption remains foundational to the cultural industries. In what has been termed today's 'attention economy', digital media content is abundant whereas audience attention is finite; proponents of attention economics conceptualize human attention itself as a scarce and, hence, valuable commodity (Goldhaber 1997; Davenport and Beck 2002). Celebrities and hits can still command attention and produce value. As such, as we saw in chapter 2, the music industries have not dispensed with the blockbuster model but instead have renovated this approach to profit generation. Encircling multiple rights or 360 deals have intensified the logics of control of creative workers and expropriation of music-related property inherited from the 'old' music industry model. Because audience attention most readily accrues to the already 'discovered' or famous, as always, new artists are placed at a considerable disadvantage.

The digital music industries, then, are marked by a combination of Fordist and post-Fordist industrial logics. Jonathan Burston makes a similar argument regarding change inside the global economy that is contemporary 'Broadway', which 'is intimately wrapped up in the changing motivations and capacities of capital, recent progress of digital technologies, and the constant movement between Fordist and "post-Fordist" moments of production in neo-liberal times' (Burston 2009: 161). Neoliberalism and intensified commodification go hand-in-hand.

The Neoliberal Turn, the Music Industries and 'Accumulation by Dispossession'

Capitalism's 'cultural turn' is closely tied to the neoliberal turn in politics and government. In *A Brief History of Neoliberalism*, Harvey (2005: 159–65) argues that processes of what Karl Marx termed 'primitive accumulation' – the capitalist enclosure of common lands and corresponding expulsion of people – have continued under neoliberalism in the form of what he terms 'accumulation by dispossession' (see also Harvey 2003: 137–82; Harvey 2006: 43–50). For Harvey, accumulation by dispossession consists of 'the corporatization, commodification, and privatization of hitherto public assets'; is 'marked by its speculative and predatory style'; and involves '[c]risis creation, management, and manipulation on the world stage' and state redistributions that 'revers[e] the flow from upper to lower classes that had occurred during the era of embedded liberalism' (Harvey 2005: 160–3). With respect to cultural production in particular, privatization, trade liberalization and deregulation have allowed for intensifying commodification across the music, film, television, radio and new media sectors. Assets that were previously publicly owned and markets that were formerly regulated have been rendered new fields for capitalist appropriation and expansion.

Neoliberal capitalism – not only a political and economic but also a cultural system – reaches farther, moves faster and commodifies more than previous capitalisms, drawing in more and more (though not all) musics on a global scale (see Taylor 2016). Following David Hesmondhalgh, it is instructive to conceptualize the commodification of culture as an instance of accumulation by dispossession, as 'forms of creativity and knowledge and culture which were not previously conceived as ownable are brought into the intellectual property system, making them available for the investment of capital and the making of profit, and helping to avoid the perennial problems of over-accumulation which haunt capitalism' (Hesmondhalgh 2008b: 97). The theory of accumulation by dispossession can help to explain the music industries' changing accumulation strategies in the neoliberal, post-Fordist era.

Whereas Fordist growth was achieved via 'expansion' and 'massification', post-Fordist growth rests on 'innovation' and 'intensification' (Lee 1993: 128). While the origins of culture as commodity can be traced to the era before Fordist capitalism, corporations today capitalize on culture more fully by launching new products and wringing additional surplus value out of existing ones, as is the case inside the contemporary music industries. The widening and intensifying commodification of culture, which has rendered new areas of social life economically productive, is related to capitalism's inherent growth orientation and the 'problem' of over-accumulation flagged by Hesmondhalgh. Growth is the lifeblood of capitalism. As Marx observes in Volume I of *Capital: A Critique of Political Economy*, classical economics is premised on '[a]ccumulation for the sake of accumulation, production for the sake of production' (Marx [1867] 1990: 742). 'In the absence of any limits or barriers', Harvey explains, 'the need to reinvest in order to remain a capitalist propels capitalism to expand *at a compound rate*. This then creates a perpetual need to find new fields of activity to absorb the reinvested capital' (Harvey 2010: 45; emphasis added). Amid the continual removal of barriers to big business, we have witnessed an especially aggressive hunt for new areas ripe for investment – no easy task given how far the reach of commodification had already extended inside advanced global capitalism. Capitalism's 'expansionary' and 'imperialistic' character explains why 'cultural life in more and more areas gets brought within the grasp of the cash nexus and the logic of capital circulation' (Harvey 1990: 344). Under post-Fordism, the inherent capitalist drive to commodify and colonize new sites and spaces has been furthered by the corporate flexibility gained from new technologies, deregulation and the declining power of workers.

With respect to the music industries, because consumers now demonstrate resistance to paying for sound recordings, music companies' drive to tighten their control over existing commodities and recording artists and to monetize new products has been especially intensive. Matt Stahl (2010) employs 'primitive accumulation analysis' to conceptualize the institutionalization of multiple rights deals. According to Stahl, the seizure of additional recording artist rights demonstrates how, 'when capital encounters an obstacle or a limit it often works aggressively to overcome it; the limit's transcendence often requires and results in the erosion of the employee's political position' (Stahl 2010: 348–9). He continues: 'Abandoned by increasing numbers of file-sharing (non-) consumers, record company capital ... [is] transcending former barriers, colonizing new regions of musical economic activity, and consolidating new dimensions of political control, particularly over legions of new artists in weak bargaining positions' (Stahl 2010: 352). The flexibility gained by record companies produces, and contractually enforces, artist dependence and vulnerability.

The binding of recording artists ever more tightly to single music companies is only one aspect of accumulation by dispossession inside the contemporary music industries, however. Another key source of capital accumulation for music companies is the (attempted) commodification of previously uncommodified aspects of subjective and affective musical experiences. Thus, record labels and consumer brands are increasingly turning to popular music as a tool intended to help commodify the *feelings* tied to 'authenticity' and 'experience'. The B2B market for music licences and recording artist endorsements represents an attempt to commodify affects and emotions that previously lay outside the reach of capital accumulation strategies; the commodity that brands and marketers purchase is not *just* popular music, but also the webs of personal associations and experiences within which music circulates. As brands partner with recording artists, they increasingly look for 'value added' or 'something more'. According to music and digital media marketing executive Vered Koren, 'exclusive artist experiences' (she provided the example of private guitar lessons with John Mayer) and other 'experiential' strategies are 'really popular with brands': 'Stuff that money can't buy – stuff that you can't get anywhere else. ... Why not sell those, monetize those experiences?' (Koren, personal communication, 2009). In a similar vein, the 'experiential' services offered by Universal Music Group's (2015) media/branding agency include 'access to artists', 'meet & greets', 'money can't buy experience' and 'live showcases'. This logic, which seamlessly rationalizes the sale of those things that 'money can't buy', is unique to an unfettered capitalism.

In the digital age, the music industries have produced new sites and modes of commodification, driving a proliferation of new products and services – many of which cater to B2B markets. The contemporaneous transformation of popular music into a promotional form means that new music commodities are not only consumed but also encourage consumption elsewhere. The use of popular music as a means of aestheticizing brands speaks to the 'design intensity' characteristic of post-Fordism.

Branding Culture: Popular Music as Design Feature

If there is merit to the argument that in the post-Fordist era 'culture is more like design: we experience it more like the inhabitations of designed spaces' (Lash and Lury 2007: 196), this shift is surely tied to the aestheticization of commerce initiated in the 1980s and 1990s. The rise of branding and branding consultancies did not simply mark the next stage of advertising, Liz Moor points out, but also was bound up with 'the mutation of many design agencies into corporate identity consultancies' during this period (Moor 2007: 8–9). In *Economies of Signs and Space*, Scott Lash and John Urry argue that, due a heightened emphasis on flexibility, design and symbolic production under post-Fordism, the '[o]rdinary manufacturing industry is becoming more and more like the production of culture' (Lash and Urry 1994: 123). They introduce the term 'reflexive accumulation' to capture the new 'reflexivity' found in the spheres of production and consumption; in their optimistic account of these developments, new 'lifestyle and consumer choice[s] are freed up' by post-Fordist accumulation strategies (Lash and Urry 1994: 61). My interest here, however, is in how design intensity and the proliferation of consumer lifestyles are tied to the concomitant rise of new branding strategies, including music-related branding.

The increasing role of design in business strategies has been tied to corporations' understanding of brands as value-generating entities that capitalize on consumer affect (Moor 2007: 37–8). Marketing literature suggests that branding has become more 'culture oriented' (Holt 2004; Ridderstråle and Nordström 2008), and that product development is more design-driven: design itself is seen as a site of 'innovation' and, hence, as a source of value (Brown 2005, 2008; Lockwood 2009). I understand the emergence of branded 'sound identities' as a product of this wider shift toward 'design thinking'. The use of uniform 'programmed' music within chain stores, for instance, serves a similar function to in-store design (Sterne 1997: 35). Such musics 'are used to mark out and aestheticize these spaces, to invest them with symbolic meaning, and to define the relations of the self, to goods and to others in ways that enhance commercial interests' (Jones and Schumacher 1992: 165; see also Sterne 1997; DeNora and Belcher 2000; Kassabian 2004; Krims 2007: 127–62). The creation of designed environments – both physical and virtual – helps to reinforce brand identities. If culture is increasingly 'designed', this indicates that utility has become a more central aspect of and consideration for culture: design is ultimately function-driven, whereas art does not *have* to be.[15]

While branding is a technique used to distinguish otherwise similar products and services, when these differences coalesce under the sign of the brand, they constitute a form of property. According to Douglas Holt, 'The economic value of a brand – its brand equity – is based on the future earnings stream the brand is expected to generate from customers' loyalty, which is revealed in their willingness to pay price premiums compared with otherwise equivalent products' (Holt 2004: 95). Brands constitute a form of 'immaterial capital' that builds on 'subjective meanings or social functions' (Arvidsson 2005: 239). They are 'slightly intangible things. ... A brand is touching your emotions' (Tunnicliffe, personal communication, 2010). Important here is how such business thinking assumes that without distinctive brand identities, commodities within the same product category are essentially equivalent; what the brand signifies for those who value it is the substance of 'difference'. As Shane Gunster observes, 'semiotic differences or brand identities increasingly bear the burden of differentiating objects that are virtually the same' (Gunster 2004: 258).

While the cultural 'essence' of brands may be somewhat ethereal, they are treated as tangible, monetizable assets on balance sheets. The importance of subjective qualities to brands has produced more and more complex systems of brand valuation, which simultaneously measure, work to produce and exploit the new economic value forms born of contemporary branding strategies (Lury and Moor 2010: 29, 43). Given that popular music is now used to forge links between brands and consumer feelings, and to fold those meanings into brand identities, music is implicated in such systems of measurement: as a tool used in service of differentiation, popular music is intended to help brands concretize and capitalize on various 'intangibles'.

Music is just one cultural field where the fundamentally qualitative is subjected to quantitative measurement techniques under new capitalization strategies. In order to shed light on the primacy of utility within the new music industries and the music-related branding paradigm, the following section examines music licensing software. Digital technologies and branding practices work together in twinned processes of customization and rationalization.

Music Licensing Software and the Rationalizing Search: Categorizing Affects, Calculating Effects

> You just have to give them something pleasant, and what can be a better tool than music? (advertising strategist, personal communication, 2011)

Amid mushrooming demand for music placements, the music search and licensing process has undergone a digital makeover. A suite of tools now exists that helps consumer brands and media companies filter and sort sound recordings with efficiency and ease. As we saw in chapter 2, music licensing is a complex process that requires licensors to clear two sets of rights with two separate corporate entities: master use rights for sound recordings from record companies and synchronization rights for the use of compositions in audiovisual media from music publishers. Music supervisors are typically responsible for selecting and clearing the rights for music placements. According to music supervisor Barry Coffing, 'There is no clear-cut way to license music. ... It's a bunch of people with a Rolodex and "good luck." ... So I set out to ... automate it' (Coffing, personal communication, 2010). Numerous other businesses joined Coffing in the rush to automate the licensing process and profit from this burgeoning music marketplace. Music branding firms, music publishers, music licensing companies and music libraries sell music with the help of specialized software that sorts songs according to various tagged keywords. Some companies offer pre-cleared music available for immediate licensing, while others still participate in the decidedly human fee negotiation and approval process, particularly when licensing music by star artists. According to music supervisor Amy Fritz, 'The market trends are ... moving so quickly. ... Instead of ... people saying "Oh, that's so last year", people are saying "Oh, that's so last week"' (Fritz, personal communication, 2009). In keeping with the overarching need for speed, some services even promise instantaneous licensing, contract generation and payment (for example, see Instant Music Licensing 2015). Music licensing software streamlines the music search and selection process.

These software systems allow would-be licensors to search and sort music catalogues according to mood, composer, genre, lyrics, era, instrumentation, metre, tempo, rhythmic complexity, gender and keyword (see Ole 2012; MusicSupervisor.com 2013). For instance, independent music publisher Ole's service sorts music by moods such as 'anthemic', 'carefree', 'cheesy', 'cynical', 'feel good', 'needy' and many more (Ole 2012). In interview, Jennifer Beavis explained that Ole's 'e-tools' allow their catalogue to be searched for certain words – 'happy' or 'wonderful', for example – in the chorus: 'You can type any type of emotion in and it will give you the list of songs immediately' (Beavis, personal communication, 2009). 'Similar artist' targeted searches are also commonly offered by music licensing firms (Black Toast Music 2013; Jingle Punks 2013; MusicSupervisor.com 2013). Many brands desire the instant recognition afforded by star artists but do not have the necessary budget, so they opt for sound-alikes.

The patented search engine and keyword tagging system developed by Jingle Punks goes one step further than tagging musical features and moods.[16] As stated in a promotional video on the company website, the Jingle Punks Jingle Player 'uses a custom Pandora-style algorithm to tag and categorize a 75,000 track library of pre-cleared songs. That algorithm makes it possible for film, television, and commercial producers to search for songs using pop culture relevant terms' (Jingle Punks 2013). Phrases such as 'getting voted off the island' (Jingle Punks 2013), 'sounds like I'm in Starbucks' (Roshkow 2010), 'sounds like an iPod commercial', or 'sounds like a show on Bravo' – even brand names such as Walmart or Target – can be used to generate music searches (Gutstadt, personal communication, 2011). 'We filed a patent so that you can describe music using non-musical terms', CEO Jared Gutstadt explained. The uses to which the music may be put, then, shape how it is listened to and assigned relevance: 'We're strictly focusing on how to extract all those emotions from the music that's sent to us. So we don't think of music as hit single/not hit single. We think, is this going to end up on a Food Network show or is this going to end up on NBC's *Minute to Win It*, and where in the spectrum of emotions, cultural contexts, does all that stuff lie?' (Gutstadt, personal communication, 2011).

These software systems are beginning to resemble those employed by stock audio companies that link the music's mood to the context in which particular moods are ostensibly appropriate. For instance, one song licensed by AudioSparx, a music library and stock audio company, is an R&B track that features 'an angular vocal in the style of Beyonce, Rihanna, Aaliyah and others', and is described as '[c]ool for pole dancing, striptease, 20-something nightclubs, chasing girls, teen fantasies, bar lounge club' (AudioSparx 2012b). While a catalogue search with the term 'evil' produced music options purportedly suited for political attack advertisements and horror movies, a search for 'happy' music yielded a 'quirky' track featuring a piano, ukulele and glockenspiel described as '[p]erfect for commercials and advertising, brand identity, YouTube videos, corporate presentations, motivational projects or kids projects', among many other similar tracks (AudioSparx 2012a). As discussed in chapter 3, happy sounds, feelings and vibes are particularly desirable from the perspective of brand partners. One 'mood' earmarked by music publisher Ole (2012) is 'driving', underscoring the short distance between the mood and that mood's function for the purposes of brands. The potential uses of music determine how it is tagged.

If music placements play a key role in the promotional apparatus underpinning the new music industries, and if music licensing software guides an increasing number of music searches, what are the consequences for musical diversity? In this wider system, it would seem, the 'sound identities' of certain brands have become so strong that the referent has become the signifier: the Walmart sound now signifies certain feelings or vibes. One critical consequence of this 'innovation' and others like it is that recording artists who wish to license their music to such companies face pressure to think about and position their work in terms of the brands it ostensibly sounds like. This software categorizes and sorts music according to perceived functions and desired effects, and produces ever more self-referential modes of rationalization. The root problem, however, is not the software. After all, individual marketers, media producers and music supervisors still determine which songs best fit their projects, regardless of how those songs are retrieved. The underlying problem is the character of the brand–music relationship. Brands' interest in popular music is instrumental, and the music licensed – via specialized software or not – is chosen due to its utility. The musical content is incidental, though its meaning is not extinguished: as 'curators', brands stake a claim to popular culture and, in effect, become owners of its symbolic force – its power to signify rich cultural, emotional and affective meanings. The meanings and rebellions linked to popular music are put to work.

In *Sonic Warfare: Sound, Affect, and the Ecology of Fear*, Steve Goodman argues that 'most branding theory has already moved on to invest in the modulation of emotion by nonverbal means, signalling a mutation of capital logic into a more subtle colonization of memory through the preemptive sonic modulation of affective tonality' (S. Goodman 2010: 148). Branded musical hooks or 'ear worms' are intended to capture our attention and invade our memory (S. Goodman 2010: 146–7). 'Affective tonality' – 'dimensions of mood, ambience, or atmosphere' (S. Goodman 2010: 195) – appears to be a guiding force behind music licensing software. These systems of classification and comparison enable the licensor to search music according to the affects it is intended to arouse: the targeted emotion takes priority and different musics can be substituted so long as they meet the licensor's key criteria. Profoundly different musics are not only rendered commensurate as objects of exchange in the marketplace for music licences; music must also conform to company-dictated, utility-driven (search) terms. Music is sorted according to its (perceived) function, with the desired effect guiding music selection.

This use of new technology to achieve the longstanding capitalist goal of maximizing efficiencies reveals a complex dialectic of old and new capital accumulation strategies inside post-Fordist, neoliberal capitalism. Music branding is premised on the calculated and efficient targeting of listener feelings in an attempt to rationalize emotions and experiences. According to Brandamp, the use of popular music allows for the stream-lining of brand messaging:

> [M]usic provides a simple way to communicate a single idea to the masses. It's good at communicating a deluge of attitudinal and demo-graphic information, targeting deeply and quickly, without images or even, necessarily, words. It can therefore communicate a brand's essence in a second, summing up its nonrational proposition and com-municating emotion, rather than logic. (Brandamp 2008: 49)

Attesting to the effectiveness of such marketing practices, in a testimonial quoted on the website of Elias Arts, a client praised the audio branding firm for 'rationaliz[ing] a subjective tool for us' (Elias Arts 2011). The actions of enterprises such as Jingle Punks illustrate capitalism's drive to commodify that which was previously uncommodified – in this case, even *search terms*. Music licensing software provides a concrete example of how the turn toward post-Fordist customization in the era of digital media abundance does not undermine but actually complements pro-cesses of calculation and rationalization typically associated with Fordism.

Popular Music, Promotion and Artist-brands: Post-Fordism and 'Ideal-type' Commodities

In the post-Fordist, neoliberal era, a 'flexible' capitalism has emerged that is supple, dynamic, and has a capacity for the hyper-targeting and measurement of consumers – tendencies only intensified and accelerated in the digital age. In *Consumer Culture Reborn: The Cultural Politics of Consumption*, Lee claims that 'if the term Post-Fordism is truly to signify important developments within capitalist production, and if these devel-opments genuinely herald major reconfigurations within contemporary culture, then in the first instance we should expect to see such transfor-mations materialised in a changing commodity-form' (Lee 1993: 119). He contends that '[q]ualitative changes to the intensity and structure of labour and means of production tend to be reflected in changes to the commodity-form' (Lee 1993: 133). A sustained analysis of artist-brands and associated music-related commodities and promotional forms, then, can provide insight into the character of the social relations embedded in them.

Lee suggests that 'ideal-type' commodity forms can be paired with the Fordist and post-Fordist regimes of accumulation. While Fordist commodities were characterized by durability, materiality, solidity, structure, collectivity, homogeneity, standardization, fixity, longevity, function and utility, post-Fordist commodities are marked by non-durability, experientiality, fluidity, flexibility, individuality, heterogeneity, customization, portability, instantaneity, form and style (Lee 1993: 128). Of course, schemas based on binary oppositions are typically simplistic, but as a starting point, this list is instructive; while certain commodity forms complement the dynamic post-Fordist marketplace, others were compatible with its more staid predecessor. Lee nominates standardized housing and automobiles as Fordism's ideal-type commodity forms, and contends that post-Fordism favours hi-tech commodities, non-physical commodities (e.g. information, data), cultural services and financial services (Lee 1993: 128). After noting the vagueness of Lee's examples of post-Fordist ideal-type commodities, Kline et al. submit the interactive video game as its exemplar:

> It is a child of the computer technologies that lie at the heart of the post-Fordist reorganization of work. In production, game development, with its youthful workforce of digital artisans and netslaves, typifies the new forms of post-Fordist enterprise and labour. In consumption, the video game brilliantly exemplifies post-Fordism's tendency to fill domestic space and time with fluidified, experiential, and electronic commodities. ... The interactive gaming business also powerfully demonstrates the increasingly intense advertising, promotional, and surveillance strategies practiced by post-Fordist marketers in an era of niche markets. In all these aspects the interactive game industry displays the global logic of an increasingly transnational capitalism whose production capacities and market strategies are now incessantly calculated and recalculated on a planetary basis. (Kline et al. 2003: 75)

In these authors' accounts, we can indeed read specific production, consumption and labour relations through a particular cultural commodity.

Parallels can be identified between the video game industry and the music industries. While it is true that as workers, recording artists exercise significant autonomy, they also experience considerable constraints and vulnerabilities – and may even be exploited – as they become bound to record companies via recording contracts (see Stahl 2013). Popular music is an 'experiential' and 'portable' commodity; aside from star artists, musical labour is generally remunerated unfairly; record companies aggressively promote a rapid turnover of 'new releases' and associated merchandise; and increasingly calculated production and marketing systems are central to the major music companies' digital business models. Trends that would eventually take hold across the cultural industries, such as P2P file sharing and later streaming, first rocked the music industries, in part due to the flexibility and portability engendered by the small file size of MP3s and the smaller amount of bandwidth required. As Jonathan Sterne points out in *MP3: The Meaning of a Format*, compression 'allow[ed] media content to proliferate in new directions, where it might not otherwise have gone' (Sterne 2012: 230).

My focus here is not only on the proliferation of music commodities and corresponding forms of work, but also on the emergence of popular music as a type of promotion or branded entertainment in particular. The promotional goods and services produced by the contemporary music industries (ranging from music placements to endorsements to newer forms of 'curated' content) meet Lee's criteria, although I make a key amendment: I find especially illuminating the, in many cases, *complementary* dynamics between the key characteristics of commodities listed above as binary oppositions. While music branding and associated promotional texts are characterized by pliability, fluidity and instantaneity, they are functional commodities. We have seen how customization is not opposite to rationalization and standardization, but instead allows for the imposition of different types of standards, and how style is not opposite to but rather has been subsumed by and is defined in terms of utility. These amalgams of music and marketing arguably constitute what Lee terms 'compound commodities': 'the merging of two or more previously discrete commodities into a single good. The unification or compression of previously discrete needs effectively opens up both the ontological and physical spaces that are required for the creation and development of new needs and therefore new use-values' (Lee 1993: 134). In such a fashion, the use of popular music as promotion in the contemporary era has allowed for the intensified capitalization of music and recordings artists' reputations, as music companies exploit musical rights in the B2B licensing marketplace, and brands exploit the associations and affects tied to music as they build brand identities.

Another noteworthy coupling is corporate flexibility and labour rigidity. While enabling maximum capitalization, the pairing of post-Fordist flexibility with Fordist rationalization has also contributed to precariousness and subordination for working artists. The type of flexibility offered by consumer brands brings with it a decided lack of commitment to building artists' careers. Brandamp's 'Bands and Brands' study likens advertising partnerships with recording artists to corporate social responsibility (CSR) initiatives, and suggests that '[t]here is a need for brands to commit to a longer-term relationship of care and nurture' (Brandamp 2008: 58). Such a commitment is rare. The institutionalization of multiple rights deals illustrates how 'the rigid enforcement powers on which companies still depend for their control of labour are not only not inimical to corporate flexibility, they are central to it' (Stahl 2010: 349). Flexibility under the new music industry model refers to an artist's willingness to comply with corporations' demands – to sign away more rights and to work for less money. The flexibility gained by music companies comes at the expense of artists. Music makers' insecurity and vulnerability to the whims of the market under the music branding paradigm – in which various corporations continue to test just how much the *recording artist* will bear – can be seen as an extension of the precarious position of workers in the neoliberal era more broadly. The dream of 'making it' – of winning the jackpot in a winner-take-all economy – motivates people to offer substantial discounts to corporations that can afford to pay.

A notable distinction between music's new and old gatekeepers is that record companies' interests align with the interests of recording artists at least in some regards, even if in a problematically unbalanced way. Quite simply, both benefited from record sales (though, again, typically overwhelmingly disproportionately). Consumer brands, on the other hand, have a very different stake in popular music. Unless brands sign artists to more formal record deals, they have no direct interest in the profitability of a given artist; their interest is limited to that artist's cultural relevance to particular target markets. As a result, non-star artists are even more exposed to the unpredictability of what has always been a trend-oriented marketplace. Partnerships with consumer brands may often come with no formal strings attached, but they typically offer little security. In addition to the ways that they delimit artists' repertoire choices, consumer brands seldom have a vested interest in providing the support necessary to cultivate career longevity.

Furthermore, there *are* tacit strings tied to branding agreements. Hayman characterizes the licensing agreement as 'an intellectual property consent form' and indicates that 'you better buy into that brand, or else you'll be called out on it' (Hayman, personal communication, 2009). Jake Hurn of Cornerstone noted on a North by Northeast conference panel that his advertising firm will 'rarely go near artists that have talked shit about brands' (Hurn 2011). The ideal recording artist within the new branding template has no political voice or must agree to be silent. He or she must endorse the capitalist status quo, even if through a type of self-censorship. The music branding trend threatens to drown out more oppositional musics, not because critical or dissenting musics do not exist (they do), but because they may be crowded out by the sounds of upbeat music that permeate media and seep into commercial spaces.

'Sharecropping the Long Tail', a blog post by Nicholas Carr on the economics of social media, captures a key dynamic also at work inside the music industries, especially among non-star artists:

> What's being concentrated ... is not content but the economic value of content. MySpace, Facebook, and many other businesses have realized that they can give away the tools of production but maintain ownership over the resulting products.
>
> One of the fundamental economic characteristics of Web 2.0 is the distribution of production into the hands of the many and the concentration of the economic rewards into the hands of the few. It's a sharecropping system. ... It's only by aggregating those contributions on a massive scale ... that the business becomes lucrative. (Carr 2006)

The amassing of wealth by a select few is as old as the industrialization of music and corresponding creation of a star system. What is unique here is how the popularization of digital recording technologies has not destroyed the financial heath of music companies. Instead, it has been a source of new efficiencies derived from cheap or free content for music companies and consumer brands alike. 'We have a world of advertising that is desperate for innovation and creative partnerships', Grant McCracken points out, and we also have 'a world of cultural producers, millions of people at this point, who are very good at producing meanings' (McCracken 2011). Again, of interest here are the purposes to which such meanings are put, not what they happen to be. Interestingly, while the 'indie' *aesthetic* remains valuable to brands, according to Panos Panay of Sonicbids, 'It's the aggregate that is interesting to them [brands], rather than the one individual small band. ... If they want to sponsor one big artist, they'll tend to go ... with a bigger name' (Panay 2011).

In the end, the economic wealth and cultural relevance generated in this capitalist system is monopolized by the aggregator – be it a music company, a consumer brand or a technology company, a point to which I return in the concluding chapter. The asymmetrical manner in which the music industries and the cultural industries more broadly mete out riches and rewards reflects what Henry A. Giroux refers to as the 'winner-take-all philosophy' of 'casino capitalism' in the neoliberal age (Giroux 2008: 55). The increasing subjugation and substitutability of *cultural* workers, labourers hitherto granted an atypical degree of autonomy (Hesmondhalgh and Baker 2011; Hesmondhalgh 2013a), speak volumes about the character of work under neoliberalism. Flexibility means that the worker must do more for less.

Music, Promotion, Zeroes and Ones: Homogenization amid Difference?

In a post-Fordist regime marked by the fragmentation of cultural markets and the proliferation of new media technologies and diverse texts, the cultural industries remain complex, and the boundary between media companies (including music companies) and promotional companies (such as advertising firms) has been redrawn. It is routinely argued that the 'culture industry' thesis no longer holds in this context. According to Krims, 'What Adorno took for an inexorable process turned out to be historically specific. ... What intervened, and what Adorno could not have theorized in his lifetime, is, of course, the advent of flexible accumulation or so-called post-Fordism' (Krims 2007: 94). Scott Lash and Celia Lury argue that it is 'not so much that they [Horkheimer and Adorno] were wrong, but that things have moved on. ... [C]ultural objects are everywhere; as information, as communications, as branded products, as financial services, as media products, as transport and leisure services, cultural entities are no longer the exception: they are the rule' (Lash and Lury 2007: 3–4). Because the dynamics of capitalist commodification, expansion, colonization and quantification surveyed above have long characterized commercial cultural production and capitalism more broadly, there are grounds for revisiting Horkheimer and Adorno's critique of the constraints produced by the commodification of culture.

At first glance, the culture industry thesis appears to be handcuffed by the radical changes to the cultural industries ushered in by post-Fordism and, more specifically, digitalization. The industrial structures examined by Horkheimer and Adorno were a product of what they refer to as 'monopoly capitalism' – an era characterized by the detailed division of labour, Taylorist Scientific Management, mass consumption and cultural homogeneity. Their account aligns with the Fordist period. Nevertheless, as we have seen, a similar drive to commodify, rationalize and instrumentalize persists in the post-Fordist era, suggesting that we might think beyond this critique's '(now) stifling association with the historical specificity of Fordist cultural production' (Gunster 2004: 26). Because Fordist and post-Fordist logics continue to coexist, and because the culture industry thesis offers a theory on the production of culture under capitalism as such, some of these arguments still resonate.

First, an Adornian critique of cultural commodification centres on the domination of the particular by a universal standard – the exchange or barter principle. Drawing on Marx, Adorno sees the forced assimilation of the individual to the universal as a defining feature of human labour as it becomes a commodity:

> The barter principle, the reduction of human labor to the abstract universal concept of average working hours, is fundamentally akin to the principle of identification. Barter is the social model of the principle, and without the principle there would be no barter; it is through barter that non-identical individuals and performances become commensurable and identical. (Adorno [1966] 1973: 146)

Much as workers are rendered commensurable or 'identical' in the labour market, the products of the culture industry are rendered identical by the exchange principle. The universalizing instrumental rationality inherent to the capitalist system is still in evidence in the contemporary music industries, now in the ways they increasingly cater to B2B markets. From the perspective of would-be business partners and licensors, the value of a vast range of music is pinned to its price, and different musics and artists are seen as largely substitutable within different price ranges. The use value of recording artists – and the leverage or 'equity' they may or may not wield – is tied to their exchange value. While the products of the music industries may not be overly standardized – indeed they can be quite diverse – today's 'artist-brands' and associated products are treated as interchangeable insofar as they are seen as profit-generating properties. Under the abstract rules of capitalist equivalence they are rendered commensurable.

In a manner arguably comparable to Harvey's approach, Horkheimer and Adorno make distinctions between different eras of capitalism as they develop a critique of capitalism. They observe that monopoly capitalism was marked by a decline in competition and a growing concentration of wealth into the hands of the few relative to the preceding liberal era (Horkheimer and Adorno [1944] 2002: 164). The culture industry thesis speaks to the oligopolistic corporate structures associated with monopoly capitalism. Though historically specific, given that logics of consolidation, concentration and conglomeration persist (see chapter 2), and that wealth and media power remain centralized into the hands of a select few, Horkheimer and Adorno's characterization of oligopolistic control over cultural production retains purchase. After all, the music industries are dominated by just three transnational corporations – Universal Music Group, Sony Music Entertainment and Warner Music Group – whose parent companies have business interests spanning the media and telecommunications industries.

Although Adorno's critique of capitalism is more conceptual than descriptive, he does offer analysis of specific production and marketing techniques still at work inside the post-Fordist cultural industries. For instance, Horkheimer and Adorno recognize the strategic function of different product categories, genres and prices, which, similar to contemporary market segmentation approaches, 'assist in the classification, organization, and identification of consumers. Something is provided for everyone so that no one can escape; differences are hammered home and propagated' (Horkheimer and Adorno [1944] 2002: 96–7). The production of 'difference' enabled the culture industry to at once cater to and quantify different tastes. According to Adorno, 'The culture industry intentionally integrates its consumers from above' not by imposing only one type of cultural product on the market, but instead by rendering the customer 'an object of calculation' (Adorno [1967] 2001b: 98–9). Then as now, market research reflects 'the competitor's desire to find out something about the type of commodities his customers like and to mold his production or his purchases according to their wishes in order to gain by means of such information an advantage over his competitors' (Adorno [1939] 2009a: 436). The relentless drive for competitive advantage and increased sales leads to a corporate aspiration to understand customer desires and purchasing habits. Post-Fordist techniques used to calculate and monetize strategic 'fits' between popular music and corporate brands only intensify this process. Music supervision software illustrates the dynamism of this feedback loop today, and appears to be the literal fulfilment of Adorno's claim that '[p]opular music becomes a multiple-choice questionnaire' (Adorno [1941] 2002b: 446).

A common criticism of the culture industry thesis is that the types of cultural rationalization, standardization, massification and pseudo-individualization described by Adorno cannot account for the aesthetic diversity characteristic of post-Fordist cultural production (for example, see Krims 2007: 89–126). According to Lash and Lury, 'In the culture industry production takes place in the Fordist and labour-intensive production of identity', whereas in today's post-Fordist 'global culture industry' 'production and consumption are processes of the construction of *difference*' (Lash and Lury 2007: 5; emphasis in original). What Lash and Lury fail to acknowledge, however, is that because corporations and brands now understand difference in terms of its commercial utility, difference itself falls under the modes of instrumental rationality and identitarian thinking – or 'thinking in equivalents' – theorized by Adorno. In 'Stars Down to Earth', a content analysis of a *Los Angeles Times* astrology column, Adorno gestured to the 'sales value' of 'rare' qualities: 'Being different ... is integrated into the pattern of universal sameness as an object of barter. Individuality itself is submerged in the process of

transformation of ends into means' (Adorno [1953] 1994: 113). Capitalist exchange relations work to quantify the qualitative. If treated as
interchangeable commodities by its licensors and deployed to the same
ends, namely grabbing consumer attention, arousing particular affects
and transferring them to brands, then the actual musical content –
diverse or not – is beside the point.

Amid the persistent drive to commodify new spaces of social and
cultural life, it appears that cultural difference is especially productive
for capital today. As Carah points out, 'Experiential branding and the
brandscape can also be thought of as a contemporary articulation of the
culture industry' (Carah 2010: 9). The cultural industries have become
increasingly 'computational' (Berry 2014), allowing for intensified production and tracking of consumption. Read in concert with the theory
of accumulation by dispossession, the culture industry thesis provides
critical insights into *why* difference constitutes an important site of value
creation in the post-Fordist era: as fodder for unfettered capitalism's
relentless drive for expansion and growth. Of course, inside the culture
industry, commodification '*directly* expresses itself through a highly specific cultural logic that maximizes certain types of difference at the
expense of others' (Gunster 2007: 311; emphasis in original). Music
companies and consumer brands alike demonstrate a preference for
market-friendly difference at the expense of less commercially viable
alternatives.

The 'sync-friendly' sounds of advertising actually speak to considerable homogeneity against a wider backdrop of musical diversity, at the
very least in terms of the sentiment most advertising music is intended
to express and harness: happiness. Market-friendly sounds are generally
cheerful or can be construed as such; in a sense, they must serve as empty
signifiers or pliable symbolic 'containers' that can be filled with advertising content. Consistent with Adorno's critique, the logic of the market
(in this case the market for music placements and branding opportunities) threatens to infiltrate the creation process itself. Recording artists
may heed advice to write music filled with happy keywords in lyrics or
with upbeat musical arrangements – or instead to write songs that offer
a general semiotic flexibility that sets the stage for easy 'occupation' by
brands.

Adorno's analysis of the commodification of culture is not hamstrung
by the dynamism characteristic of post-Fordism and digitalization, then,
because the same technological and economic means that have ushered
in the current era of media abundance also have allowed for the expansion of commodification overall. As argued more recently by Steven
Shaviro (who, it should be noted, distances himself from Adorno's
theories),

The proliferation of variations, and of consumer choices, is underwritten by a more fundamental homogeneity. Money and credit make it possible for anything to be exchanged with anything else. In the realm of digital media, binary code functions in a similar manner. Everything can be sampled, captured, and transcribed into a string of ones and zeroes. This string can then be manipulated and transformed, in various measured and controllable ways. Under such conditions, multiple differences ramify endlessly; but none of these differences actually *makes a difference*, since they are all completely interchangeable. (Shaviro 2010: 133; emphasis in original)

It is still essential to offer careful analysis of the logics that make the cultural industries and cultural commodities contradictory and complex. However, also tending to the overriding commercial and promotional pressures that these industries work with and against – forces originating in capitalism itself – can offer a fuller picture of *why* popular music has taken on a more promotional and intensively commodified character.

No Way Out or Opportunities for Change: The Task Ahead for Working Artists

The flexible capitalism founded on market fundamentalism discussed above may seem all-powerful and impenetrable. Indeed, the account I have provided of the perils of the new music industries is bleak. This unjust system is not inevitable, however. Change is possible. Questioning the problematic 'common sense' regarding the viability and acceptability of the music branding paradigm – seeing the ways this system is not advancing most recording artists' interests and instead is placing new constraints on them – is an important first step. I acknowledge that music makers themselves would be the best source for learning about the potential for creating positive change. Given that interviewing musicians fell outside the scope of this research – whose focus was on industry perspectives – I will draw on my critique of the industry view on music and brands in order to make some practical suggestions for strategies and tactics that might help to improve conditions for music makers moving forward.

In order to shift away from the 'sharecropping system' that underpins musical labour and begin to think about more just models of remuneration, as a starting point, we must insert the working artist squarely into the file sharing, and more recently, music streaming debates that largely are framed as battles between corporations and consumers. Consistent with neoliberal values more broadly, there is a tendency not to look beyond one's own self-interest:

> Most positions in the file-sharing debate are unable to articulate a strong ethical position beyond self-interest. The interests in the recording industry speak for themselves as copyright holders, and not for the musicians they claim to represent or for music itself. But the same must be said of the people who enable or participate in file-sharing. Often enough, they too have themselves in mind, either as industries who affect music transectorially and find profit as recordings slip out from inside the money economy, or as users who simply get something for free because they do not want to pay for it and do not have to (though they pay for the tools and network access that enables file-sharing). (Sterne 2012: 217)

Although it may be an unpopular conversation, and although strict enforcement of copyrights very well may be the wrong way forward, fans ought to listen to and consider taking on board working artists' concerns regarding the difficulties associated with making a living in the post-CD era. Unless we only want to hear the voices of heavily promoted artist-brands on the one hand, or of self-sufficient artists with trust funds on the other, we must think about the consequences of existing commercial structures for the career longevity of working artists. Unfortunately, artists have been put in a difficult position. In the culture of 'free' content (free for consumers but not for cultural labourers), even asking to be paid can come across as pro-corporation and, hence, anti-freedom and simply uncool, though this has begun to change.

Substantive change will not come from consumers, however. Indeed, such an expectation would simply reinscribe problematic neoliberal rhetoric regarding 'consumer choice' and 'consumer sovereignty' that works to mask uneven power relations under capitalism; consumer solutions cannot remedy the ills of consumer capitalism. Instead, progressive change must be systemic, coming from cultural and social policy and from collective action. Conversation regarding the potential for change must consider how music makers might be compensated fairly for their work without the 'assistance' of record labels or consumer brands. If neoliberalism's strength has been, in part, built on the dismantling of union power, then the revitalization of existing and creation of new collectives is potentially one way forward. Working with artist-centred organizations could allow for artists' voices to be heard and experiences to be considered in the struggle for equitable remuneration (even as all involved acknowledge that new forms of recompense will invariably have to take our changing digital circumstances firmly into account). If these organizations decide that working with brands and other corporate partners is indeed the best way forward, they might produce – and agree to stick to – specific guidelines for fair remuneration for particular types of work and uses of music, in keeping with practices found in artists' guilds for other cultural industries (for actors, writers and so forth).

On a smaller scale, given that the axes of brands' power and influence inside neoliberal capitalism are also built on a reputation economy, recording artists might consider honestly and publicly discussing how corporations treat them under this system, thereby potentially generating negative publicity for and tarnishing the 'cool' image of such brands. The response of Ex Cops to McDonald's (discussed in chapter 3) is instructive. By sharing their experience with fans, speaking with the popular and business press, and grabbing the digital megaphone, they motivated one of the world's richest companies to do an about-face on its own policies and practices involving music makers. According to Giroux, 'As the prevailing discourse of neoliberalism seizes the public imagination, there is no vocabulary for progressive social change' (Giroux 2008: 55). By actively participating in and changing the tone of the dominant conversations about the new music industries, recording artists can help to rewrite the new 'common sense'.

This type of action is much more achievable if artists have not signed non-disclosure agreements with brands and corporations (a typical practice), which is why recording artists also might want to consider my next recommendation: say 'no'. The music and promotional industries take advantage of the position of those who feel that they have no other option but to say yes to whatever terms are offered – be it for recording contracts, music licensing fees, or otherwise. If the fees available are low or non-existent, and if the marketing exposure promised is questionable (as explored in chapter 3), there is actually very little to lose by saying no. Such an approach depends on solidarity between working artists. A collective 'no' packs a much bigger punch than a more individualistic approach.

Interestingly, even some of the biggest winners from the artist-brand based system have started to redraw the eroded boundary between culture and promotion. For instance, reflecting on why she had wanted to quit music at one point, Stefani Germanotta, better known by stage name Lady Gaga, offered the following:

> Well, I really don't like selling these, you know, ... fragrances, perfumes. I don't like ... wasting my time spending days just shaking people's hands and smiling and taking selfies. It feels shallow to my existence. I have a lot more to offer than my image. I don't like being used to make people money. ... It feels sad when ... I'm overworked

and that I just become a money making machine, and that my passion and my creativity take a back seat. That makes me unhappy. So what did I do? I started to just say no. I'm not doing *that*. I don't want to do *that*. I'm not taking that picture. I'm not going to that event. I'm not standing by that because that's not what I stand for. And slowly but surely I remembered who I am. ... That person has integrity. That person has an opinion. That person just doesn't say yes. (Germanotta 2015)[17]

It is always easier for the wealthy or those in financially stable positions to pass on opportunities to earn a payday, of course. Nevertheless, by shining a light on the vexing aspects of promotional work inside the new music industries, we might begin to consider what the work of music makers *ought to* entail.

Conclusion

The challenges facing music makers today are complex. They are intimately connected to the structural forces shaping not only cultural production, but the spheres of production and consumption more broadly inside contemporary capitalism. Thus, developing a critique that focuses on constraints tied to capitalism as such can serve as a nice complement to a cultural industry-specific analysis. This chapter combined insights gleaned from critical theory with Harvey's analysis of flexible accumulation and accumulation by dispossession in order to conceptualize and understand popular music's transformation into a form of promotion. The culture industry thesis retains purchase in the digital age (albeit with modifications, given its inadequate account of aesthetic experience) not because the cultural industries have not changed, but rather because the fundamental impulse of capitalism and its growth imperative have not.

This chapter situated the changing relationship between the music industries and the promotional industries within a longer trajectory of the commodification of culture, and identified the persistence of both Fordist and post-Fordist logics today. Popular music has been increasingly instrumentalized and rationalized, even as the wider music marketplace offers considerable semiotic diversity – a dialectic not contrary to, but rather firmly in step with, capitalism's accelerating expansion and extension in the neoliberal era. A range of strategies are used toward the aim of maximizing profits and, hence, growth. Drawing on and opening up Lee's conception of 'ideal-type' commodities, I proposed that the artist-brand and the corresponding music branding paradigm can help us to understand the character of post-Fordist capitalism, precisely because they capture this regime's industrial and cultural complexity. This complexity notwithstanding, under new music branding models, popular music is rendered equivalent and substitutable in terms of the affects and effects it is intended to provoke. Not only is music thoroughly commodified, but music licensing software has begun to produce ever more self-referential modes of rationalization. Collective forms of action, transparent communication about brands' treatment of working artists and the potential to say 'no' might help working artists to forge a path that allows for more autonomy, fairer remuneration and, hopefully, career longevity.

5

Conclusions

This book has argued that in the digital age the music industries have undergone a transformation not simply in terms of how they distribute music products to listeners. Significantly, the corporations that dominate the commercial production of popular music have shifted their conceptualization and positioning of what constitutes the primary basis of monetization in the first place: the core popular music commodity is no longer viewed as the sound recording, but instead as the artist-brand. Major record companies, remade as *music* companies, have compensated for declining CD revenues in the era of digital downloads and music streaming by expanding B2B revenues, a move enabled by increasing corporate diversification, the acquisition of competitors and the use of restrictive and all-encompassing contracts for recording artists ('360 deals'). As we saw in chapter 2, a new blockbuster model underpins corporate decision-making and the allocation of financial and promotional resources within this rights-driven enterprise: corporate reliance on stars has deepened, with artist-generated profits across a range of music-related products now falling under the remit of a handful of corporate powerhouses. Overarching dynamics of corporate consolidation and integration have enabled the 'Big Three' (Sony, Universal and Warner) to retain positions of dominance within what remains an oligopolistic marketplace.

In many respects, the power structure inherited from the 'old' music industries remains intact in the era of digital distribution. A select few transnational conglomerates continue to monopolize the wealth generated by music; at a time when more music is being released by more recording artists than ever before, we have seen profound music industry concentration and the deepening of the 'winner-take-all' market. As reported by Paul Resnikoff (2012b) of *Digital Music News*, in 2011, roughly 2 per cent of new releases in the United States produced 90 per cent of new album sales. According to Glenn Peoples (2011a) of *Billboard*, in 2010, 60,000 new US releases sold only 1 to 100 units. Generous marketing budgets and refined marketing strategies are of paramount importance inside the digital music system. Intense competition for audiences and declining compensation for music makers means that celebrity remains fundamental to the music business, and the top stars continue to receive the lion's share of artist revenues deriving not only from recordings and live performances, but also licensing, branding and endorsement deals. By mapping how profits accrue and to whom within this emerging model, it becomes clear that 'common sense' assertions that the new music industries offer a democratizing, open playing field are entirely misleading, and are better understood as legitimizing rhetoric serving to obscure deeper forms of cultural commodification. The more fundamental change, which promises to shape the music industries moving forward, is the emergence of new corporate gatekeepers, including consumer brands.

The rise of the artist-brand has produced important shifts in terms of how music marketing is understood among music companies and recording artists. According to Keith D'Arcy (2012), a music licensing specialist who formerly worked for Universal Music Publishing, radio programmers now ask A&R executives, ' "Who's this artist touring with?" ... "What press has gotten on to them?" ... and "What placements have they had?" It's actually part of the story that we need to tell to radio these days to get them to pay attention to a new record.' 'We're in the artist brand management business', Steve Stoute of advertising firm Translation claims. 'It's about finding corporate partners and matching them with artists to tell their brand story' (quoted in High 2009). Music companies seeking to promote artists and advertising firms wishing to differentiate consumer brands speak the same artist-brand language. Under this approach, artists are rendered branding vehicles, which has, in effect, transformed much popular music into a form of promotion.

As we saw in chapter 3, music placements in advertisements, television programmes and video games have been positioned as cross-promotional media, although as I demonstrated, promotion typically leans more one way than the other: a possessive promotional dynamic is apparent. As music supervisor Barry Coffing warns, 'everyone look[s] to licensing as their saviour and we're not' (Coffing, personal communication, 2010). We have even seen branded record labels and branded music festivals emerge as ways for consumer brands to cash in on the cultural currency provided by popular music. The shrinking spaces between music and brands do not speak to business 'partnerships' characterized by shared interests, despite the language employed, as is evidenced by these corporations' drive for cost-savings and the corresponding drop in fees for non-star artists. Precarious labour conditions have been foisted on recording artists from two directions: via restrictive new contracting conventions from music companies *and* (in theory) hands-off partnerships with consumer brands. What is more, the bias toward happy music embedded in this promotional system places parameters around the range of music that even garners the attention of would-be 'partners', a dynamic that works against popular musical diversity by circulating sounds amenable to brand messages.

Behind the nexus of music and branding, we see the alignment of the interests of a wide range of corporate players, including record companies, music publishers, music branding firms, advertisers and music supervision companies. These various entities in the B2B network each in different ways have contributed to the cross-sector promotional apparatus that underpins the production, licensing and marketing of popular music and recording artists as brands. The argument advanced in this book is supported by a synthesis of trade publication coverage, industry conference discussions and interviews that centre on these executives and their involvement in connecting recording artists and brands. By drawing on these industry perspectives, I revealed the business thinking behind these new modes of monetization and attitudes toward promotion. The emergence of popular music as a form of advertainment or branded entertainment points not just to a type of convergence but instead dependence: cultural logics are subordinated to branding logics. The asymmetrical power relations characteristic of the new music industries – both between recording artists and corporations and across a stratified pool of artists – can be seen as an extension of those of the old music industries. The difference is that brands have joined entertainment corporations. Within this system, I argue, popular music has been colonized by brands, which attempt to seize its symbolic force.

While the mutation of the music industries and the promotional industries has been bound up with the disruption to 'business-as-usual' ushered in by digital technologies, this reconfiguration has also been connected to larger shifts in capitalism and culture. The explanatory power of critical theory when combined with more recent scholarship on both post-Fordism and the cultural industries provides a critical lens for understanding the structural forces that have contributed to the business trends examined. As we saw in chapter 4, the story of change across these industries, and the explosion of branding and related practices, is intricately linked to changes accompanying post-Fordism and neoliberalism. As David Harvey argues, during this era we have seen 'the tension that has always prevailed within capitalism between monopoly and competition, between centralization and decentralization of economic power, ... being worked out in fundamentally new ways' (Harvey 1990: 159). In what has become a 'reputation' economy, a premium is placed on brands. The analysis provided suggests that although we have witnessed a radical expansion of cultural diversity in the digital age, there has also been a rationalization of that diversity, as popular music has been tethered to brand objectives. Consumer and media brands attempt to capitalize on the market for meaning and to commodify affects tied to popular culture.

In this context, the culture industry thesis, introduced in chapter 1, remains applicable, albeit with qualification: the positioning of popular music as branded entertainment marks a new stage in culture's intensifying commodification. The overarching instrumentalizing logic is tied to the dominance of the capitalist principle of exchange. The critique provided by Horkheimer and Adorno helps us to theorize not only the collapse between popular music and advertising, but also the more recent turn toward capitalizing on 'difference' inside promotional culture. Popular music has been transformed into a largely utilitarian and substitutable product to be harnessed by consumer brands and media companies inside 'flexible' capitalism – a dynamic illustrated by the example of music licensing software. The culture industry framework is less helpful for theorizing culture in terms of aesthetic qualities, pleasure and what music may mean to people despite such constraints, however; consumer brands have taken an interest in popular music precisely because it continues to be such a rich source of meaning. Harvey's concept of 'accumulation by dispossession', which examines the expanded and escalating reach of commodification under neoliberalism, serves as a critical complement to the culture industry thesis.

In chapter 4, I slightly amended Martyn J. Lee's description of post-Fordism's 'ideal-type' commodity form, and nominated popular music in its contemporary promotional form as one such commodity, highlighting the ways that the capitalization of popular music and 'artist-brands' reflects a combination of Fordist rigidity and post-Fordist flexibility. A combination of business strategies and techniques has rendered them especially productive for corporations. Overall, the deepening commodification of popular music speaks to new depths of subordination for working artists and for culture. Forces of rationalization work to counter the semiotic diversity ostensibly given a voice with the affordance of the music industries' digitalization. Popular music has been positioned as the soundtrack to what Andrew Wernick (1991) first termed 'promotional culture'.

Though expansive and powerful, this wider promotional system is far from seamless or inevitable, however, and the effectiveness of popular music-related branding can be uneven. In fact, if a spot featuring a recording artist becomes too popular, it can backfire and the music used can become a source of annoyance. For example, in 2010, YouTube-based indie group Pomplamoose were featured singing Christmas carols in holiday advertisements for Hyundai. These television commercials, which were filmed in the group's own garage and show the band members frolicking around the car, were initially lauded as effective alternative music marketing (see Lefsetz 2010). However, according to Grant McCracken (2011), the spot 'went from odd to charming to familiar to contemptible to irritating in about 3 weeks'. In his *Seattle Times* blog entry, 'How Pomplamoose Made Me Hate Christmas, Hyundai, and Pomplamoose', Mike Seely (2010) criticizes the singer's 'generic-*Grey's Anatomy*-chick-voice', among other things. Sexist language aside, this complaint suggests that the formerly novel, 'sync-friendly' *Grey's Anatomy* sound had become too expected, homogeneous and bland. In a trend-driven marketplace, media and consumer brands continue the hunt for the 'latest sound'. Indeed, brands' search for 'credible' content has led to a radical widening of previously established models of artist endorsement. No longer singularly focused on celebrities, brands also seek out various partnerships with independent and lesser known artists in an effort to gain cultural legitimacy. The increasingly calculated choice of music is driven by brands' desire for the patina of 'authenticity'.

Cultural Industries as Promotional Industries?

These promotional logics and new business models are not unique to the music industries, however. Popular music is an exemplary case of a much broader phenomenon. Under neoliberalism, values tied to individualism, logics of branding and corresponding practices of 'self-branding' have spread throughout promotional culture, influencing the spheres of politics and civil society in addition to the cultural industries and consumer goods industries (Davis 2013). For instance, parallel to the transformation of popular music into a form of promotion, we have seen the erosion of the boundary between journalism and public relations. As Jim Macnamara explains in a discussion of new forms of 'sponsored content',

> These go by a range of names (or euphemisms) including 'paid content', 'content integration', 'editorial integration', 'native advertising' and 'embedded marketing'. The key characteristic of these formats is that they 'embed', so as to partially hide or render invisible, paid promotional messages and products in media content and internet news and information sites. (Macnamara 2014: 746)

Such 'advertorial' content not only blurs boundaries, but also attempts to obscure its promotional intent. Under new 'corporate publishing' models, journalists might even be hired to write 'bespoke digital publications under the editorial direction or even full control of the client organization' (Macnamara 2014: 747), raising serious ethical concerns.

We have also seen the growth of forms of advertainment or branded entertainment whose focus is not on veiling the brand behind the message, but instead on making promotional content itself more entertaining. For example, *Variety* provided a listing of 'The Best Branded Entertainment of 2014', which ranged from *The Lego Movie* to a viral video that paired Nissan with YouTuber T.J. Smith to an Audi-sponsored reunion of the cast of *Breaking Bad* (Graser 2014). Such arrangements assume a variety of forms, but all attempt to tap into popular culture as a source of cultural relevance, legitimacy, credibility and talent.

As such, it is important to revisit what makes cultural industries that are *primarily* invested in the communicative content of symbolic texts distinct from those industries whose interest in producing such texts is based first and foremost on their function: the promotional industries. By keeping these two discrete sets of sectors separate, even if only for analytic purposes, we might come to better understand what happens when films, television shows, songs and even journalism must play by the rules that govern advertising, branding, marketing and public relations. A key way that the promotional industries are distinct is the basis of revenue generation, which is also one of the reasons why they have not been challenged by digitalization in the same way as other core cultural industries. They do not sell content to audiences. They sell content to clients. In other words, the growing B2B market that is shaping the music industries and other cultural industries has always underpinned the promotional industries. When we see the cultural industries behaving more like promotional industries, I suggest, it is not because it is now 'all culture': on the contrary, such a dynamic suggests that it is business and promotion through and through. Thus, moving forward, it will be important to revisit debates regarding the autonomy of creative workers across the cultural industries, and the ways these workers are – and are not – able to exercise what they understand as professional integrity amid new commercial and promotional constraints.

A range of political, economic, technological and cultural forces, then, have contributed to the erosion of the boundary between popular music worlds and brand worlds. Digitalization, promotionalism and globalization have shaped changing ideas about 'selling out' in the music industries, even as the values associated with cultural autonomy and artistic integrity persist (see Klein et al. 2016). According to Vered Koren,

> Ten years ago, if you went to a label and you said 'I want to give away … 100,000 tracks to users for free on Pepsi cans', they would say, 'No way – our artists don't want to be associated with Pepsi. That's a sell-out.' … They were really precious about where their artists were seen and what products they were endorsing. And now it's an opportunity. (Koren, personal communication, 2009)

It could be argued that the overt and unabashed commercialism we see today had been held in check by cultural and social forces and attitudes in previous decades. The stigma associated with 'selling out' that formerly lay at the heart of rock culture helped govern the distance between popular music and advertising (albeit contingently, precariously, and at times hypocritically), especially across genres that aspire to art status. However, as Keir Keightley points out, the relationship between rock and commercialism always has been contradictory:

> One of the great ironies of the second half of the twentieth century is that while rock has involved millions of people buying a mass-marketed, standardised commodity (CD, cassette, LP) that is available virtually everywhere, these purchases have produced intense feelings of freedom, rebellion, marginality, oppositionality, uniqueness and authenticity. (Keightley 2001: 109)

As we have seen, those intense feelings flagged by Keightley, available for purchase in commodity form, have proven especially appealing to advertisers looking to animate and differentiate brand identities.

However, when records were profitable, merchandising and licensing revenue remained ancillary. What is distinctive about the post-CD marketplace is that these commodities and rights have moved from the periphery to the centre, meaning that shifting attitudes do not suggest that opportunistic or cynical artists are betraying some sacrosanct notion of selling out, but rather that the need to breach the promotion–culture divide now lies at the foundation of music industry business models. Changes in business thinking have informed cultural assumptions within popular music circles – among both artists and fans. Due to the challenges and vulnerabilities tied to what is, as always, a highly stratified industry, working artists have become more receptive to music licensing, endorsement and branding deals, often from a place of resignation.

It turns out that the stigma associated with selling out actually had a market value insofar as it served to limit the number of artists interested in such opportunities. An artist's willingness to participate in these promotional arrangements formerly commanded high fees. In the era of brand–music partnerships, however, popular music is readily available to advertisers. Bargain-hunting brands offer deals to recording artists on a 'take it or leave it' basis, and because the number of artists hungry for marketing exposure far exceeds the number of opportunities available, negotiation is often unnecessary. As suggested in chapter 4, working artists might want to reconsider what is actually gained and what is lost through such arrangements, and organize collectively in ways that might allow for fairer compensation and negotiation arrangements.

The tension between creativity and commerce in the cultural industries has always been complex. The autonomy of culture vis-à-vis industry is contingent and at times fragile. Changing attitudes are not indicative of a simple narrative about supposedly greedy artists or corporations co-opting art that had previously been untainted by commercial considerations. As Tiziana Terranova suggests of ongoing 'economic experimentation with the creation of monetary value out of knowledge/culture/affect' (Terranova 2000: 38) more generally:

> This process is different from that described by popular, left-wing wisdom about the incorporation of authentic cultural moments: it is not, then, about the bad boys of capital moving in on underground subcultures/subordinate cultures and 'incorporating' the fruits of their production (styles, languages, music) into the media food chain. ... Incorporation is not about capital descending on authentic culture but a more immanent process of channeling collective labor (even as cultural labor) into monetary flows and its structuration within capitalist business practices. (Terranova 2000: 38–9)

Under capitalist systems of cultural production, popular music is always already commodified, and as such, subject to strong commercial pressures. Yet Bethany Klein is right to argue that '[d]ismissing the art versus commerce divide as constructed and the "sell-out" debates as antiquated conceals the importance of acknowledging and investigating tensions within and between the popular music and advertising worlds. When fans and critics perceive this line to be crossed, it is not necessary to redraw or reject the line, but to assess who is in control and to what end' (Klein 2009: 139).

As we have seen, major music companies, consumer brands and media companies are firmly in control of such arrangements, and use popular music and recording artists as profit-generating properties and vehicles for achieving strategic branding objectives. This set of corporations has been joined by another group of music gatekeepers that are especially adept at succeeding within, if not controlling, the new digital realities shaping cultural production: technology companies.

Future Challenges, New Dependencies: Enter 'Big Tech'

This book contends that the dominant idea that music placements and other branding arrangements constitute the 'new radio' has provided advertisers with a new source of leverage vis-à-vis recording artists: access to a highly sought-after media audience. Importantly, the independence gained by music makers is tied to a new dependence not only on advertisers but also on technology companies, which command new levers of control (see Hesmondhalgh and Meier 2015). In fact, the dynamic of gatekeeping presented by the case of lifestyle brands pales in comparison to the capacities of 'big tech': Apple, Amazon and Google. Given the important intersection between the information technology and consumer electronics industries and the cultural industries, it is not surprising that these technology giants have entered the fold. They have direct access to users of digital content *and* purchasers of hardware and devices. At present, it is very difficult to circumvent the digital oligopoly controlled by these companies. Furthermore, leveraging social media as a marketing tool in ways that promise substantial reach entails working with Facebook and Twitter.

Much as consumer brands have a different interest in music content than do music companies (the former use popular music as a means to achieving promotional ends rather than necessarily directly profiting from the content itself, as we have seen), technology giants' use of content also reflects the specificities of their business models, which differ from those underpinning the cultural industries in notable ways. Content helps to sell devices for Apple and to generate user data for Google, while Amazon sells devices as a way of driving content sales (Mulligan 2014). In the words of music industry analyst Mark Mulligan (2014),

For each of them music is a means to an end. All are willing to some degree to loss lead on music to achieve ulterior business objectives. All of which is great for labels and publishers as they get their royalties, advances and equity stakes. But for the pure play start up it means competing on an uneven footing with giant companies who don't even need music to generate a revenue return for them.

In a digital economy that favours 'free' or advertising-subsidized content, the big tech oligopoly is able to use cultural content as a loss leader and promotional medium in efforts to drive sales elsewhere. The power of these companies is staggering because they are not only the dominant *sellers* of cultural products to end consumers, but also the dominant *purchasers* of those cultural products from creators and media companies; they can 'dictate terms at both ends of the equation' (Mulligan 2015a). While the major music companies are currently benefiting from business arrangements with these companies, in a so-called 'attention economy' (Goldhaber 1997; Davenport and Beck 2002), any real threat to the old guard of the music industries would surely come from these technology giants. They dominate B2B and consumer markets and can generate revenue from content, hardware, consumer data and advertising.

Regardless of the industry, corporations are built to maximize returns on investments, not share those rewards with workers in an equitable way. This parsimonious orientation has become apparent as various brands have taken increasing interest in producing their own content and have exercised their power to drive down fees paid to recording artists. For example, according to Marc Altshuler of sound design firm Human Music, Microsoft's Xbox brand previously licensed music, but has since done an about-face on music licensing and is no longer interested in this strategy for proprietary reasons: 'They don't want to borrow equity off a band. … They don't want to share any equity. … They really strongly believe that they have the platform to build their own equity and have the music stand for what they want to do' (Altshuler 2012). As we have seen, amid declining revenues from CD and digital download sales, recording artists and record companies have become dependent on brands as a source of income. Significantly, the *brand* develops the strategy, chooses the artist and sets the terms of the relationship. Gabe McDonough, vice president and music director at Leo Burnett, declared that '[s]omebody's got to pay the bills' and 'brands are one of the few entities in human culture that are willing to pony up' (quoted in Beltrone 2012). This claim seems disingenuous. Emboldened by the harsh force of supply and demand, brands are often no longer willing to 'pony up' quite simply because they no longer *have* to. As profit-maximizing entities, corporations make decisions based on self-interest, and seek the best possible terms for their own bottom lines. It would be ill-advised to think that technology companies will be any different than lifestyle or media brands.

Over a decade ago, Andrew Leyshon et al. made the incisive observation that

> music has become an increasingly important part of the infrastructure of capitalist society, and is now an essential crutch to all manner of acts of consumption (DeNora and Belcher 2000). But, significantly, this development has actually served to *weaken* the music industry as popular music is decreasingly valued for itself, but is, instead, increasingly valued more for the ways in which it is consumed in relation to other things. (Leyshon et al. 2004: 182–3; emphasis in original)

The argument forwarded in this book suggests that as a brand-building tool, popular music and the associations and affects linked to it are being used to encourage consumption inside neoliberal, post-Fordist capitalism. It also appears that a perhaps unexpected byproduct of popular music's ubiquity within this promotional culture has been the unstable economic value assigned to it. Under the music-related branding paradigm, this instability has been exacerbated by advertisers' overreliance on novelty and thirst for the ever new (see Meier 2011: 409–10). My analysis suggests that these shifts actually have not done irreparable damage to the music industries, however, because the major companies at the helm have made the adjustments necessary to adapt to the new digital economy. Instead, individual artists, especially the aspiring and lesser known, have borne the brunt of these changes. Discussions regarding the future of the music industries must put the circumstances of working artists front and centre, if we as fans and listeners hope to benefit from exciting new music and ideas.

Notes

1 Taking my cue from Mike Tunnicliffe, an advertising expert and, as of December 2014, Universal Music Group's first US Head of Brand Partnerships (Hampp 2014b), I see popular media such as television programmes as effectively functioning as 'media brands' (Tunnicliffe, personal communication, 2010).

2 Music supervisors are those executives responsible for selecting and clearing the rights for music licensed for use in television programmes, commercials, films and video games (see Klein and Meier forthcoming).

3 According to statistics reported by the International Federation of the Phonographic Industry (IFPI) (a worldwide recording industry lobby group), due to unauthorized downloading, '[t]he trade value of recorded-music sales has fallen from about $7 billion in 2005 to $4.6 billion in 2009' (quoted in Peoples 2010b). Specific recording industry statistics should not necessarily be taken at face value, however; lobby organizations and trade associations such as the IFPI and the Recording Industry Association of America (RIAA) have an obvious interest in perpetuating the idea that the recording industry has been unduly harmed by 'piracy' in order to pressure governments to police unauthorized online distribution of music.

4 However, note that according to IFPI (2015) figures, on a global scale, physical formats still generated as much revenue as digital formats in 2015 (US$6.85 billion).

5   Devon Powers underlines consequences of this version of independence for working musicians: 'Examples such as Palmer suggest that label-less musicians are actually doing *more* work, but nonetheless it remains seductive to idealize them as the pinnacle of DIY' (Powers 2015: 127; emphasis in original; see also Meier 2015).

6   This is not to suggest that the notion of 'selling out' vanished altogether in the wake of the Telecommunications Act of 1996. When the Shins licensed 'New Slang' to McDonald's in 2002, for instance, fans and rock journalists censured the band; the 'unwritten rules and boundaries' regarding the appropriate distance between popular music and advertising 'bubbled to the surface' (Klein 2009: 123). The licensing of indie rock in particular was still relatively rare in 2002, and partnering with global fast food franchise McDonald's was seen as particularly egregious. Pop/R&B singer Justin Timberlake's performance of the slogan in the McDonald's 'I'm Lovin' It' jingle (2003), which was subsequently released as a Timberlake single, was more expected. Reflecting on the widespread shift toward licensing original songs and away from commissioning jingles, Nygren suggested that 'I'm Lovin' It' is 'probably the last example of the truly great jingle' (Nygren, personal communication, 2009).

7   'Performance on the Grammy Awards', 'performance during Super Bowl halftime show' and 'homepage placement on iTunes' ranked first, second and third, respectively (Mitchell 2011) – a testament to the continued importance of mass audiences to effective popular music promotion.

8   Interestingly, Death Cab for Cutie bassist Nick Harmer cited the Flaming Lips *90210* appearance in order to justify his band's decision to work with *The O.C.*: 'When people were saying, "Are you guys comfortable with either being on the show, or the references that the show makes to you guys?" We would just say, "Well, The Flaming Lips were on 90210"' (quoted in McFarland 2005). An 'alternative' cool precedent had been set.

9   Wrigley suspended the advertisements and eventually terminated the deal after Brown assaulted pop/R&B/reggae singer and then-partner Rihanna (Kreps 2009).

10   Interestingly, Mountain Dew's use of this type of approach dates back to its 'early sponsorship of extreme sports in the early 1990s', which helped the brand 'become perceived as cultural producers ... rather than mere cultural parasites that appropriate valued popular culture' (Holt 2002: 84).

11   In this context, 'all in' means 'writing, publishing, no royalties. This is all you get, essentially. I don't care if we press five billion of them. You're not getting another dime. This is it' (Coffing, personal communication, 2010).

12   'Pumped Up Kicks' may seem to be a strange fit for advertisers, given that it contains a sinister and threatening lyric about a gun. Lyrics can be important, but they are not necessarily the primary consideration of advertisers, who do not assume that audiences listen attentively to commercials in any case. The popular music inserted into television commercials, typically snippets of songs, is often distilled into a key rhythmic groove, melodic hook or an overall 'vibe'. Furthermore, given what media and cultural studies scholarship tells us about polysemy, it bears remembering that songs are

open to multiple interpretations and that for some audiences, musical content may trump lyrical content.

13   Thanks to David Hesmondhalgh for an especially productive conversation around this topic.

14   See Hesmondhalgh (1996) for a review of misleading assumptions and problematic policy implications for the cultural industries in literature on post-Fordism and 'flexible specialization'.

15   According to Malcolm Barnard, design 'possesses communicative or functional intent', and while aesthetic considerations are important, they serve and yield to 'the job there is to do' (Barnard 1998: 15).

16   Interestingly, Ole acquired Jingle Punks in spring 2015, consistent with the dominant logic of consolidation found elsewhere in the music industries (Christman 2015a).

17   Thanks to the Future of Music Coalition's Kristin Thomson via Bethany Klein for passing on information about the Talk at Emotion Revolution Summit, hosted by the Yale Center for Emotional Intelligence and Born This Way Foundation, at which Lady Gaga spoke.

References

Unpublished Materials

Interviews

Advertising creative director. 2009. Interview by author. Toronto, ON. 13 May.
Advertising strategist. 2011. Interview by author. New York, NY. 9 May.
Beavis, Jennifer. 2009. Interview by author. Toronto, ON. 15 May.
Campanelli, John. 2010. Interview by author. New York, NY. 9 November.
Canadian major record label executive A. 2009. Interview by author. Toronto, ON. 19 June.
Canadian major record label executive B. 2009. Interview by author. Toronto, ON. 19 June.
Coffing, Barry. 2010. Interview by author. New York, NY. 13 November.
Danzig, Ian. 2009. Interview by author. Toronto, ON. 7 September.
Digital marketing project manager. 2011. Interview by author. New York, NY. 13 May.
Director of licensing at video game publisher. 2010. Interview by author. Los Angeles, CA. 15 November.
Ferneyhough, Jodie. 2009. Interview by author. Toronto, ON. 28 September.
Fritz, Amy. 2009. Interview by author. Toronto, ON. 8 June.
Grierson, Don. 2010. Interview by author. Los Angeles, CA. 16 November.

Gutstadt, Jared. 2011. Interview by author. New York, NY. 13 April.
Hayman, David. 2009. Interview by author. Toronto, ON. 4 June.
Independent label licensing executive. 2011. Interview by author. New York, NY. 26 April.
Jansson, Peter. 2010. Interview by author. Los Angeles, CA. 17 November.
Kenzer, Amy. 2010. Interview by author. Los Angeles, CA. 16 November.
Koren, Vered. 2009. Interview by author. Toronto, ON. 29 April.
Lifestyle advertising account executive. 2011. Interview by author. New York, NY. 5 May.
Martin, Ari. 2010. Interview by author. New York, NY. 10 October.
Nygren, Bill. 2009. Interview by author. Toronto, ON. 28 October.
Outhit, Allison. 2009. Interview by author. Toronto, ON. 21 April.
Potocic, Tim. 2009. Interview by author. Toronto, ON. 5 May.
Quinlan, Neville. 2009. Interview by author. Toronto, ON. 22 September.
Sound branding executive. 2010. Interview by author. Los Angeles, CA. 16 November.
Tunnicliffe, Mike. 2010. Interview by author. New York, NY. 23 November.
White, Emily. 2011. Interview by author. New York, NY. 19 April.

Additional Interviews (not cited)

Canadian entertainment attorney. 2011. Interview by author. Toronto, ON. 16 August.
Dryden, Richard. 2011. Interview by author. New York, NY. 15 May.
Hoffert, Paul. 2009. Interview by author. Toronto, ON. 5 June.
Kuruvilla, Sue. 2009. Interview by author. Toronto, ON. 15 October.
LeBel, André. 2010. Interview by author. Toronto, ON. 12 January.
Mobile cross-media agency CEO. 2009. Interview by author via telephone. Vancouver, BC. 4 May.
Tobias, Tony. 2009. Interview by author. Toronto, ON. 8 September.
Yannopoulos, Vangelis. 2010. Interview by author. New York, NY. 7 November.

Books, Articles and Other Published Materials

Access Industries. 2016. Holdings by industry. http://www.accessindustries.com/industry/ (accessed 1 May 2016).
Adams, Gregory. 2014. 'Happy' (Beats by Dre Beat Pill commercial). *Exclaim.ca*, 2 January. http://exclaim.ca/music/article/pharrell_williams-happy_beats_by_dre_beat_pills_commercial (accessed 1 October 2015).
Adorno, Theodor W. 1945. A social critique of radio music. *The Kenyon Review* 7, no. 2 (Spring): 208–17.
Adorno, Theodor W. [1966] 1973. *Negative dialectics*, trans. E.B. Ashton. New York: Continuum.

Adorno, Theodor W. [1959] 1993. Theory of pseudo-culture, trans. Deborah Cook. *Telos* 95 (Spring): 15–38.

Adorno, Theodor W. [1953] 1994. The stars down to earth: The *Los Angeles Times* astrology column. In *Stars down to earth and other essays on the irrational in culture*, ed. Stephen Crook, 46–171. New York: Routledge.

Adorno, Theodor W. [1960] 2001a. Culture and administration. In *The culture industry: Selected essays on mass culture*, ed. J.M. Bernstein, 107–31. New York: Routledge.

Adorno, Theodor W. [1967] 2001b. Culture industry reconsidered. In *The culture industry: Selected essays on mass culture*, ed. J.M. Bernstein, 98–106. New York: Routledge.

Adorno, Theodor W. [1938] 2002a. On the fetish-character in music and the regression of listening. In *Essays on music*, trans. Susan H. Gillespie, ed. Richard Leppert, 288–317. Berkeley: University of California Press.

Adorno, Theodor W. [1941] 2002b. On popular music [with the assistance of George Simpson]. In *Essays on music*, trans. Susan H. Gillespie, ed. Richard Leppert, 437–69. Berkeley: University of California Press.

Adorno, Theodor W. [1941] 2002c. The radio symphony. In *Essays on music*, trans. Susan H. Gillespie, ed. Richard Leppert, 251–70. Berkeley: University of California Press.

Adorno, Theodor W. [1939] 2009a. The problem of experimentation in music psychology. In *Current of music: Elements of a radio theory*, ed. Robert Hullot-Kentor, 413–50. Malden, MA: Polity.

Aglietta, Michel. 1979. *A theory of capitalist regulation*. London: New Left Books.

Alexomanolaki, Margarita, Catherine Loveday and Chris Kennett. 2007. Music and memory in advertising: Music as a device of implicit learning and recall. *Music, Sound, and the Moving Image* 1, no. 1 (Spring): 51–71.

Altshuler, Marc. 2012. Advertising IS the new radio! Conference panel at South by Southwest, Austin, TX. 15 March. http://schedule.sxsw.com/2012/events/event_MP10725 (accessed 30 March 2012).

Anderson, Chris. 2006. *The long tail: How endless choice is creating unlimited demand*. London: Random House.

Anderson, Tim. 2014. *Popular music in a digital music economy: Problems and practices for an emerging service industry*. New York: Routledge.

Angus, Ian H. and Sut Jhally. 1989. Introduction. In *Cultural politics in contemporary America*, ed. Ian Angus and Sut Jhally, 1–14. New York: Routledge.

Aronczyk, M. 2013. *Branding the nation: The global business of national identity*. Oxford: Oxford University Press.

Aronczyk, Melissa and Devon Powers, eds. 2010. *Blowing up the brand: Critical perspectives on promotional culture*. New York: Peter Lang.

Arvidsson, Adam. 2005. Brands: A critical perspective. *Journal of Consumer Culture* 5, no. 2: 235–58.

AudioSparx. 2012a. Happiness, corporate music, download music, stock music. http://www.audiosparx.com/sa/summary/play.cfm/crumb.3/crumc.0/sound_iid.562641 (accessed 15 October 2012).

AudioSparx. 2012b. I'm on fire, RnB music. http://www.audiosparx.com/sa/summary/play.cfm/crumb.30/crumc.0/sound_iid.329240 (accessed 15 October 2012).

Austin, Helen. 2010a. 4 steps to film and TV placement. *Passive Promotion*, 3 September. http://passivepromotion.com/4-steps-to-film-and-tv-placement (accessed 15 September 2012).

Austin, Helen. 2010b. Happy lyrics. http://www.helenaustin.com/lyricssow.html (accessed 15 September 2012).

Babe, Robert. 2009. *Cultural studies and political economy: Toward a new integration*. Toronto: Lexington Books.

Banet-Weiser, Sarah. 2012. *Authentic TM: Politics and ambivalence in a brand culture*. New York: New York University Press.

Barker, Andrew. 2013. Branding deals with pop stars go beyond the casual endorsement. *Variety*, 16 April. http://variety.com/2013/music/features/endorsement-deals-1200334594/ (accessed 7 January 2016).

Barnard, Malcolm. 1998. *Art, design and visual culture: An introduction*. London: Macmillan Press.

Barnhard, Rachel. 2009. The power play: Connecting brands and bands. *Billboard.biz*, 5 June.

Barnhard, Rachel and Jack Rutledge. 2009. Advertising is the new radio. *Billboard.biz*, 4 June.

Barshad, Amos. 2011. Can Mountain Dew save the music industry? *Vulture.com*, 12 August. http://www.vulture.com/2011/08/can_mountain_dew_save_the_musi.html (accessed 7 September 2012).

Baxendale, John. 1995. '... into another kind of life in which anything might happen ...': Popular music and late modernity, 1910–1930. *Popular Music*, 14, no. 2: 137–54.

Beltrone, Gabriel. 2012. Behind the music: Call it borrowed authenticity or just plain good marketing, but brands are reaching out to indie bands, and both are coming out ahead. *Adweek*, 20 March. http://www.adweek.com/news/advertisingbranding/behind-music-138995 (accessed 29 May 2012).

Ben-Yehuda, Ayala. 2008. Exclusive: The Fray debuting single on ABC. *Billboard.biz*, 14 November.

Berman, Cheryl R. 2010. View from the top: The ad agency angle. Conference panel at NARIP: Bands, Brands & Beyond, New York. 15 November.

Bernstein, J.M. 2001. *Adorno: Disenchantment and ethics*. New York: Cambridge University Press.

Berry, David. 2014. *Critical theory and the digital*. New York: Bloomsbury Academic.

Billboard. 2009. The decade in music: Business trends – top 10 trends of the decade. *Billboard.biz*, 19 December.

Billboard. 2010. Top 25 tours of 2010. *Billboard.com*, 8 December. http://www.billboard.com/#/news/top-25-tours-of-2010-1004134022.story (accessed 15 January 2011).

Billboard. 2012. What really happened to Sony and Universal's 2 billion missing YouTube views. *Billboard.biz*, 21 December. http://www.billboard.com/biz/

articles/news/1483721/what-really-happened-to-sony-and-universals-2-billion-missing-youtube (accessed 1 October 2015).

Billboard. 2016. Billboard's 2016 branding power players: Meet the masters of marketing. *Billboard.com*, 14 March. http://www.billboard.com/articles/business/7256268/2016-billboard-branding-power-list-marketing (accessed 18 March 2016).

Black Toast Music. 2013. Search our music catalogue. http://blacktoastmusic.com/my/searches/new (accessed 3 May 2013).

Born, Georgina. 1993. Against negation, for a politics of cultural production: Adorno, aesthetics, the social. *Screen* 24, no. 3: 223–42.

Boyer, Robert. 1988. *The search for labour market flexibility: The European economies in transition*. Toronto: Oxford University Press.

Brandamp. 2008. Bands and brands: How music communicates with people. WPP and Universal Music.

Brandle, Lars. 2008. Bacardi, Groove Armada toast to 360 deal. *Billboard*, 28 March.

Braverman, Harry. 1974. *Labor and monopoly capital: The degradation of work in the twentieth century*. New York: Monthly Review Press.

Brita. 2012. FilterForGood: Our partners. http://www.brita.com/filter-for-good/ourpartners/ (accessed 5 July 2012).

Brown, Tim. 2005. Strategy by design. *Fast Company Magazine* 95 (June): 52–4.

Brown, Tim. 2008. Design thinking. *Harvard Business Review* (June): 84–92.

Bruno, Antony. 2009. Maximum exposure. *Billboard*, 26 September.

Bruno, Antony. 2010. @ Music & money: Execs steering clear of sponsorships. *Billboard.biz*, 4 March.

Bruno, Antony, Ed Christman, Mariel Concepcion, Ann Donahue and Cortney Harding. 2010. Maximum Exposure 2010. *Billboard*, 2 October.

Bundy, June. 1954. Title tunes cut for picture and disks. *Billboard*, 18 September.

Bundy, June. 1961. Movie theme wax adds spark to disk-flick ties. *Billboard*, 13 November.

Burkart, Patrick and Tom McCourt. 2006. *Digital music wars: Ownership and control of the celestial jukebox*. Toronto: Rowman and Littlefield.

Burston, Jonathan. 2009. Recombinant Broadway. *Continuum: Journal of Media and Cultural Studies* 23, no. 2: 159–69.

Butler, Jeremy G. 2007. *Television: Critical methods and applications*. 3rd ed. Mahwah, NJ: Lawrence Erlbaum Associates.

Buxton, David. [1983] 1990. Rock music, the star system, and the rise of consumerism. In *On record: Rock, pop, and the written word*, ed. Simon Frith and Andrew Goodwin, 427–40. New York: Routledge.

Carah, Nicholas. 2010. *Pop brands: Branding, popular music, and young people*. New York: Peter Lang.

Carah, Nicholas. 2015. Algorithmic brands: A decade of brand experiments with mobile and social media. *New Media and Society*, DOI: 10.1177/1461444815605463.

Carr, Nicholas. 2006. Sharecropping the long tail. Rough Type blog, 19 December. http://www.roughtype.com/?p=634 (accessed 5 July 2011).

Christman, Ed. 2012a. Analysis: Edgar Bronfman's big statements about Universal/EMI deal are business as usual—but much more public. *Billboard. biz*, 2 February. http://www.billboard.biz/bbbiz/others/analysis-edgar-bronfman-s-bigstatements-1006079952.story (accessed 3 February 2012).

Christman, Ed. 2012b. Billboard power 100: Hartwig Masuch. *Billboard.biz*, 26 January. http://www.billboard.biz/bbbiz/others/billboard-power-100-hartwig-masuch-1006004962.story (accessed 15 March 2012).

Christman, Ed. 2012c. It's official: Sony-led acquisition of EMI Music Publishing approved by EU. *Billboard.biz*, 19 April. http://www.billboard.biz/bbbiz/industry/publishing/it-s-official-sony-led-acquisition-of-emi-1006815552 .story (accessed 5 September 2012).

Christman, Ed. 2015a. Publishing briefs: Spirit picks up StyleSonic catalog, ole takes Jingle Punks and John Denver to Kobalt. *Billboard*, 23 March. http://www.billboard.com/articles/business/6509430/publishing-briefs-spirit-stylesonic-ole-jingle-punks-john-denver (accessed 3 September 2015).

Christman, Ed. 2015b. Publishers Q2 report: Sony/ATV is holding onto the no. 1 spot – but barely. *Billboard*, 20 August. http://www.billboard.com/articles/business/6670986/publishers-q2-report-sony-atv-warner-chappell-universal-kobalt (accessed 23 October 2015).

Christman, Ed. 2016. Sony to buy out Michael Jackson estate's half of Sony/ATV Music Publishing. *Billboard*, 14 March. http://www.billboard.com/articles/business/7256367/sony-michael-jackson-estate-sony-atv-music-publishing-deal (accessed 17 March 2016).

Cobo, Leila. 2014. Fiat debuts global ad campaign featuring Pharrell's 'Happy'. *Billboard*, 12 February. http://www.billboard.com/articles/news/5901241/fiat-debuts-global-ad-campaign-featuring-diddy-pharrells-happy-exclusive (accessed 1 October 2015).

comScore. 2012. U.S. digital future in focus 2012. Key insights from 2011 and what they mean for the coming year. http://www.comscore.com/Press_Events/Presentations_Whitepapers/2012/2012_US_Digital_Future_in_Focus (accessed 16 February 2012).

CQ Transcriptions, LLC. 2011. Q4 2010 Live Nation Entertainment, Inc. Earnings conference call – final. *CQ FD Disclosure*, 28 February.

Creswell, Julie. 2008. Nothing sells like celebrity. *New York Times*, 22 June. http://www.nytimes.com/2008/06/22/business/media/22celeb.html?pagewanted=all (accessed 24 August 2012).

D'Arcy, Keith. 2012. Advertising IS the new radio! Conference panel at South by Southwest, Austin, TX. 15 March. http://schedule.sxsw.com/2012/events/event_MP10725 (accessed 30 March 2012).

Davenport, Thomas H. and John C. Beck. 2002. *The attention economy: Understanding the new currency of business*. Boston: Harvard Business Press.

Davis, Aeron. 2013. *Promotional cultures: The rise and spread of advertising, public relations, marketing and branding*. Cambridge: Polity.

Davis, Melissa. 2009. *The fundamentals of branding*. Lausanne: AVA Publishing.

Day, Bart. 2009. Net profit deals: A recent alternative to the traditional record deal. *Music Biz Academy.com*, October. http://www.musicbizacademy.com/articles/netprofitdeals1.htm (accessed 26 March 2011).

Deery, June. 2004. Reality TV as advertainment. *Popular Communication* 2, no. 1: 1–20.

Denisoff, R. Serge and William D. Romanowski. 1991. *Risky business: Rock in film*. New Brunswick, NJ: Transaction Publishers.

DeNora, Tia and Sophie Belcher. 2000. 'When you're trying something on you picture yourself in a place where they are playing this kind of music' – Musically sponsored agency in the British clothing retail sector. *Sociological Review*, 48, no. 1: 80–101.

Donahue, Ann. 2008. The Billboard Q&A: Jordan Schur. *Billboard*, 8 March.

Donaton, Scott. 2003. The story behind a landmark music commercial. *Advertising Age*, 22 September. http://adage.com/article/viewpoint/advertising-landmark-jaguarsting-tv-commercial/38400/ (accessed 7 January 2012).

Donaton, Scott. 2004. *Madison & Vine: Why the entertainment & advertising industries must converge*. New York: McGraw-Hill (eBook).

Donnelly, K.J. 2002. Tracking British television: Pop music as stock soundtrack to the small screen. *Popular Music* 21, no. 3: 331–43.

Elberse, Anita. 2008. Should you invest in the Long Tail? *Harvard Business Review* 86, no. 7/8: 88–96.

Elberse, Anita. 2013. *Blockbusters: Why big hits – and big risks – are the future of the entertainment business*. New York: Faber and Faber.

Elias Arts. 2011. Audio identity insights. http://eliasarts.com/?page_id=810 (accessed 1 March 2011).

Elliot, Stuart. 2010a. Better days ahead for branded entertainment, report says. *New York Times*, 29 June. http://mediadecoder.blogs.nytimes.com/2010/06/29/betterdays-ahead-for-branded-entertainment-report-says/ (accessed 4 February 2012).

Elliot, Stuart. 2010b. Brita whets concertgoers' appetites with Jack Johnson tour. *New York Times*, 2 July. http://mediadecoder.blogs.nytimes.com/2010/07/02/brita-whetsconcertgoers-appetites-with-jack-johnson-tour/ (accessed 5 June 2012).

Erdman, Justin. 2011. The changing experience of music. Conference panel at North by Northeast Interactive, Toronto. 16–18 June.

Erwin, Stephen T. 2010. What's the deal? Conference panel at Artist Management Conference (AMCON) 2010, New York. 14–15 October.

Fiske, John. 1987. *Television culture*. London: Routledge.

Fiske, John. 1989. *Understanding popular culture*. New York: Routledge.

Fixmer, Andy. 2012. Taking music in ads beyond jingles. *Businessweek*, 23 February. http://www.businessweek.com/articles/2012-02-23/taking-music-in-ads-beyondjingles (accessed 29 May 2012).

Fixmer, Andy and Jon Erlichman. 2012. California said to probe effect of EMI Music's sale. *Businessweek*, 28 March.

Frank, Jay. 2012. Guest post: Jay Frank on NRP's Emily White vs. David Lowery: Is stealing music really the problem? *Billboard.biz*, 21 June. http://www.billboard.biz/bbbiz/industry/record-labels/guest-post-jay-frank-on-npr-s-emily-white1007388552.story (accessed 5 September 2012).

Frith, Simon. 1981. *Sound effects: Youth, leisure, and the politics of rock 'n' roll*. New York: Pantheon Books.

Frith, Simon. 1988a. Copyright and the music business. *Popular Music* 7, no. 1: 57–75.

Frith, Simon. 1988b. The industrialization of music. In *Music for pleasure: Essays in the sociology of pop*, ed. Simon Frith, 11–23. New York: Routledge.

Frith, Simon. 2001. The popular music industry. In *The Cambridge companion to pop and rock*, ed. Simon Frith, Will Straw and John Street, 26–52. New York: Cambridge University Press.

Gardner, Eriq. 2009. Termination rights: A blast from the past. *IP Law and Business* 7, no. 10.

Garnham, Nicholas. 1979. Contribution to a political economy of mass-communication. *Media, Culture and Society* 1, no. 2: 123–46.

Garnham, Nicholas. 1990. *Capitalism and communication: Global culture and the economics of information*. London: Sage.

Garnham, Nicholas. 2005. From cultural to creative industries: An analysis of the implications of the 'creative industries' approach to the arts and media policy making in the United Kingdom. *International Journal of Cultural Policy* 11, no. 1: 15–29.

Garrity, Brian. 2007. Influential music supervisor forms record label. *Reuters*, 26 March. http://www.reuters.com/article/2007/03/27/music-label-dc-idUSN2624160920070327 (accessed 15 September 2012).

Germanotta, Stefani. 2015. Talk at Emotion Revolution Summit. Hosted by Yale Center for Emotional Intelligence and Born This Way Foundation. 24 October. https://www.youtube.com/watch?v=_49G4dU56T0 (accessed 30 October 2015).

Gillett, Charlie. [1970] 1996. *The sound of the city: The rise of rock and roll*. 2nd ed. New York: Da Capo.

Gilmore, James H. and B. Joseph Pine II. 2007. *Authenticity: What consumers really want*. Boston: Harvard Business School Press.

Giraldi, Bob. 2009. Director recalls Michael Jackson's contribution to advertising. *Advertising Age*, 26 June. http://adage.com/article/news/director-recalls-jacksons-contribution-advertising/137618/ (accessed 7 August 2012).

Giroux, Henry A. 2008. *Against the terror of neoliberalism: Politics beyond the age of greed*. London: Paradigm Publishers.

Global Media Online. 2011. 2011–2012 film & TV music salary and rate survey. *Film Music Magazine*.

Goldhaber, Michael H. 1997. Attention shoppers! *Wired*, December. http://www.wired.com/wired/archive/5.12/es_attention.html?pg=1&topic= (accessed 2 January 2012).

Gomes, Lee. 2006. It may be a long time before the long tail is wagging the web. *Wall Street Journal*, 26 July. http://online.wsj.com/public/article/

SB115387606762117314-WwmoACNV7rjYDAvcwpe8vMpMYs_20070725
.html (accessed 9 November 2009).

Goodman, David. 2010. Distracted listening: On not making sound choices in the 1930s. In *Sound in the era of mechanical reproduction*, ed. David Suisman and Susan Strasser, 15–46. Philadelphia: University of Pennsylvania Press.

Goodman, Fred. 2008. Special report: Rock's new economy: Making money when CDs don't sell. *Rolling Stone*, 29 May.

Goodman, Steve. 2010. *Sonic warfare: Sound, affect, and the ecology of fear.* Cambridge, MA: MIT Press.

Goodwin, Andrew. 1992. *Dancing in the distraction factory: Music television and popular culture.* Minneapolis: University of Minnesota Press.

Gordon, Steve. 2015. A simple guide to signing the best sync deal possible. *Digital Music News*, 25 May. http://www.digitalmusicnews.com/2015/05/25/a-simple-guide-to-signing-the-best-sync-deal-possible/ (accessed 5 October 2015).

Gracyk, Theodore. 1996. *Rhythm and noise: An aesthetics of rock.* Durham, NC: Duke University Press.

Graser, Marc. 2014. The best branded entertainment of 2014. *Variety*, 22 December. http://variety.com/2014/biz/news/the-best-branded-entertainment-of-2014-1201373904/ (accessed 1 July 2015).

Greenburg, Zack O'Malley. 2012a. Jay-Z's Made in America Festival: A crosspromotional bonanza. *Forbes*, 4 September. http://www.forbes.com/sites/zackomalleygreenburg/2012/09/04/jay-zs-made-in-america-festival-a-crosspromotional-bonanza/

Greenburg, Zack O'Malley. 2012b. Lil Wayne debuts multi-million dollar DEWeezy campaign at SXSW. *Forbes*, 16 March. http://www.forbes.com/sites/zackomalleygreenburg/2012/03/16/lil-wayne-debuts-multi-million-dollar-deweezy-campaign-at-sxsw/ (accessed 5 April 2012).

Greenburg, Zack O'Malley. 2012c. Nicki Minaj to earn millions as face of new Pepsi beverage. *Forbes*, 19 March. http://www.forbes.com/sites/zackomalleygreenburg/2012/03/19/nicki-minaj-to-earn-millions-as-face-of-new-pepsi-beverage/ (accessed 5 April 2012).

Groves, John. n.d. Sound branding: A short history. http://www.groves.de/presse/information/history_of_SB_v3.1.pdf (accessed 5 April 2010).

Grow, Kory. 2015. McDonald's responds to indie-pop duo's viral complaint. *Rolling Stone*, 5 March. http://www.rollingstone.com/music/news/mcdonalds-responds-to-indie-pop-duos-viral-complaint-20150305 (accessed 1 October 2015).

Gunster, Shane. 2004. *Capitalizing on culture: Critical theory for cultural studies.* Toronto: University of Toronto Press.

Gunster, Shane. 2007. A world of difference: Adorno and cultural studies. In *Adorno and the need in thinking: New critical essays*, ed. Donald Burke, Colin J. Campbell, Kathy Kiloh, Michael Palamarek and Jonathan Short, 296–315. Toronto: University of Toronto Press.

Hampp, Andrew. 2012a. Dolla-palooza: Why more brands than ever are flocking to Lolla. *Billboard.biz*, 4 August. http://www.billboard.biz/bbbiz/others/

dollapalooza-why-more-brands-than-ever-1007751152.story (accessed 14 October 2012).

Hampp, Andrew. 2012b. Steve Stoute on uniting Budweiser & Jay-Z for Made In America: 'Brands are becoming much closer to the content'. *Billboard.biz*, 31 August. http://www.billboard.biz/bbbiz/others/steve-stoute-on-uniting-budweiser-jay-z-1007916952.story (accessed 14 October 2012).

Hampp, Andrew. 2014a. SXSW: Lady Gaga plays offbeat set, tells fans 'you don't need a f—king record label'. *Billboard*, 14 March. http://www.billboard.com/articles/events/sxsw/5937422/sxsw-lady-gaga-plays-offbeat-set-tells-fans-you-dont-need-a-f-king (accessed 1 October 2015).

Hampp, Andrew. 2014b. UMG appoints Mike Tunnicliffe as first U.S. head of brand partnerships. *Billboard*, 5 December. http://www.billboard.com/articles/business/6363573/umg-mike-tunnicliffe-head-brand-partnerships (accessed 19 August 2015).

Hampp, Andrew. 2015. McDonald's to pay performers at its SXSW showcase. *Billboard.biz*, 10 March. http://www.billboard.com/biz/articles/news/6495176/mcdonalds-to-pay-performers-at-its-sxsw-showcase (accessed 1 October 2015).

Hampp, Andrew and Jennifer Netherby. 2011. The art of the neojingle: Apple's way with music in advertising. *Billboard*, 15 October.

Hancock, Herbie. 2014. *Herbie Hancock: Possibilities*. With Lisa Dickey. New York: Viking Books.

Hanley, Andrew. 2011. Sound capital (music supervisor panel). Conference panel at North by Northeast Interactive, Toronto. 16–18 June.

Hanlon, Patrick. 2012. Marketers master their three P's: Push, pull and portal. *Forbes*, 22 March. http://www.forbes.com/sites/patrickhanlon/2012/03/22/marketersmaster-their-3ps-push-pull-and-portal/ (accessed 15 April 2012).

Harding, Brian. 2015. *Ex Cops*. [Facebook]. 4 March. https://www.facebook.com/excopsband/posts/892840547444887:0 (accessed 1 October 2015).

Harding, Cortney. 2008a. License to thrill; Is synch exposure worth giving away songs for free?' *Billboard*, 24 May.

Harding, Cortney. 2008b. The Maximum Exposure list. *Billboard*, 27 September.

Harding, Cortney. 2010. Amanda Palmer: Cult of personality. *Billboard*, 14 August.

Harding, Cortney and Jonathan Cohen. 2008. New Nine Inch Nails album hits the web. *Billboard.biz*, 2 March. http://www.billboard.biz/bbbiz/content_display/industry/news/e3ie188ab48abcdb0497e8c7946dc3fd240 (accessed 18 August 2011).

Hardy, Jonathan. 2014. *Critical political economy of the media: An introduction*. London: Routledge.

Harvey, David. 1990. *The condition of postmodernity: An enquiry into the origins of cultural change*. Cambridge, MA: Blackwell.

Harvey, David. 2003. *The new imperialism*. Oxford: Oxford University Press.

Harvey, David. 2005. *A brief history of neoliberalism*. Oxford: Oxford University Press.

Harvey, David. 2006. *Spaces of global capitalism: Towards a theory of uneven geographical development*. New York: Verso.

Harvey, David. 2010. *The enigma of capital*. New York: Oxford University Press.

Hau, Louis. 2007. The new radio? More fans finding music on TV. *Forbes.com*, 19 July. http://today.msnbc.msn.com/id/19836755/ns/today-entertainment/t/newradio-more-fans-finding-music-tv/#.T7K9n-1yHww (accessed 2 May 2012).

Hearn, Alison. 2008. 'Meat, mask, burden': Probing the contours of the branded 'self'. *Journal of Consumer Culture* 8, no. 2: 197–217.

Hearn, Alison. 2010. Structuring feeling: Web 2.0, online ranking and rating, and the digital 'reputation' economy. *Ephemera* 10, no. 3/4: 421–38.

Heartbeats International. 2009. Social music revolution: A white paper on music and social media. http://www.soundslikebranding.com/pdf/hb_whitepaper_web.pdf (accessed 7 April 2010).

Hebdige, Dick. 1979. *Subculture: The meaning of style*. London: Methuen.

Herrara, Monica. 2009. Michael Jackson, Pepsi made marketing history. *Reuters*, 3 July. http://www.reuters.com/article/2009/07/03/industry-us-jackson-pepsi-idUSTRE56252Z20090703 (accessed 12 November 2011).

Hesmondhalgh, David. 1996. Post-Fordism, flexibility and the music industries. *Media, Culture and Society* 18, no. 3: 468–88.

Hesmondhalgh, David. 2008a. Towards a critical understanding of music, emotion and self-identity. *Consumption, Markets and Culture* 11, no. 4: 329–43.

Hesmondhalgh, David. 2008b. Neoliberalism, imperialism and the media. In *The media and social theory*, ed. David Hesmondhalgh and Jason Toynbee, 95–111. New York: Routledge.

Hesmondhalgh, David. 2013a. *The cultural industries*. 3rd ed. Los Angeles: Sage.

Hesmondhalgh, David. 2013b. *Why music matters*. Chichester: Wiley Blackwell.

Hesmondhalgh, David and Sarah Baker. 2011. *Creative labour: Media work in three cultural industries*. London: Routledge.

Hesmondhalgh, David and Leslie M. Meier. 2015. Popular music, independence and the concept of the alternative in contemporary capitalism. In *Media independence: Working with freedom or working for free*, ed. James Bennett and Niki Strange, 94–116. New York: Routledge.

High, Kamau. 2008. With the brand: Despite the buzz, corporate vanity labels remain a work in progress. *Billboard*, 20 December.

High, Kamau. 2009. The Billboard Q&A: Steve Stoute. *Billboard*, 28 February.

Holt, Douglas B. 2002. Why do brands cause trouble? A dialectical theory of consumer culture and branding. *Journal of Consumer Research* 29, no. 1: 70–90.

Holt, Douglas B. 2004. *How brands become icons: The principles of cultural branding*. Boston: Harvard Business School Press.

Horkheimer, Max. [1947] 2004. *Eclipse of reason*. New York: Continuum.

Horkheimer, Max and Theodor W. Adorno. [1944] 2002. *Dialectic of enlightenment: Philosophical fragments*. Stanford: Stanford University Press.

Hutfless, Laura. 2010. Branding and sponsorships in live events. Conference panel at Billboard Touring Conference, New York. 3–4 November.

Hurn, Jake. 2011. Product of a label – Selling out? Hell no ... We're buying in! Conference panel at North by Northeast Interactive, Toronto. 16–18 June.

Huron, David. 1989. Music in advertising: An analytic paradigm. *Musical Quarterly* 73, no. 4: 557–74.

IBISWorld. 2012. Global music production and distribution. IBISWorld industry report Q8712-GL, March.

IFPI. 2015. IFPI digital music report 2015: Charting the path to sustainable growth. http://www.ifpi.org/digital-music-report.php (accessed 3 February 2016).

IMDb. 2016. Alexandra Patsavas – IMDb. http://www.imdb.com/name/nm0666031/ (accessed 5 July 2016).

Ingham, Tim. 2015a. $25 billion: The best number to happen to the global music business in a very long time. *Music Business Worldwide*, 10 December. http://www.musicbusinessworldwide.com/25-billion-the-best-number-to-happen-to-the-music-business/ (accessed 15 January 2016).

Ingham, Tim. 2015b. Independent labels trounce UMG, Sony and Warner in US market shares. *Music Business Worldwide*, 29 July. http://www.musicbusinessworldwide.com/independent-label-us-market-share-trounces-universal-sony-warner/ (accessed 23 October 2015).

Instant Music Licensing. 2015. How it works. http://www.instantlicensing.com/#anchor-howitworksvid (accessed 1 October 2015).

Jameson, Fredric. 2007. *Late Marxism: Adorno or the persistence of the dialectic*. 2nd ed. New York: Verso.

Jingle Punks. 2013. Creative audio services. http://jinglepunks.com/services/ (accessed 15 May 2013).

Jones, Rhian. 2015. How to completely mess up a sync deal. *Music Business Worldwide*, 2 October. http://www.musicbusinessworldwide.com/how-to-completely-mess-up-a-sync-deal/ (accessed 5 October 2015).

Jones, Simon C. and Thomas G. Schumacher. 1992. Muzak: On functional music and power. *Critical Studies in Mass Communication* 9, no. 2: 156–69.

Jurgensen, John. 2012. Making an impression in just four notes. *Wall Street Journal*, 28 January. http://online.wsj.com/article/SB10001424052970203718 504577182951405815364.html (accessed 15 February 2012).

Kassabian, Anahid. 2002. Ubiquitous listening. In *Popular music studies*, ed. David Hesmondhalgh and Keith Negus, 131–42. London: Arnold.

Kassabian, Anahid. 2004. Would you like some world music with your latte? Starbucks, Putumayo, and distributed tourism. *Twentieth-Century Music* 1, no. 2: 209–23.

Kassabian, Anahid. 2013. *Ubiquitous listening: Affect, attention, and distributed subjectivity*. Berkeley: University of California Press.

Keightley, Keir. 2001. Reconsidering rock. In *The Cambridge companion to pop and rock*, ed. Simon Frith, Will Straw and John Street, 109–42. New York: Cambridge University Press.

Kellaris, James J., Anthony D. Cox and Dena Cox. 1993. The effect of background music on ad processing: A contingency explanation. *Journal of Marketing* 57, no. 4: 114–25.

Kelly, Kevin. 2008a. 1,000 True Fans. The Technium blog, 4 March. http://www.kk.org/thetechnium/archives/2008/03/1000_true_fans.php (accessed 9 November 2009).

Kelly, Kevin. 2008b. The case against 1,000 True Fans. The Technium blog, 27 April. http://www.kk.org/thetechnium/archives/2008/04/the_case_agains.php (accessed 9 November 2009).

Kelly, Kevin. 2008c. The reality of depending on True Fans. The Technium blog, 21 April. http://www.kk.org/thetechnium/archives/2008/04/the_reality_of.php (accessed 9 November 2009).

Khicha, Preeti. 2008. India turns up the volume on sonic branding. *Brandchannel*, 4 August. http://www.brandchannel.com/features_effect.asp?pf_id=433 (accessed 22 February 2012).

Klein, Bethany. 2009. *As heard on TV: Popular music in advertising*. Burlington, VT: Ashgate.

Klein, Bethany and Leslie M. Meier. Forthcoming. In sync? Music supervisors, music placement practices, and industrial change. In *Routledge companion to screen music and sound*, ed. Miguel Mera, Ron Sadoff and Ben Winters. New York: Routledge.

Klein, Bethany, Leslie M. Meier and Devon Powers. 2016. Selling out: Musicians, autonomy, and compromise in the digital age. *Popular Music and Society*, DOI: 10.1080/03007766.2015.1120101.

Klein, Bethany, Giles Moss and Lee Edwards. 2015. *Understanding copyright: Intellectual property in the digital age*. Los Angeles: Sage.

Kline, Stephen, Nick Dyer-Witheford and Greig de Peuter. 2003. *Digital play: The interaction of technology, culture, and marketing*. Montreal: McGill-Queen's University Press.

Knight, Mark. 2015. When bands meet brands: The mutual benefits of music partnerships. *The Guardian*, 14 October. http://www.theguardian.com/media-network/2015/oct/14/bands-brands-benefits-music-industry-partnerships (accessed 15 March 2016).

Knopper, Steve. 2007. Reinventing record deals. *Rolling Stone*, 29 November.

Knopper, Steve. 2011. The new economics of the music industry: How artists really make money in the cloud – or don't. *Rolling Stone*, 25 October. http://www.rollingstone.com/music/news/the-new-economics-of-the-music-industry-20111025 (accessed 6 February 2012).

Kozinn, Allan. 2007. Still needing, still feeding the muse at 64. *New York Times*, 3 June. http://www.nytimes.com/2007/06/03/arts/music/03kozi.html?_r=0 (accessed 19 September 2012).

Kreps, Daniel. 2009. Chris Brown officially out as Wrigley gum pitchman. *Rolling Stone*, 7 August. http://www.rollingstone.com/music/news/chris-brownofficially-out-as-wrigley-gum-pitchman-20090807 (accessed 1 July 2012).

Krims, Adam. 2007. *Music and urban geography*. New York: Routledge.

Kulash, Damian Jr. 2010. The new rock-star paradigm. *Wall Street Journal*, eastern edition, 17 December. http://online.wsj.com/article/SB100014240527 48703727804576017592259031536.html (accessed 25 January 2011).

Laing, Dave. 2009. World music and the global music industry: Flows, corporations and networks. *Collegium* 6: 14–33. https://helda.helsinki.fi/bitstream/handle/10138/25811/006_03_Laing.pdf?sequence=1 (accessed 15 May 2016).

Laing, Dave. 2012. Live Music Exchange blog: What's it worth? Calculating the economic value of live music. *Live Music Exchange*. http://livemusicexchange.org/blog/whats-it-worth-calculating-the-economic-value-of-live-music-dave-laing/ (accessed 12 September 2012).

LaPolt, Dina and Max Resnick. 2009. Multiple rights deals in the US: 360° and beyond. Excerpted from multiple rights deals in the music industry, MIDEM International Music Business Conference, Cannes, France, January. International Association of Entertainment Lawyers. http://www.lommen.com/pdf/SXSW-2011/What-You-Get-and-Give-Up-in-Today-s-Recording-Agr.aspx (accessed 7 February 2011).

Lash, Scott and Celia Lury. 2007. *Global culture industry: The mediation of things*. Malden, MA: Polity.

Lash, Scott and John Urry. 1994. *Economies of signs and space*. Thousand Oaks, CA: Sage.

LeBeau, Philip. 2003. Rock songs are hits with auto makers. *CNBC*, 21 February. http://www.msnbc.msn.com/id/3072893/t/rock-songs-are-hits-auto-makers/#.T9uLwY5OTww (accessed 15 May 2012).

Lee, Martyn J. 1993. *Consumer culture reborn: The cultural politics of consumption*. New York: Routledge.

Lefsetz, Bob. 2010. Pomplamoose/Hyundai. Lefsetz Letter blog, 25 November. http://lefsetz.com/wordpress/index.php/archives/2010/11/25/pomplamoosehyundai/ (accessed 5 August 2012).

Lefsetz, Bob. 2012. The David Lowery screed. Lefsetz Letter blog, 18 June. http://lefsetz.com/wordpress/index.php/archives/2012/06/18/the-david-loweryscreed/ (accessed 5 September 2012).

Lehu, Jean-Marc. 2007. *Branded entertainment: Product placement and brand strategy in the entertainment business*. Philadelphia: Kogan Page.

Leland, John. 2001. For rock bands, selling out isn't what it used to be. *New York Times*, 11 March. http://www.nytimes.com/2001/03/11/magazine/11SELLOUT.html?pagewanted=all (accessed 14 November 2011).

Leyshon, Andrew. 2014. *Reformatted: Code, networks, and the transformation of the music industry*. Oxford: Oxford University Press.

Leyshon, Andrew, Peter Webb, Shawn French, Nigel Thrift and Louise Crewe. 2005. On the reproduction of the musical economy after the Internet. *Media, Culture and Society* 27, no. 2: 177–209.

Lieb, Kristin J. 2013. *Gender, branding, and the modern music industry: The social construction of female popular music stars*. New York: Routledge.

Lipietz, Alain. 1986. New tendencies in the international division of labour: Regimes of accumulation and modes of regulation. In *Production, work, ter-*

ritory: The geographical anatomy of industrial capitalism, ed. Allen J. Scott and Michael Storper, 16–40. Boston: Allen & Unwin.

Litwak, Glenn. 2010. The money trail. Conference panel at Artist Management Conference (AMCON) 2010, New York. 14–15 October.

Lockwood, Thomas, ed. 2009. *Design thinking: Integrating innovation, customer experience, and brand value*. New York: Allworth.

Logan, Tim. 2012. Budweiser turns to music in bid to attract younger beer consumers. *Los Angeles Times*, 4 September. http://articles.latimes.com/2012/sep/04/business/la-fi-bud-young-drinkers-20120904 (accessed 13 October 2012).

Lury, Celia and Liz Moor. 2010. Brand valuation and topological culture. In *Blowing up the brand: Critical perspectives on promotional culture*, ed. Melissa Aronczyk and Devon Powers, 29–52. New York: Peter Lang.

Macnamara, Jim. 2014. Journalism-PR relations revisited: The good news, the bad news, and insights into tomorrow's news. *Public Relations Review* 40: 739–50.

Made in America. 2012. Budweiser Made in America. http://www.madeinamericafest.com/ticketing.html (accessed 14 October 2012).

Marshall, Lee. 2013. The 360 deal and the 'new' music industry. *European Journal of Cultural Studies* 16, no. 1: 77–99.

Marx, Karl. [1867] 1990. *Capital, Volume I: A critique of political economy*. Trans. Ben Fowkes. Toronto: Penguin Books.

McAllister, Matthew P. and Emily West, eds. 2013. *The Routledge companion to advertising and promotional culture*. London: Routledge.

McCourt, Tom and Eric Rothenbuhler. 1997. SoundScan and the consolidation of control in the popular music industry. *Media, Culture and Society* 19, no. 2: 201–18.

McCracken, Grant. 2011. Grant McCracken: Cracking the Pomplamousse – Hyundai Case. *CultureBy.com*, 2 January. http://cultureby.com/2011/01/cracking-the-pomplamoosehyundai-case.html (accessed 2 November 2012).

McFall, Liz. 2004. The language of the walls: Putting promotional saturation in historical context. *Consumption, Markets and Culture* 7, no. 2: 107–28.

McFarland, Melanie. 2005. Seattle's own Death Cab for Cutie to appear on 'The O.C.' *Seattle Post-Intelligencer*, 20 April. http://www.seattlepi.com/ae/tv/article/Seattle-s-Own-Death-Cab-for-Cutie-to-appear-on-1171355.php (accessed 2 June 2012).

Meier, Leslie M. 2011. Promotional ubiquitous musics: Recording artists, brands, and 'rendering authenticity'. *Popular Music and Society* 34, no. 4: 399–415.

Meier, Leslie M. 2015. Popular music making and promotional work inside the new music industry. In *The Routledge companion to the cultural industries*, ed. Kate Oakley and Justin O'Connor, 402–12. Abingdon: Routledge.

Mencher, Brian. 2010. The money trail. Conference panel at Artist Management Conference (AMCON) 2010, New York. 14–15 October.

Metzner, Paul. 1998. *Crescendo of the virtuoso: Spectacle, skill, and self-promotion in Paris during the Age of Revolution.* Berkeley: University of California Press.

Michaels, Sean. 2010. Damon Albarn aims to release Gorillaz album before Christmas. *The Guardian,* 12 November. http://www.theguardian.com/music/2010/nov/12/damon-albarn-gorillaz-album-christmas (accessed 1 October 2015).

Middleton, Richard. 1990. *Studying popular music.* Milton Keynes: Open University Press.

Miège, Bernard. 1989. *The capitalization of cultural production.* New York: International General.

Mitchell, Gail. 2011. Maximum exposure. *Billboard,* 26 November.

Mock, Vanessa and Ethan Smith. 2012. EU clears Universal-EMI merger, sets tough conditions. *Wall Street Journal,* 21 September. http://online.wsj.com/article/SB10000872396390444165804578009780588806980.html (accessed 25 September 2012).

Moor, Elizabeth. 2003. Branded spaces: The scope of 'new marketing'. *Journal of Consumer Culture* 3, no. 1: 39–60.

Moor, Liz. 2007. *The rise of brands.* New York: Berg.

Mophonics. 2012. Music: Songwriters: Mark Foster. http://www.mophonics.com/music/songwriter/mark_foster_writer (accessed 31 July 2012).

Morris, Christopher. 2012. Sony-led group closes EMI pub buy: Acquisition was cleared by FTC. *Variety,* 29 June. http://www.variety.com/article/VR1118056117 (accessed 18 July 2012).

Morris, Jeremy Wade. 2015. *Selling digital music, formatting culture.* Oakland: University of California Press.

Morris, Jeremy Wade and Devon Powers. 2015. Control, curation and musical experience in streaming music services. *Creative Industries Journal* 8, no. 2: 106–22.

Mulligan, Mark. 2014. Digital ascendency: The Future Music Forum keynote - highlights. *Music Industry Blog,* 29 September. https://musicindustryblog.wordpress.com/2014/09/29/digital-ascendency-the-future-music-forum-keynote/ (accessed 25 July 2015).

Mulligan, Mark. 2015a. Apple, the indies and the rise of the digital monopsony. *Music Industry Blog,* 19 June. https://musicindustryblog.wordpress.com/2015/06/19/apple-the-indies-and-the-rise-of-the-digital-monospony/ (accessed 25 July 2015).

Mulligan, Mark. 2015b. *Awakening: The music industry in the digital age.* CreateSpace Independent Publishing.

MusicSupervisor.com. 2013. Take a tour. http://www.musicsupervisor.com/need-music/#take_a_tour (accessed 15 May 2013).

Nagi, Paul. 2010. What's the deal? Conference panel at Artist Management Conference (AMCON) 2010, New York. 14–15 October.

Nashel, Peter. 2012. Advertising IS the new radio! Conference panel at South by Southwest, Austin, TX. 15 March. http://schedule.sxsw.com/2012/events/event_MP10725 (accessed 30 March 2012).

Negus, Keith. 1992. *Producing pop: Culture and conflict in the popular music industry*. New York: E. Arnold.

Negus, Keith. 1999. *Music genres and corporate cultures*. New York: Routledge.

New York Times. 1989. How MTV has rocked television commercials. *New York Times*, 9 October.

Nuwame, Jacqueline. 2011. The changing experience of music. Conference panel at North by Northeast Interactive, Toronto. 16–18 June.

Ole. 2012. Ole: syncnow. http://www.majorlyindie.com/search?search_type =synch (accessed 15 September 2012).

O'Reilly, Terry. 2012. Big Chill marketing: Under the influence with Terry O'Reilly. *CBC.ca*, 12 February. http://www.cbc.ca/undertheinfluence/season-1/2012/02/12/big-chill-marketing/ (accessed 5 October 2012).

Owen, Frank. 1998. Electronica arrives via Madison Ave; Underground techno music is a hit in the land of jingles. *The Washington Post*, 12 July.

Page, Will. 2010. Interview with Will Page, music industry economist. *Techdirt*, 29 April. http://techdirt.com/articles/20100429/0116199232.shtml (accessed 15 June 2010).

Page, Will and Eric Garland. 2009. The long tail of P2P. *Economic Insight*, 14: 1–8. http://www.prsformusic.com/creators/news/research/Documents/The%20 long%20tail%20of%20P2P%20v9.pdf (accessed 15 June 2010).

Pakinkis, Tom. 2013. PJ Bloom on changing sync revenues and opportunities for rights-holders. *Music Week*, 21 March. http://www.musicweek.com/news/ read/pj-bloom-on-changing-sync-revenues-and-opportunities-for-rights-holders/054069 (accessed 1 October 2015).

Panay, Panos. 2011. How brands are using emerging music to reach consumers. Conference panel at South by Southwest., Austin, TX. 17 March. http:// schedule.sxsw.com/2011/events/event_MP8143 (accessed 30 March 2012).

Passman, Donald S. 2015. *All you need to know about the music business*. 9th ed. New York: Simon & Schuster.

Peoples, Glenn. 2009. *In tune with consumers: How brands and artists can get the most out of using music in campaigns*. Corporate White Paper, *Billboard/ Nielsen*.

Peoples, Glenn. 2010a. @ Leadership Music Digital Summit Day 2: Genuine optimism. *Billboard.biz*, 1 October. http://www.billboard.biz/bbbiz/content_ display/industry/news/e3ifd62d5f2cdeae60e1cb0f11647ac0d9b (accessed 18 January 2011).

Peoples, Glenn. 2010b. The new D.I.Y. *Billboard*, 10 July.

Peoples, Glenn. 2010c. TicketsNow, 360 deals a drag for Live Nation. *Billboard*, 10 May. http://www.billboard.com/biz/articles/news/touring/1207078/ticketsnow-360-deals-a-drag-for-live-nation (accessed 25 March 2011).

Peoples, Glenn. 2011a. Business matters: 75,000 albums released in U.S. in 2010 – down 22% from 2009. *Billboard.biz*, 18 February. http://www.billboard.com/ biz/articles/news/1179201/business-matters-75000-albums-released-in-us-in-2010-down-22-from-2009 (accessed 19 February 2013).

Peoples, Glenn. 2011b. What you didn't know about Live Nation's growth in 2010. *Billboard.biz*, 7 March. http://www.billboard.biz/bbbiz/industry/

legal-and-management/what-you-didn-t-know-about-live-nation-s
-1005059352.story (accessed 8 March 2011).

Peoples, Glenn. 2015a. This $25 billion global music industry isn't everything. *Billboard*, 11 December. http://www.billboard.com/articles/business/6805318/25-billion-global-music-industry-not-everything (accessed 15 January 2016).

Peoples, Glenn. 2015b. Record label revenue flat in first half of 2015. *Billboard*, 21 September. http://www.billboard.com/articles/business/6700811/record-label-revenue-flat-in-first-half-of-2015 (accessed 2 October 2015).

Peters, Mitchell. 2011. Foster the People: how a free download begat a business. *Billboard*. 3 October. http://www.billboard.com/articles/news/467011/foster-the-people-how-a-free-download-begat-a-business (accessed 17 August 2016).

Peterson, Richard A. and David G. Berger. 1975. Cycles in symbol production: The case of popular music. *American Sociological Review* 40, no. 2: 158–73.

Peterzell, Marcus. 2010. View from the top: The ad agency angle. Conference panel at NARIP: Bands, Brands & Beyond, New York. 15 November.

Pham, Alex. 2013. YouTube confirms Vevo deal. *Billboard*, 2 July. http://www.billboard.com/biz/articles/news/digital-and-mobile/1568816/youtube-confirms-vevo-deal (accessed 1 October 2015).

Plambeck, Joseph. 2010. Product placement grows in music videos. *New York Times*, 5 July. http://www.nytimes.com/2010/07/06/business/media/06adco.html?_r=2&ref=business (accessed 15 July 2011).

Pollard, Garland. 2009. Interview: Singer songwriter Jake Holmes, America's most memorable jingle writer. *BrandlandUSA*. 15 August. http://www.brandlandusa.com/2009/08/15/singer-songwriter-jake-holmes (accessed 17 August 2016).

Powers, Devon. 2010. Strange powers: The branded sensorium and the intrigue of musical sound. In *Blowing up the brand: Critical perspectives on promotional culture*, ed. Melissa Aronczyk and Devon Powers, 285–306. New York: Peter Lang.

Powers, Devon. 2015. Intermediaries and intermediation. In *The Sage handbook of popular music*, ed. Andy Bennett and Steve Waksman, 120–34. Los Angeles: Sage.

PQ Media. 2015. PQ Media update: US product placement revenues up 13% in 1H15; pacing for 6th straight year of accelerated growth as value of TV, digital & music integrations surge. PQ Media press release. June. http://www.pqmedia.com/about-press-20150615.html (accessed 1 October 2015).

Price, Jeff. n.d. Music industry survival manual: How to not get screwed: The six legal rights that drive the music business. Tunecore Music & Video Distribution. http://www.tunecore.com/guides/sixrights (accessed 5 February 2012).

Prince, David J. 2010. K'Naan: The real thing. *Billboard*, 29 May.

Prindle, Gregory M. 2003. No competition: How radio consolidation has diminished diversity and sacrificed localism. *Fordham Intellectual Property, Media and Entertainment Law Journal* 14: 279–325.

PR Newswire. 2007. Tim McGraw and Faith Hill's Jeep(R) story launches 'Share Your Favorite Jeep Story' contest on June 7 as Jeep presents Soul2Soul tour 2007 debuts. Jeep press release. *PR Newswire*. http://www.prnewswire.com/ news-releases/tim-mcgraw-and-faith-hills-jeepr-story-launches-share-your-favorite-jeep-story-contest-on-june-7-as-jeep-presents-soul2soul-tour-2007-debuts-57922952.html (accessed 17 January 2010).

Rabinowitz, Josh. 2008. Parting shots: Branding columnist wraps up six-month tenure with words of wisdom to tack on your bulletin board. *Billboard*, 19 July.

Rabinowitz, Josh. 2010. View from the top: The ad agency angle. Conference panel at NARIP: Bands, Brands & Beyond, New York. 15 November.

Resnikoff, Paul. 2010. The latest stat: Less than 30,000 artists are actually earning a living. *Digital Music News*, 7 November. http://www.digitalmusicnews .com/stories/110510newnoisebreaking?layout=flat#idCdKlC_9UEXucpBUeT T4ARg (accessed 10 November 2010).

Resnikoff, Paul. 2012a. I'm a successful artist and here's why things have never been worse. *Digital Music News*, 14 February. http://www.digitalmusicnews.com/ permalink/2012/120214cracker (accessed 8 March 2012).

Resnikoff, Paul. 2012b. Longtail #FAIL: In 2011, 90% of new album sales came from 2% of releases. *Digital Music News*, 12 January. http://www. digitalmusicnews.com/permalink/2012/120112longfail (accessed 7 May 2013).

Reynolds, Matthew. 2016. OK Go's latest video was filmed entirely in zero gravity. *Wired*, 12 February. http://www.wired.co.uk/news/archive/2016-02/12/weightless-music-video (accessed 15 March 2016).

Richeri, Giuseppe. 2011. The media amid enterprises, the public, and the state. In *The handbook of political economy of communications*, ed. Janet Wasko, Graham Murdock and Helena Sousa, 129–39. Malden, MA: Wiley-Blackwell.

Ridderstråle, Jonas and Kjell Nordström. 2008. *Funky business forever: How to enjoy capitalism*. Toronto: Prentice Hall.

Ripley, Kathleen. 2011a. Low fidelity: Though strong, digital music sales fail to offset declining CD sales. IBISWorld Industry Report 51222 Major Label Music Production in the US, July.

Ripley, Kathleen. 2011b. Moving to the beat: Digital media and changing tastes will force publishers to change strategies. IBISWorld Industry Report 51223 Music Publishing in the US, December.

Robert, Klara. 2010. I'm with a celebrity, get me out of here! *Mediaweek* 20, no. 10: 13.

Roberts, Johnnie L. 2011. Lady Gaga's 360 ways to save the music industry. *MSN Entertainment Music News*, 20 May. http://music.msn.com/music/ article.aspx?news=648668 (accessed 20 August 2011).

Robinson, Frances. 2012. Sony/ATV submits EMI Publishing to EU antitrust regulators. *Wall Street Journal*, 28 February. http://online.wsj.com/article/ BTCO-20120228-711063.html (accessed 5 March 2012).

Roc Nation. 2015. Budweiser Made In America Festival 2015 line-up announced. http://rocnation.com/budweiser-made-in-america-festival-2015-line-up-announced/ (accessed 8 December 2015).

Rogers, Jim. 2013. *The death and life of the music industry in the digital age*. London: Bloomsbury.

Rosenbaum, Steve. 2010. Content is no longer king: Curation is king. *Business Insider*, 15 June. http://articles.businessinsider.com/2010-06-15/tech/30097151_1_content-creation-king-curation (accessed 5 March 2012).

Roshkow, Matt. 2010. A fresh (and cheap!) sound for TV soundtracks. *CNN Money*, 2 March. http://money.cnn.com/2010/03/02/smallbusiness/jingle_punks/ (accessed 9 September 2012).

Rothenbuhler, Eric W. and Tom McCourt. 1992. Commercial radio and popular music: Processes of selection and factors of influence. In *Popular music and communication*, ed. James Lull, 2nd ed., 101–15. Newbury Park, CA: Sage.

Ryan, Bill. 1991. *Making capital from culture: The corporate form of capitalist cultural production*. New York: de Gruyter.

Sanburn, Josh. 2012. Advertising killed the radio star: How pop music and TV ads became inseparable. *Time*, 3 February. http://business.time.com/2012/02/03/advertising-killed-the-radio-star-how-pop-music-and-tv-ads-becameinseparable/ (accessed 25 July 2012).

Sandoval, Greg. 2007. When rockers cut ties from labels. *CNET News*, 2 November. http://news.cnet.com/When-rockers-cut-ties-from-labels/2100-1027_3-6216704.html?tag=mncol;txt (accessed 29 March 2011).

Schmelzer, Randi. 2005. RPM's new urban marketing tool: The DJ made me do it. *Adweek*, 14 March. http://www.adweek.com/news/advertising-branding/rpmsnew-urban-marketing-tool-dj-made-me-do-it-78306 (accessed 11 December 2011).

Schultz, Mark F. 2009. Live performance, copyright, and the future of the music business. *University of Richmond Law Review* 43, no. 2: 685–764.

Seeking Alpha. 2011. Warner Music Group's CEO discusses F3Q2011 results – Earnings call transcript. *Seeking Alpha*, 6 August. http://seekingalpha.com/article/285352-warner-music-group-s-ceo-discusses-f3q2011-results-earningscall-transcript (accessed 18 January 2012).

Seely, Mike. 2010. Pomplamoose's Christmas Hyundai commercials cause hatred of Pomplamoose, Hyundai and Christmas. *Seattle Weekly* blogs, 21 December. http://blogs.seattleweekly.com/reverb/2010/12/pomplamooses_christmas_hyundai.php (accessed 23 October 2012).

Seybold, Patricia. 2011. The next big thing: Content curation. *Customers.com Technologies*, 13 January. http://blogs.customers.com/technologies/2011/01/thenext-big-thing-content-curation.html (accessed 17 February 2011).

Shaviro, Steven. 2010. *Post-cinematic affect*. Washington: Zero Books.

Sherbow, David. 2010. One for the road. Conference panel at Artist Management Conference (AMCON) 2010, New York. 14–15 October.

Shuker, Roy. 2002. *Popular music: The key concepts*. 2nd ed. New York: Routledge.

Siegel, Ed. 1989. Madonna sells her soul for a song. *Boston Globe*, 2 March.

Sisario, Ben. 2010. Looking to a sneaker for a band's big break. *New York Times*, 10 October. http://www.nytimes.com/2010/10/10/arts/music/10brand.html?pagewanted=all (accessed 4 April 2011).

Sisario, Ben. 2011. A new Madonna album, on a new label. *New York Times*, 15 December. http://artsbeat.blogs.nytimes.com/2011/12/15/a-new-madonna-album-on-anew-label/ (accessed 7 January 2012).

Sisario, Ben. 2012. U.S. and European regulators approve Universal's purchase of EMI. *New York Times*, 21 September. http://www.nytimes.com/2012/09/22/business/global/universal-takeover-of-emi-music-is-approved.html?pagewanted=all&_r=0 (accessed 22 September 2012).

Smirke, Richard. 2013. IFPI digital music report 2013: Global recorded music revenues climb for the first time since 1999. *Billboard*, 26 February. http://www.billboard.com/biz/articles/news/digital-and-mobile/1549915/ifpi-digital-music-report-2013-global-recorded-music (accessed 3 March 2016).

Smith, Ethan. 2002. Organization Moby. *Wired*, May. http://www.wired.com/wired/archive/10.05/moby.html (accessed 15 January 2010).

Smith, Ethan and Julie Jargon. 2008. Chew on this: Hit song is a gum jingle. *Wall Street Journal*, 28 July. http://online.wsj.com/article/SB121721123435289073.html (accessed 7 January 2012).

Smith, Jeff Paul. 1998. *The sounds of commerce: Marketing popular film music.* New York: Columbia University Press.

Smith, P.R. and Ze Zook. 2011. *Marketing communications: Integrating offline and online with social media.* 5th ed. London: Kogan Page.

Sony/ATV. 2013. Sony/ATV Music Publishing: Search. https://www.sonyatv.com/search/index.php/search (accessed 8 May 2013).

Sony. 2012. Sony USA: U.S. businesses & operations. http://www.sony.com/SCA/outline/atv.shtml (accessed 2 August 2012).

Sony. 2016. Corporate info: Organization data. http://www.sony.net/SonyInfo/CorporateInfo/Data/organization.html (accessed 1 May 2016).

South by Southwest. 2016. SXSW schedule. http://schedule.sxsw.com/?conference=music&lsort=name&event_type=sessions&day=ALL&category=bands+%26+brands (accessed 1 April 2016).

Stahl, Matt. 2010. Primitive accumulation, the social common, and the contractual lockdown of recording artists at the threshold of digitalization. *Ephemera* 10, no. 3/4: 337–55.

Stahl, Matt. 2013. *Unfree masters: Recording artists and the politics of work.* Durham, NC: Duke University Press.

Stahl, Matt and Leslie M. Meier. 2012. The firm foundation of organizational flexibility: The 360 contract in the digitalizing music industry. *Canadian Journal of Communication* 37, no. 3: 441–58.

Starcount Squared. 2012. Facebook, Twitter, YouTube social media statistics: Famecount. http://www.starcountsquared.com/ (accessed 31 March 2012).

Sterne, Jonathan. 1997. Sounds like the Mall of America: Programmed music and the architectonics of commercial space. *Ethnomusicology* 41, no. 1: 22–50.

Sterne, Jonathan. 2012. *MP3: The meaning of a format.* Durham, NC: Duke University Press.

Stone, Steven. 2011. Do record labels matter? *Audiophile Review*, 17 October. http://audiophilereview.com/audiophile-music/do-record-labels-matter.html (accessed 17 January 2012).

Sullivan, Hudson. 2011. Product of a label – Selling out? Hell no … We're buying in! Conference panel at North by Northeast Interactive, Toronto. 16–18 June.

Taylor, Timothy D. 2007. The changing shape of the culture industry; Or, how did electronica music get into television commercials? *Television and New Media* 8, no. 3: 235–58.

Taylor, Timothy D. 2009. Advertising and the conquest of culture. *Social Semiotics* 19, no. 4: 405–25.

Taylor, Timothy D. 2012. *The sounds of capitalism: Advertising, music, and the conquest of culture.* Chicago: University of Chicago Press.

Taylor, Timothy D. 2016. *Music and capitalism: A history of the present.* Chicago: University of Chicago Press.

Terranova, Tiziana. 2000. Free labor: Producing culture for the digital economy. *Social Text* 18, no. 2: 33–58.

Topping, Alexandra. 2011. Record labels are not dinosaurs of the music industry. *The Guardian*, 13 May. http://www.guardian.co.uk/business/2011/may/13/recordlabels-not-dinosaurs-music-industry (accessed 1 March 2012).

Toynbee, Jason. 2000. *Making popular music: musicians, creativity and institutions.* London: Arnold.

Toynbee, Jason. 2002. Mainstreaming, from hegemonic centre to global networks. In *Popular music studies*, ed. David Hesmondhalgh and Keith Negus, 149–63. London: Arnold.

Tunnicliffe, Mike. 2008. Music: The brand-band love in. *Campaign*, 7 November. http://www.campaignlive.co.uk/article/860785/music-brand-band-love-in (accessed 28 May 2012).

Universal Music Group. 2015. Universal Music Group & Brands. http://www.universalmusicandbrands.com/#Our-Work (accessed 1 October 2015).

Universal Music Publishing. n.d. Inside UMPG. Company overview. http://www.umusicpub.com/#contentRequest=insideumpgcompanyoverview&contentLocation=sub&contentOptions= (accessed 2 February 2012).

Vivendi. 2013. Vivendi in brief. http://www.vivendi.com/vivendi-en/vivendi-in-brief-2/# (accessed 1 May 2016).

Waddell, Ray. 2010a. Across the aisle: Talks about label investment in AEG Live point to market changes. *Billboard*, 3 July.

Waddell, Ray. 2010b. Tough times on the road: The year that live business growth hit the brakes. *Billboard*, 18 December.

Waddell, Ray. 2011. Resurgence on the road: Hard lessons learned the touring business rebounds. *Billboard*, 17 December.

Waksman, Steve. 2011. Selling the nightingale: P.T. Barnum, Jenny Lind, and the management of the American crowd. *Arts Marketing: An International Journal* 1, no. 2: 108–20.

Warner Music Canada. 2015. Services: For brands. http://www.warnermusic.ca/services/for-brands/ (accessed 5 July 2015).

Warner Music Group. 2011. Warner Music Group: Timeline. http://www.wmg.com/timeline (accessed 5 August 2012).

Weiser, Mark. 1991. The computer for the twenty-first century. *Scientific American* 265, no. 3: 94–104

Wernick, Andrew. 1991. *Promotional culture: Advertising, ideology, and symbolic expression.* Newbury Park, CA: Sage.

White, Emily. 2012. In defense of Emily White (the NPR intern). *Hypebot
.com*, 19 June. http://www.hypebot.com/hypebot/2012/06/in-defense-of-emily-
whitethe-npr-intern.html?cid=6a00d83451b36c69e2016767adfe56970b
(accessed 5 September 2012).

Wikström, Patrik. 2009. *The music industry: Music in the cloud.* Cambridge:
Polity.

Williamson, John and Martin Cloonan. 2007. Rethinking the music industry.
Popular Music 26, no. 2: 305–22.

Worstall, Tim. 2012. Where David Lowery goes wrong: We don't care about
producers, not even musicians. *Forbes*, 8 July. http://www.forbes.com/sites/
timworstall/2012/07/08/where-david-lowery-goes-wrong-we-dont-care-about-
producers-not-even-musicians/ (accessed 4 September 2012).

Young, Sherman and Steve Collins. 2010. A view from the trenches of Music
2.0. *Popular Music and Society* 33, no. 3: 339–55.

Index